Geopolitics of the Knowledge-Based Economy

T0330880

We live in the era of the knowledge-based economy, and this has major implications for the ways in which states, cities and even supranational political units are spatially planned, governed and developed. In this book, Sami Moisio delves deeply into the links between the knowledge-based economy and geopolitics, examining a wide range of themes, including city geopolitics and the university as a geopolitical site. Overall, this work shows that knowledge-based "economization" can be understood as a geopolitical process that produces territories of wealth, security, power and belonging.

This book will prove enlightening to students, researchers and policymakers in the fields of human geography, urban studies, spatial planning, political science and international relations.

Sami Moisio is Professor of Spatial Planning and Policy in the Department of Geosciences and Geography at the University of Helsinki, Finland. His research interests include political geographies of Europeanization, state spatial transformation and urban political geographies.

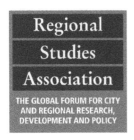

Regions and Cities

Series Editor in Chief
Joan Fitzgerald, Northeastern University, USA

Editors
Ron Martin, University of Cambridge, UK
Maryann Feldman, University of North Carolina, USA
Gernot Grabher, HafenCity University Hamburg, Germany
Kieran P. Donaghy, Cornell University, USA

In today's globalized, knowledge-driven and networked world, regions and cities have assumed heightened significance as the interconnected nodes of economic, social and cultural production, and as sites of new modes of economic and territorial governance and policy experimentation. This book series brings together incisive and critically engaged international and interdisciplinary research on this resurgence of regions and cities, and should be of interest to geographers, economists, sociologists, political scientists and cultural scholars, as well as to policy-makers involved in regional and urban development.

For more information on the Regional Studies Association visit www.regionalstudies.org

There is a 30% discount available to RSA members on books in the **Regions and Cities** series, and other subject related Taylor and Francis books and e-books including Routledge titles. To order just e-mail Joanna Swieczkowska, Joanna.Swieczkowska@tandf.co.uk, or phone on +44 (0)20 3377 3369 and declare your RSA membership. You can also visit the series page at www.routledge.com/Regions-and-Cities/book-series/RSA and use the discount code: RSA0901

Geopolitics of the Knowledge-Based Economy

Sami Moisio

Routledge
Taylor & Francis Group

LONDON AND NEW YORK

First published 2018
by Routledge
2 Park Square, Milton Park, Abingdon, Oxon OX14 4RN

and by Routledge
711 Third Avenue, New York, NY 10017

Routledge is an imprint of the Taylor & Francis Group, an informa business

© 2018 Sami Moisio

The right of Sami Moisio to be identified as author of this work has
been asserted by him in accordance with sections 77 and 78 of the
Copyright, Designs and Patents Act 1988.

The Open Access version of this book, available at www.taylorfrancis.
com, has been made available under a Creative Commons Attribution-
Non Commercial-No Derivatives 4.0 license.

Trademark notice: Product or corporate names may be trademarks
or registered trademarks, and are used only for identification and
explanation without intent to infringe.

British Library Cataloguing-in-Publication Data
A catalogue record for this book is available from the British Library

Library of Congress Cataloging-in-Publication Data
Names: Moisio, Sami, author.
Title: Geopolitics of the Knowledge-Based Economy / Sami Moisio.
Description: 1 Edition. | New York: Routledge, [2018] |
Series: Regions and cities; 125
Identifiers: LCCN 2017046198 (print) | LCCN 2017056706 (ebook) |
ISBN 9781315742984 (ebook) | ISBN 9781138821996 (hardback)
Subjects: LCSH: Knowledge management. | Technological
innovations–Economic aspects. | Economic policy. | Geopolitics.
Classification: LCC HD30.2 (ebook) | LCC HD30.2 .M65 2018
(print) | DDC 303.48/33–dc23
LC record available at https://lccn.loc.gov/2017046198

ISBN: 978-1-138-82199-6 (hbk)
ISBN: 978-0-367-87131-4 (pbk)

Typeset in Bembo
by Deanta Global Publishing Services, Chennai, India

I dedicate this book to my two lovely daughters. The next round of knowledge-based economization may be exciting and politically significant but the presence of Elli and Liisi reminds me of what really matters.

Contents

List of illustrations

Figures

Tables

Acknowledgements

Writing this book took longer than I estimated. In the course of writing it I have benefited enormously from many connections, conversations, encounters and friendships. I began to write the book when I was still working at the University of Oulu, and finalized the project in the Department of Geosciences and Geography at the University of Helsinki. Both of these institutions have provided me with a stimulating environment to work. The Academy of Finland Centre of Excellence RELATE has enabled some of the activities without which this book project would have been difficult to accomplish. I thank The Association of Finnish Non-fiction Writers for a grant to write this book.

I want to express my most sincere thanks to my human geography colleagues and friends at the Goethe University in Frankfurt am Main for accepting me to visit their department and enjoy its great atmosphere on a regular basis since 2014. Furthermore, I wish to extend warm thanks to all my colleagues who have kindly helped me with my efforts by commenting on some of the draft chapters: Toni Ahlqvist, Veit Bachmann, Bernd Belina, Andy Jonas, Anni Kangas, Juho Luukkonen, Reijo Miettinen, Anssi Paasi, Ugo Rossi, Heikki Sirviö and the late Perttu Vartiainen. On a practical level, I am also indebted to Andrew Pattison, Rachel Cook and Arttu Paarlahti for their help with the manuscript. Warm thanks are due to my editors at Taylor & Francis for their help, advice and encouragement. I am also grateful to John Wiley & Sons for allowing me to use previously published material. Part of Chapter 6 draws upon my article, co-authored by Anni Kangas, entitled "Reterritorializing the global knowledge economy: an analysis of geopolitical assemblages of higher education", published in *Global Networks* in 2016.

1 Introduction

A quick internet search reveals that the term geopolitics is hardly ever associated with the term knowledge-based economy. Journalists, debaters and politicians do not make such a link in their articulations and the textbooks of geopolitics, political geography, economic geography and urban studies are equally silent on the issue (see, however, Salter 2009). Yet, the air is full of popular and scholarly argumentation concerning how we are currently living in an era marked by the prominence of knowledge in all societal, economic and cultural developments, as well as pronouncements about the knowledge-intensive form of capitalism as an important subtext for inter-state relations and inter-spatial competition. Hence, it seems it is high time to begin pondering what the interconnections between the knowledge-based economy and geopolitics look like. The purpose of my inquiry is analytical and conceptual: the goal is to raise new questions rather than answering old concerns.

When I began this project I soon realized the ambiguous nature of the term knowledge-based economy and some related terms such as knowledge economy, information economy, new economy or the like. The fact that the knowledge-based economy has become an idée fixe in political debates within the past two decades does not give proof of its value as a scholarly concept. Indeed, one may argue that the knowledge-based economy is a somewhat popular and hollow policy term and that the competition state, neoliberalism, global capitalism, financialization, information capitalism or the like would work better in a geopolitical analysis of the contemporary political–economic condition.

My solution to this conceptual issue has been to think through the concept of *knowledge-based economization*. I thus shift attention from the economy toward processes of economization (see, in particular, Çalişkan and Callon 2009). The concept of knowledge-based economization refers both to the material processes of knowledge-intensive capitalism (including subject formation), and to the processes whereby this form of capitalism is constructed discursively through imageries and objectifying social practices. My central claim is that the phenomenon of knowledge-based economization includes significant geopolitical dimensions that can be exposed through an act of conceptualization and with the help of different research materials ranging from expert interviews to popular academic literature, observations, policy documents and statistics.

Geopolitics is almost invariably conjoined with the notion of territorial control of natural resources and territorial expansion as states vie for power and seek to exert influence on other states. Accordingly, geopolitics typically focuses on international power relations and power plays based on military influence within a set geographical area. Indeed, the very concept of geopolitics is often associated with a dangerous militaristic form of political reasoning which may lead to all manner of violent events. Stefano Guzzini (2014), for instance, proclaims that the effect of a geopolitical world view is a fundamental militarization of states' foreign policies.

In an orthodox view, geopolitics is treated as a synonym for politics of territorial force (and spheres of influence) and in particular for states as primary users of such "hard force" (see, e.g. Mead 2014, 69). More often than not, geopolitics is still understood to denote drawing state borders, building nations as definite territories, constructing domestic social order through spatial techniques of coercion and consent, controlling territorial spaces through new military technologies within and beyond a given state, as well as geographical and historical justifications of territorial claims (Moisio 2013). The concept of geopolitics is therefore almost without exception associated with the idea of the purportedly territorially consolidated twentieth-century European state and the wider system of military strategy and power which still characterizes the powerful imaginary of the "Westphalian" inter-state system. As a persistent form of reasoning, the classical geopolitical perspective discloses some of the key political characteristics of the "industrial era" of the nineteenth and twentieth century: command of territory and natural resources were understood as pivotal dimensions of inter-state rivalry and as fundamental constituents of territories of wealth, power, status, security and belonging (cf. Maier 2016).

Today, variants of classical geopolitics persist in the ways in which politicians, foreign and security policy experts, military strategists, scholars and the general public make sense of international affairs. However, it is similarly stressed that inter-state competition over territories belongs to the past, and that "democratic governments" operate through a qualitatively entirely new set of state strategies. Geoff Mulgan (2009, 2), the former director of policy under the British Prime Minister Tony Blair, states how

> Past states wanted to grow their territory, crops, gold, and armies. Today the most valuable things which democratic governments want to grow are intangible: like trust, happiness, knowledge, capabilities, norms, or confident institutions. These grow in very different ways to agriculture or warfare. Trust creates trust, whether in markets or civil societies. Knowledge breeds new knowledge. And confident institutions achieve the growth and societal success that in turn strengthens the confidence of institutions. Much of modern strategy is about setting these virtuous circles in motion, whether through investments or programmes or by creating the right laws, regulations and institutions.

This narrative on the shift from tangible to intangible "things" discloses a great deal of the key aspects of the transformation from natural resource-based national economies toward the so-called knowledge-based economies. The book at hand is an attempt to conceptualize the geopolitical in the latter context. I argue that knowledge-based economization emerged gradually from the 1980s onwards as a result of the turbulent era in world economy and politics (which began already in the early 1970s; for this crisis, see Hobsbawm 1996), and took an increasingly geopolitical form in the 1990s.

Towards a political geography of economic geographies

Developing a geopolitical perspective on the knowledge-based economy requires adopting a theoretically sophisticated notion of geopolitics which transcends its pervasive orthodox connotations. Since the late 1980s, critical scholars began to broaden the narrow understanding of classical geopolitics. John Agnew and Stuart Corbridge (1995, 211), to name but one example, referred to a geopolitical struggle which they conceptualized as an effort "by dominant states and their ruling social strata to master space – to control territories and/or the interactional flows through which modern terrestrial spaces are produced". In such a view, geopolitics is about mastering both territorial and relational spaces and producing spatial orders through discourses and practices.

Notwithstanding the significant conceptual developments in the field of critical geopolitics over the past 30 years, it is not uncommon today to see the narrow territorial definition of geopolitics in scholarly literature – to say nothing of public discourse. To illustrate, the annexation of Crimea by Russia and the political developments in eastern Ukraine in 2014 were rapidly scripted in terms of geopolitics. Politicians, commentators, journalists, civil servants and scholars in the Organisation for Economic Co-operation and Development (OECD) world and beyond were quick to classify the conflict as geopolitical. But in so doing, they also tended to place the term geopolitics in the past. While the crisis itself was interpreted in terms of twentieth-century geopolitics, this form of political action was nonetheless understood as entirely anachronistic. It was argued that some states such as China, Iran and Russia (as opposed to the US and the EU) had never given up practicing hard territorial power and were now making "forceful attempts" to overturn the "geopolitical settlement that followed the Cold War", as Mead (2014, 70) put it in *Foreign Affairs*. Mead continues revealingly how

> So far, the year 2014 has been a tumultuous one, as geopolitical rivalries have stormed back to center stage. Whether it is Russian forces seizing Crimea, China making aggressive claims in its coastal waters, Japan responding with an increasingly assertive strategy of its own, or Iran trying to use its alliances with Syria and Hezbollah to dominate the Middle East, old-fashioned power plays are back in international relations. The United States and the EU, at least, find such trends disturbing. Both would rather

move past geopolitical questions of territory and military power and focus instead on ones of world order and global governance.

(Mead 2014, 69–70)

This quote is exemplary, not exceptional, of a logic according to which "geopolitical competition" and "liberal world order" are opposite developments. In such a temporal articulation, whereas the twentieth century was characterized by the "dark geopolitics" of inter-state rivalry and "territorialized" friend–foe relations, the contemporary era is experienced in Europe and the US as if it were marked by a relative inapplicability of state territory with respect to territorial conflicts and inter-state competition. This fact notwithstanding, it has been remarkably rare to discuss the concept of the geopolitical in the context of those political imaginaries that frame the world in terms of economic expansion, connectivity and pace or global integration and connectivity (cf. Sparke 2007). And yet, these imaginaries have become increasingly salient in state-centric political debates on national interests, national security, national identity and foreign policy. In such a perspective, the world is increasingly becoming a network consisting of urban hubs, wider "network-regions" and what Ong (2006) calls economic zones in which surplus value is formed and which are pivotal in controlling the movement of money, information, talent and innovative human behavior. This perspective, therefore, effectively reveals the geopolitics of relational spaces that partly, but definitely not entirely, characterizes the early twenty-first century and which is the topic of this treatise (Figure 1.1).

In public policy and mainstream academic spatial planning discourse, the nodes and hubs of the global networks through which the "global flows" are being actively re-territorialized have been, particularly since the 1990s,

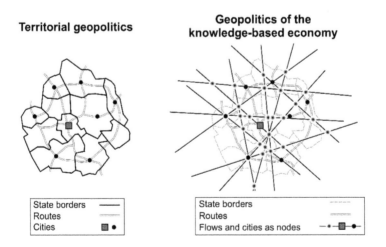

Figure 1.1 Simplified visualizations of the parallel worlds of the contemporary geopolitical condition.

understood as cities, city-regions and urban spaces and related micro-spaces which together contribute to the building of "global cities", "smart cities", "creative cities" or "happy cities". The development of these new spaces would not only significantly contribute to capital accumulation in the future but also render obsolete "geopolitics" such as the military control of vast territorial spaces and strategic locations. Accordingly, the preceding state-centered era epitomized by the term geopolitics has been replaced by the notion of the international competitiveness of the state based on generating competitive advantages (of nations) through different kinds of spatial formations as well as through new kinds of citizen subjectivities.

Examples of this kind of geopolitical logic are not difficult to find. Indeed, a sort of global knowledge-production industry dealing with the novelty of the relational global political order has emerged concomitantly with the so-called knowledge-based economy. Khanna (2016a) writes in *The New York Times* how the US is actually reorganizing itself around "regional infrastructure lines" and "metropolitan clusters that ignore state and even national borders", and that the problem is that a political system which still conceives of the US through its fifty member states "hasn't caught up". Arguing against such a territorial view, Khanna (2016a) goes on to say that these fifty states "aren't about to go away, but economically and socially, the country is drifting toward looser metropolitan and regional formations, anchored by the great cities and urban archipelagos that already lead global economic circuits". This serves as the rationale for Khanna (2016a) to make a normative policy recommendation. The author suggests that rather than channeling investments into "disconnected backwaters", the US federal government should focus on helping the "urban archipelagos" or "super-regions" to prosper.

It is interesting that this kind of geopolitical narrative, whereby particular infrastructural and economic connections are viewed as superseding traditional state-centered geopolitical markers, has become increasingly popular since the 1990s (see, e.g. Ohmae 1993). Indeed, Khanna's (2016b) *Connectography* is just one among the many attempts to tell a story about the ways in which the future is being shaped less by states/nations than by connectivities of hubs and flows in the age of knowledge-intensive capitalism. Accordingly, connectivity becomes a crucial resource in the emerging "global network civilization" in which "mega-cities compete over connectivity" and in which state borders are increasingly irrelevant. It is a de-territorialized world marked by conflict over internet cables, advanced technologies and market access; a new world where novel energy solutions and innovations more generally eliminate the need for resource wars:

> The 21st century will not be a competition over territory, but over connectivity – and only connecting American cities will enable the United States to win the tug of war over global trade volumes, investment flows and supply chains. More than America's military grand strategy, such an

economic master plan would determine if America remained the world's leading superpower.

(Khanna 2016a)

This view of the world goes to the heart of what in the book at hand is conceptualized as the geopolitics of the knowledge-based economy. From the perspective of "connectography", national interest is today defined differently than in the past, both socially and spatially. It is a new world in which the state is not only challenged, for instance, by global cities, global city-regions and megaregions (for a discussion of these, see Harrison and Hoyler 2015; Moisio and Jonas 2017), but also re-constructed through these spaces. It is a world in which large cities and urban agglomerations are conceived as crucial sites of a new type of global governance. So pervasive has the hub-centered imaginary grown that scholars are increasingly comprehending the new social organization of the world as indicative of a geopolitical shift from sovereign territorial states to relational city networks (Jonas and Moisio 2016). Peter Taylor (2011, 201) states revealingly how

> The prime governance instrument of the modern world-system has been the inter-state system based upon mutually recognized sovereignties of territorial polities. It is possible that we are just beginning to experience an erosion of territorial sovereignties and their replacement by new mutualities expressed through city networks. This is what the rise of globalization as a contemporary, dominant 'key word' might be heralding.

These processes may already be under way. But the preceding articulation is also a form of productive power: it reveals some of the dominant ways in which political agents in the OECD sphere in particular comprehend the transformation of global political conditions in the age of globalization. These agents also act upon such a comprehension. In other words, the "connectography" view of the world is in essence a geopolitical one, and it plays an increasingly important role in the context of contemporary strategies and ideas of state territorial restructuring.

I will argue that the hub and flow imaginary is at the heart of contemporary geopolitics. The link between these imaginaries, knowledge-based economization and the restructuration of the state is however rarely debated. This is the case because the geopolitical is often seen to be separate from the issue of regional development and policy, and because the distinction between geoeconomics and geopolitics is still pervasive. Furthermore, the economic geographical literature since the 1990s has more or less naturalized the relational view that the shift toward a knowledge-based economy implies that the capability of regions and their nodal cities to support learning and innovation is a key source of competitive advantage of the state or nation (for a useful discussion, see MacKinnon, Cumbers and Chapman 2002).

The economic geographical understanding of the hub and flow nature of the contemporary world has played a tremendously productive role in the political–economic developments that have taken place during the past three decades. This understanding is driven in particular by the needs of the purportedly knowledge-driven and conceivably global (understood often as existing above the nation state) economy. This is also disclosed by the fact that new urban formations and associated social experiments have been given a prominent place in the political and policy agendas in the OECD states and beyond during the past decades.

One of the key claims of this book is that the contemporary geopolitical condition is characterized by two processes and related imaginaries. The first is centered on issues of territorial power and the associated purportedly old-fashioned territorial power plays which take their motivation from military strategy, natural resources and territorially rooted identity politics. The second is structured around "hub and flow imaginaries" concerned with the state and world that seem to make state territory and military conquest increasingly obsolete. This process and related imaginary touch less on natural resources and military calculation and conquest but also contain a significant amount of territorial politics: it can be understood as a historically contingent process to produce territories of wealth, security, power and belonging. More importantly, the twin processes of the contemporary geopolitical condition are not mutually exclusive but take place simultaneously and may be entangled – generating various context-specific spatial formations, as well as tensions and contradictions. In other words, territorial competition and the purportedly liberal world of knowledge-intensive capitalism are not mutually exclusive but rather parallel developments that co-constitute the contemporary geopolitical condition. In sum, it is analytically untenable to conflate the ongoing territorial power plays solely with the ostensibly geopolitical world of the twentieth century, but it is equally problematic to comprehend the contemporary processes associated with hubs and flows as signaling some sort of post-geopolitical "geoeconomic" condition. Questioning the teleological explanation of the progression toward the post-geopolitical geoeconomic condition is the first prerequisite for analyzing the geopolitics of the knowledge-based economy in general and knowledge-based economization in particular (Sellar *et al.* 2017).

This book seeks to geopoliticize the purportedly geoeconomic present, particularly as it unfolds in the strategies of knowledge-intensive capitalism and associated societal developments. The goal is therefore to conceptualize the geopolitical in a manner that highlights the entanglement of the economic and the political. I go on to argue that one of the critical challenges of contemporary critical urban and regional studies is to conceptualize the focal geopolitical constituents of the ongoing knowledge-based economization, since it is arguably this facet of the contemporary geopolitical condition which furnishes the very rationale for many of the key contemporary processes and reforms of foreign policy, as well as regional and urban development and planning.

My approach is characterized by what might be called a method of constant observation. The analysis in the chapters which follow is informed by actively experiencing and observing the rapid emergence of the discourses, practices, subjects and various material dimensions of the knowledge-based economy in the Finnish and in a wider European context for almost two decades. There is arguably much relevance in the Finnish context with respect to the wider geopolitical theorization of knowledge-based economization. First, it represents a geographical "site" where the governments since the 1990s have operated on the basis of a view that intangible assets and related innovation capital are the primary drivers of economic growth and national success (see, e.g. Ståhle 2016). So pervasive has the idea of an innovation–led growth been in the Finnish context that it is today a commonplace to argue that Finland has gone through agrarian and industrial stages and is now witnessing a stage of development which is characterized by a society of services, knowledge and experiences.

Second, Finland has been, for quite some time already, internationally acknowledged as an exemplary "information society", combining aspects of the neo-corporatist welfare state and knowledge intensive capitalism. Manuel Castells and Pekka Himanen (see, e.g. 2004) have made the "Finnish model" popular in their writings which highlight Finland as a sort of political business site which is characterized by exceptional rates of innovation. Third, the development toward a new society in Finland has been very rapid. Indeed, as Mulgan (2009, 2) writes, "Finland began the 1990s with its GDP declining by 7 per cent in a single year but ended it as a technological powerhouse". Fourth, it is often retrospectively highlighted that in the Finnish context the knowledge-based economy was constructed as a sort of national survival strategy (cf. Castells and Himanen 2004) and that this strategy proved to be very successful for a "small state".

Finally, what makes this context interesting is also that a rapid restructuring of the knowledge-intensive and high-technology dominated economy has taken place in Finland since 2007. This process has severely affected numerous locales, the national economy and the subjects of knowledge-intensive capitalism. As part of this process, the life of skilled labor has become increasingly characterized by job insecurity, and many of the Finnish locales have experienced deepening economic and social problems.

But simultaneously with these rather challenging developments caused by economic restructuring, a new and a more pervasive form of knowledge-based economization has emerged both in Finland and in many other geographical contexts. Accordingly, Finland is in the process of moving through the different stages of knowledge-intensive capitalism. It was first at the stage of producing the requisite machines and technologies. Second, it entered a new stage which was characterized by earning through the use of information and communication technologies. According to the narrative, the entire nation state now seeks to enter the third stage in which economic success is based on a kind of omnipresent entrepreneurship, digitalization, global orientation and the production of ideas which sell. This latest phase is articulated as a new start-up culture or start-up economy and the associated capability of the new growth-oriented entrepreneurs to commodify digital formats and contents (a kind of copyright economy based on the internet) as successful businesses for the success of the nation state. What is interesting in such a narrative on the shift of the political community called Finland from technology to content is that it gives rise to new city-and metropolis-centered spatial imaginaries of the state. Indeed, the start-up phenomenon is more often discussed and measured in the context of cities than states (see, e.g. the Startup Cities Index by Nestpick).

As there have been many different state developments in history that may be subsumed under the heading "Keynesian welfare state", there are equally many "knowledge-based economies". In order to trace some of the common geopolitical constituents of knowledge-intensive capitalism, I do not limit my analysis to the Finnish case. I also elaborate a particular type of geopolitical knowledge-production by branded international guru scholars and highlight the constitutive role of this knowledge-production in the wider process of knowledge-based economization. I thus argue that within such knowledge-production certain seductive concepts and guiding imaginaries have condensed together as powerful discursive "instruction sheets" (Blyth 2013) and have become powerful manuals that contribute to knowledge-based economization in different geographical contexts.

Highlighting the geopolitical in the context of knowledge-based econo-mization underscores that such an economy is neither apolitical nor a process whose final form is predestined. Rather, it can be understood as a geopoliti-cal structuration which is premised on certain ways of knowing and thinking about the way the world works and how the world should work. It is for this reason why "knowledge" has three meanings in the context of knowl-edge-based economization. First, knowledge refers to the role of ideas and related innovations in generating value in the production chain. Second, the attempts to commodify knowledge are coupled with knowledge-production by experts, professionals, academics and institutional actors on the knowledge-intensive form of capitalism itself. This knowledge-production plays a cru-cial constitutive role in knowledge-based economization. This is why Jessop (2005) connects the knowledge-based economy with what he calls a new economic imaginary which has performative and constitutive force. Third, knowledge refers to the ceaseless gathering of data on the development and performance of political communities as knowledge-based economies. This data is constantly employed in policy-making and territorial governance of political communities.

The discursive power of the knowledge-based economy is partly based on an active but not autonomous agency which tends to reify the imaginaries of the envisioned future systems of capital accumulation as if they already existed. The knowledge-based economy is hence tremendously future oriented in its representational aspects. The ways in which the knowledge-based economy is scripted at present as a future-oriented strategic world in which actors need to internalize particular types of action or conform to certain types of spatial understandings are hence crucial research foci of the book at hand.

The structure of the book

The present book examines the geopolitical constituents of knowledge-based economization in different kinds of social practices and through particular ideational elements. It also scrutinizes the subtle ways in which the knowledge-based economy seeks to affect the interior lives of citizens through, for instance, higher education.

The book proceeds through eight chapters. Chapter 2 integrates key ideas and literature from various fields and offers conceptual clarifications of what I call knowledge-based economization. The chapter thus brings together elements from discursive and material readings of the knowledge-based economy and concludes with a consideration of the cultural political economy approach (see, in particular, Sum and Jessop 2013), which can be understood as a central theoretical foundation of the book at hand. Chapter 3 discusses the relationship between knowledge-based economization and the increasingly transnational state apparatus. Chapter 3 also lays a foundation for comprehending the geopolitics of knowledge-based economization through three constitutive dimensions: geopolitical discourses, the production of geopolitical objects in calculative practices and geopolitical subjects. As such, Chapters 2 and 3 establish a theoretical and methodological framework for the book.

Chapter 4 begins the analysis of the constitutive role of expert knowledge-production in knowledge-based economization. It scrutinizes the founding geopolitical discourses of the knowledge-based economy through an interrogation of imaginaries of territorial competition, competitiveness and global value chains. These discourses profoundly constitute knowledge-based economization as a major spatial accumulation strategy. In order to accentuate this claim, Chapter 4 interrogates Michael Porter's seminal contributions on the ways in which political communities succeed in generating competitive advantages in the age of knowledge-intensive capitalism. One of the goals of the chapter is therefore to demonstrate that management knowledge and related ideas have not only been disseminated into the realm of politics during the past decades, but also that management knowledge and related ideas are in itself deeply geopolitical by nature.

Many of the theories of knowledge-intensive capitalism actually argue that the transformation from "industrial societies" to "knowledge societies" also indicates a shift from particular survival values to more individualistic and entrepreneurial values of self-direction (e.g. Inglehart and Wetzel 2010), or that developing a society under the knowledge-based economy actually requires the emergence of a new type of political subject or human figure (e.g. Castells 2005). Chapter 5 scrutinizes geopolitical subjects of the knowledge-intensive form of capitalism. By using the concept of the geopolitical subject, I refer to an organized set of human figures, understood to be equipped with particular desired skills, behaviors and orientations which can be harnessed in the production of territories of wealth, competition, status, power, security and belonging in the context of knowledge-intensive capitalism.

In the process of knowledge-based economization, the skill problem hence appears like a society-wide 'we' concern (Jones 2008, 391). The process of knowledge-based economization involves re-working people's conduct, perceptions, actions, motivations, skills and weaknesses vis-à-vis the purported requirements of global competition. In Chapter 5, I underline the constitutive interplay between knowledge-based economization, subjectivity/subject formation and political space, and thus elaborate the ways in which the "useful" citizen-subject is geopolitically positioned in knowledge-based economization. I approach the above-mentioned thematic through the well-known academic theories of Manuel Castells on the nature of the networked world in the age of knowledge-intensive capitalism and concomitant technological advances.

Chapter 6 turns to the geopolitics of the knowledge-based economy in higher education, and furthers the analysis of the production of geopolitical subjects as a central issue in knowledge-based economization. Higher education is here understood as a site in which subjectivities are reshaped through participation in a geopolitical assemblage (cf. Dittmer 2014, 495). Institutions of higher education are in the post-Fordist economy often considered fundamental sites within which human capital and related subjects and subjectivities (capitalist laborers) are forged both for the purposes of knowledge-intensive capitalism and the state. Indeed, the reshaping of subjectivities vis-à-vis the knowledge-intensive form of capitalism is arguably one of the central processes of contemporary state spatial transformation. In order to exemplify the interplay between geopolitical subjects and the knowledge-based economy, Chapter 6 examines the ways in which nationally scaled professional citizens have been qualitatively re-inscribed within new spaces of higher education in Finland.

The case of Aalto University is analyzed to demonstrate the fundamental role of higher education within the knowledge-based economy and its re-territorialization. Chapter 6 demonstrates how previously nationally scaled Finnish universities are in a process of being turned into transnational sites of learning – while still paradoxically serving national–territorial interests. The chapter thus provides an example of the kind of back-and-forth remaking of political spaces and associated subjectivities that characterizes the geopolitics of the knowledge-based economy.

Instead of juxtaposing mobility, flow and change of the urban space with the purported fixity of the territorial state, Chapter 7 discusses city–state relations through some of the highly popular urban theories of the link between creativity, knowledge and the post-Fordist capitalist era. I first go on to conceptualize "city geopolitics" before interrogating Richard Florida's theory of the creative class from a geopolitical perspective. I argue that pervasive ideas such as creative class or creative city are not objective universal markers of progress but rather contribute geopolitically to knowledge-based economization. I analyze the ways in which cities and knowledge-based economization come together and inquire into the ways in which the theory of the creative class constitutes the purportedly knowledge-intensive form of economy geopolitically. This chapter also includes an analysis of the Solomon R. Guggenheim Foundation's attempt to build a museum in Helsinki, and the peculiarities of this project from the perspective of knowledge-based economization. Chapter 7 closes with a discussion of the spatial efforts to constitute the EU as a knowledge-based economy. It builds on the previous work which has examined political space making in the EU context from the perspective of governmentality (see, e.g. Barry 1993; Moisio and Luukkonen 2015).

The concluding chapter presents a synthesis of the two forms of the geopolitical which characterize the contemporary condition: "territorial geopolitics" and "geopolitics of the knowledge-based economy". The final chapter also singles out the basic geopolitical dimensions of the knowledge-based economy. Furthermore, it discusses the relationship between neoliberalization and knowledge-based economization, and makes some notes on the limits, possible policy failures, tensions, contradictions, crisis tendencies and issues of socio-spatial equality inherent in knowledge-based economization. This question is pertinent given that as "knowledge" has become the key "resource" in efforts which seek to secure territorial competitiveness and maximize wealth creation, we may be witnessing the rise of a tyranny of a particular type of social relation related to the generation and use of knowledge. This tyranny may well emerge within the multiform processes of harnessing knowledge and skills (human capital in a broad sense), as well as in related practices of education and work which serve the needs of the market players.

2 Three readings of the knowledge-based economy

From economy to economization

This chapter acts as a springboard to Chapter 3 which will inquire into the geopolitics of knowledge-based economization. It would be altogether impossible, I believe, to deal with the geopolitics of knowledge-intensive capitalism without first delving into the concept of the knowledge-based economy. This economy is, as will be shown, not only a capitalist social formation but also an inescapably political process which structures socio-spatial practices, related political decision-making and different kinds of strategy work across multiple scales and sites. This kind of knowledge-based *economization* structures the ways in which political actors perceive what drives economic growth and development, as well as overall societal development, and how these actors seek to enhance, regulate and govern this "economy" (cf. Leslie and Rantisi 2012, 458). The knowledge-based economy has thus gradually become a sort of inescapable condition and a global social fact. In this capacity, it fundamentally influences policymaking.

The knowledge-based economy can be understood and defined in several ways. It is abstract yet concrete, a thing and a process, structured by practices and structuring practices, imagined and material, theorized and experienced. It refers to knowledge-intensive capitalism which has been debated under many other rubrics such as knowledge capitalism, learning economy, new economy, information economy, creative economy and knowledge economy (for altogether 57 different definitions of the knowledge-based economy, see Carlaw *et al.* 2006). The goal of this chapter is not to find the best definition of the concept of the knowledge-based economy in the academic literature or to correctly present its development path in academic and policy discourse from the 1950s onwards, a task which has been undertaken elsewhere (see, e.g. Peters 2009). What seems to be typical of the many academic and policy definitions is however that they tend to

> highlight the growing relative significance of knowledge compared with traditional factors of production – natural resources, physical capital, and low-skill labour – in wealth creation and the importance of knowledge creation as a source of competitive advantage to all sectors of the economy, with a special emphasis on R&D, higher education and knowledge-intensive industries such as the media and entertainment.
>
> (Peters 2009, 4)

In this chapter, I seek to build a foundation for the concept of knowledge-based economization. For this purpose, I elucidate the various processes, discourses and imaginaries of the knowledge-intensive economy through an inquiry into a selective set of literature which either implicitly or explicitly discuss the knowledge-based economy as a particular economic and political order. I highlight throughout that knowledge-intensive capitalism is constituted, through discourses and practices, not only as a particular kind of novel economic strategy but also, and perhaps more importantly, as a political process with enormous societal and socio-spatial implications. I use the concept of knowledge-based economization to refer to this process. As a future-oriented political–economic process, knowledge-based economization affects the everyday lives of people as well as institutional structures within firms, states, cities and regions.

Within the following pages, my aim is to tease out some of the basic dimensions of knowledge-based economization. In order to make sense of the unavoidable complexity, ambiguity and slipperiness of the concept of the knowledge-based economy in both scholarly and policy discourses, I address three partly overlapping ways to comprehend it as a particular process of economization. I begin by discussing such an economy as a discursive construct. This is then followed by an examination of the knowledge-based economy as a material process. Thereafter, I will scrutinize knowledge-intensive capitalism from the so-called Cultural Political Economy (CPE) perspective. The latter approach brings together the discursive and the material and can be understood as a loose theoretical-methodological frame through which the concept of the geopolitics of the knowledge-based economy is developed in subsequent chapters.

The knowledge-based economy as a discursive construct

As a process, knowledge-based economization proceeds through the practices of knowledge production by multiple actors operating within and through different institutional settings. These actors range from individual academics to powerful think tanks, business associations and international organizations. From this angle, knowledge-based economization can be dated back to the early 1990s. This was also a decade when academic scholars not only started to associate the term "knowledge economy" with "a new economic era" but also began to articulate its fundamental components and statistical features as an actually existing economy.

Interpenetration of scholarly concepts and policy discourses

The 1990s was a decade which witnessed the interpenetration of policy discourses and the theoretical discourses of the knowledge-based economy (see, e.g. Miettinen 2002). A kind of knowledge-based economy reportage began to circulate within a loop of expertise that brought together academics, policymakers and consultants, for instance. This was an important development in the emergence of knowledge-based economization as a social and political phenomenon: theoretical, policy-relevant and interest-driven articulations were increasingly amalgamated and began to form a sort of knowledge-based economy talk. One may thus argue that knowledge-based economization, as it gradually developed in the 1990s, was discursively produced. This production involved expert definitions and related scoreboards of indicators (Godin 2006, 21). A range of societal processes, ideas and substances such as level of education, skills, human capital, investment patterns, research and development investments and, more broadly, particular government interventions were associated with the knowledge-intensive form of capitalism in general and with the term knowledge-based economy in particular.

Even if the phenomenon of knowledge-based economization was arguably characterized by a relative conceptual fuzziness (see Godin 2006), since the mid-1990s policymakers in many geographical contexts and in many powerful international organizations have increasingly used terms such as the information economy and learning economy or the knowledge economy to guide political, social and economic strategies. Knowledge-based economization thus refers to a seemingly future-oriented policymaking which highlights the ways in which success can be both achieved and analyzed on the basis of its "knowledge-base". As such, knowledge-based economization can be understood as proceeding through a set of strategic initiatives which include the tempting promise of limitless growth: an antidote to the various material and environmental limits to economic growth which had become obvious already in the 1970s. In this capacity, the discourses of knowledge-based economization are firmly bound to the ways in which capitalism has been represented since the 1990s as the only societal system capable of providing infinite growth and profit.

The first metrics and indicators directly linked to knowledge-based economization were made by the Organisation for Economic Co-operation and Development (OECD), an organization which had identified critical problems in the Atlantic Fordist accumulation system already in the 1970s. In the 1990s, the response of the OECD to the changing economic circumstances was a recommendation to prioritize transition to the knowledge-based economy as the logical next level in capitalist development (Sum and Jessop 2013, 277). As a policy organization, the OECD, together with a plethora of international organizations and consultant companies, has hence played a pivotal role in condensing and furthering the ideational basis of knowledge-intensive capitalism and increasing its persuasive qualities as a policy paradigm. The OECD alone has produced tens of reports and hundreds of factsheets on the knowledge-based economy. In so doing, the OECD and other actors have since the 1990s fed policymakers, scholars, pundits and media a particular type of comparative information on the substances, nuances and development trajectories of such an economy across geographical contexts.

Academic circles have played a key role in the consolidation of the idea of the knowledge-based economy as a distinct system of capital accumulation.

In the 1990s, the OECD collaborated with several individual scholars whose conceptual work became central to the emergence of the idea of the knowledge-based economy. The consolidation of knowledge-based economization in the 1990s was inherently tied up with economic ideas and scholarly sister concepts of the knowledge-based economy. One central notion was the concept of the National System of Innovation, or National Innovation System (hereafter the NIS), the dynamics of which were in policymaking comprehended as the key to effectively harnessing innovation to national economies. It was through the NIS and other related concepts that the processes of knowledge-based econo-mization trickled down to policy-worlds as a constitutive statist idea, discourse and a broader system of thought. In short, from the 1990s, knowledge-based economization has been characterized by the mutually influencing and inter-penetrating theoretical ideas and policy paradigms (cf. Jessop 2008, 20).

The NIS epitomizes the discursive power of theoretical ideas inherent in knowledge-based economization. These ideas play a central constitutive role in the constitution of knowledge-intensive capitalism as a spatial phenomenon that can be acted upon. The NIS can be understood as an ideational manifes-tation of space for economy, a particular representation of space as Lefebvre (1991) would have it. The term NIS was originally developed by Bengt Åke Lundvall (together and separately with economist Christopher Freeman), who had worked with the concept already in the late 1980s and developed what would later become another widely influential policy concept: the learning economy (see Lundvall 1992).

The NIS is an example of what Reijo Miettinen (2002, 138) has referred to as a transdiscursive term. It embodies a capacity to draw together, subsume or connect seemingly separate things and knowledge in new ways. One of the key features of transdiscursive terms is their capacity to bring together or subsume the world of firms and political communities. This is an important dimension of knowledge-based economization. Miettinen argues that in the Finnish context the NIS evolved in the 1990s as a manifestation of the times, and regards the NIS as a thesis about sources of success and survival in the changing world (ibid., 139). Indeed, NIS theorizing provided policymakers in many geographical contexts with a world view and associated tenets that could be used to tailor policies for states, cities and regions in a supposedly new world of knowledge-intensive capitalism.

As a novel discursive element of the process of knowledge-based economi-zation, the NIS soon became a productive state-centered imaginary for under-standing and framing the relational spatial structure of the territorial state. It took hold as an alternative way to politically rationalize state space and its func-tional hierarchy. Already in the 1990s, the NIS was adopted in Sweden and Finland, for instance, where it arguably became one of the key ideas through which the "urban" as a state territorial issue was re-articulated and activated in regional policy programs and wider state strategies.

Although he had an official position within the institutional fabric of the OECD, in this context it is nevertheless more relevant to recognize the key message which Bengt Åke Lundvall developed in his peculiarly nation–state-centered book *National Systems of Innovation*: "the most fundamental resource in the modern economy is knowledge and, accordingly, the most important process is learning" (1992, 1). This highly state-centered argument on the fundamentally social and, indeed, political nature of the NIS would come to characterize the academic and policy discourses constitutive of knowledge-based economization for decades to come.

Why did conceptual developments constitutive of the ideas and practices of the knowledge-based economy take place in the early 1990s? Some authors have suggested that the rise of the concept of the knowledge-based economy was part of a larger discursive and material re-working of the political economy and associated social relations in the early 1990s. Accordingly, it has been seen as a political process that *manifested itself* as new economic and spatial terminology, spatial discourses and spatial practices. Some critics of the concept of the knowledge-based economy have thus pointed out that nothing tremendously novel took place in the early 1990s with regard to the centrality of knowledge in the economy and that the concept was largely aimed at directing "the attention of the policy-makers to science and technology issues and to their role in the economy" (Godin 2006, 17; see also Miettinen 2002).

It is nonetheless easy to agree with those who highlight the productive nature of the ideas, concepts and discourses related to the knowledge-intensive economy. From the 1990s onwards, knowledge-based economization has proceeded through public policymaking in many geographical contexts. The central ideas of the knowledge-based economy continue to have significant appeal among politicians, developers and planners across the globe. Knowledge-based economization therefore also refers to a peculiar discursive entrenching and to the capacity of these discourses to exclude alternative ideas as representing irrational behavior or negative development (cf. Laclau 1990). In this capacity, the discourses of knowledge-based economization form a regulative structure which conditions policy practices across many geographical contexts. As a result, the knowledge-intensive economy is politically understood and framed as "the only option". In other words, even if one may justifiably argue that the concept of the knowledge-based economy itself has remained analytically fuzzy and all-encompassing, or that it is merely a label or rhetorical concept, as a family of political ideas and processes knowledge-based economization embodies tremendous power and societal relevance.

The unique conceptual fuzziness of the knowledge-based economy and its sister terms is indeed constitutive of the power of knowledge-based economization. Knowledge-based economization has major implications with respect to the ways in which societies are conceived, planned, designed and re-worked both socially and spatially. As Godin (2006, 23) correctly argues, the knowledge-based economy is not only fertile theoretically and empirically for many contemporary scholars who practice mainstream economic analysis but also hugely relevant politically because it can be used for any issue of science and technology and for society more generally.

The above arguments point to the fact that knowledge-based economization can be understood as referring to both a historically contingent system of accumulation and a discursive process. A discursive reading of knowledge-based economization considers knowledge-intensive capitalism as a process that integrates institutional as well as administrative mechanisms with the production of knowledge. In such a conceptualization, knowledge-based economization renders the social reality of a given political community in a particular way.

Even though knowledge-based economization is a political phenomenon which has no clearly identifiable command centers and yet seems to be almost omnipresent, Western Europe and North America have functioned as the key geographical contexts of its discursive production and institutional bolting. The OECD, the World Bank and the EU have played a crucial role as well. Even individual universities such as Harvard University can be identified as particularly significant hubs in the process of knowledge-based economization. And in many geographical contexts, fostering innovation-led economy became a sort of policy common sense in the late 1990s.

The basic discursive components of knowledge-based economization have remained relatively intact since the 1990s. The 1990s was characterized by discursive construction of knowledge-intensive capitalism, which took place within a gamut of state-authored restructuring projects which strongly emphasized science and technology. During the past decade or so, this has been followed by a period of continued consolidation of these technological and science-centered discourses in various political projects across scales and sites. But the discourses of knowledge-based economization have also been slightly reformulated in such a manner that today they permeate a broad spectrum of social practices beyond purely technological and scientific matters. The contemporary discursive omnipresence of knowledge-based economization can hence be regarded as a significant source of its political–economic power. In a sense, knowledge-intensive economy has been normalized, routinized and depoliticized, and has fundamentally expanded beyond technology and science circles.

As part of the process of normalization, knowledge-based economization has gradually become more pervasive, all-encompassing and ubiquitous in the context of accumulation strategies but also in the context of managing and re-working political communities and producing human subjects and human capital. Thus, if knowledge-based economization of the 1990s represented a particular state-orchestrated, firm-supported and technology-driven attempt to respond to an economic (growth) and political (legitimacy and governance) crisis through "pure science and innovation", the 2000s have witnessed a profound stretching of the policy repertoire of this economization.

As a discursive process, knowledge-based economization has a self-actualizing quality. It produces a world which the discourses of such economization present as inevitable and which thus depoliticizes attendant societal development (see Moisio and Kangas 2016). The discourses of knowledge-based economization thus project a particular kind of future of necessity that is rooted in a conceived crisis of the present. In this capacity, the various structured projections of the knowledge-based economy have inspired (and imposed) many far-reaching political programs of state spatial restructuring across a great number of regions and localities and thus set limits to policy thought and action. Nonbelievers of the knowledge-based economy are often dismissed as representing a false understanding and outmoded interpretation of the present.

Some discursive specificities of knowledge-based economization

As a dominant discursive process of state policy at least in Western capitalist polities since the mid-1990s, knowledge-based economization has some specificities which reshuffle the relationship between the state, regions and places. As such, this discourse shapes spatial policy paradigms and policy fields more broadly (cf. Jessop 2008).

One particular discursive element of knowledge-based economization has remained largely unchanged and unchallenged. Since the 1990s, knowledge-based economization as a set of social, discursive and calculative practices and interwoven representations, as well as material arrangements, has been essentially connected to the issue of economic growth. In the 1990s, knowledge-based economization was already premised on particular theories of economic growth which take "knowledge base" as an important factor of production. Already in the 1990s, a standard OECD definition framed knowledge-based economies as "economies which are directly based on the production, distribution and use of knowledge and information" (OECD 1996, 3).

The discourses of knowledge-based economization are therefore first and foremost geared around the issue of innovation-led economic growth. The dominant theories on the growth of national economy since the 1920s up until the 1980s were typically predicated on the idea that the construction and effectiveness of production is based on bringing together labor, natural resources and capital through available technologies. The dominant theories of economic growth from the 1990s onwards have, in turn, highlighted the sheer importance of human capital and knowledge creation in particular as both the central means of production and as the end products on which economic growth and the success of the national economy are premised. Human capital and the issue of productivity have also been tightly tied together (see, e.g. Porter 1990). Both scholarly and public discourse thus often portray the knowledge-based economy as denoting an economy in which a significant share of the employees (often more than 40 percent) are working in high technology manufacturing and knowledge-intensive services, and in which the number and proportion of high-skilled jobs is rising. Since the 1990s, telecom, software, biotechnology, research, financial services, aerospace, health and educational services and many more, have become typical sectors in these framings. In the 2000s, these sectors have been forcefully accompanied by economic sectors that together form the so-called "creative economy" (for an interesting narrative on the rise and significance of this economy, see Howkins 2001) or even "start-up economy": advertising, toys and games, video games, film, fashion, design, crafts, art, architecture, TV/radio, software, publishing and performing arts. Some of these sectors have become pivotal constituents of the emerging entrepreneurial start-up politics which highlights the capacities of individuals to exercise their imagination "fully" and to exploit its economic value. Indeed, the rise of the start-up politics in the 2000s marks a qualitative shift within knowledge-based economization, and denotes an increasingly intensifying relationship between human "creativity" and economic value.

The public and scholarly discourses constitutive of knowledge-based economization more often than not underline the primacy of the private sector in the economic success of political communities. Rising employment in the financial services sector, particular skills of population, booming high tech industry, the ICT sector, media and the associated new media economy, broad cultural entrepreneurship, as well as "lifelong learning" (Jones 2008, 387, 394–395) are often picked up as indicators of success within the discourses of the knowledge-based economy.

Moreover, the discourses of the knowledge-based economy highlight the strategic role of higher education institutions and the production of scientific knowledge in generating both economic and political success. Knowledge-based economization thus connects institutions of higher education firmly with the process of endless innovation. In an age of financial instability, sagging production, credit crises and deepening environmental problems, the strategic role of institutions of higher education has only heightened. In the 2000s, and particularly since 2008, the discursive power of knowledge-intensive capitalism has thus become increasingly evident in the ways in which universities and even individual disciplines, and the "intellectual capital" they produce, are being explicitly positioned as particular agents for both the conceived and real needs of the knowledge-based economy as well as the associated production of innovations. A particular consensus as to the "primacy of ideas" as the key source of innovation and productivity is thus located at the heart of knowledge-based economization as a discursive phenomenon (Peters 2009). The White Paper *Success as a Knowledge Economy* published by the British Government in 2016 revealingly states how "for every £1 spent by the Government on research and development, private sector productivity rises by 20p annually, by perpetuity" (The British Government 2016, 16). Universities have also sought to conform to these new circumstances, and have thus gradually occupied a qualitatively new position within state strategies in the knowledge-intensive system of accumulation. In other words, universities in different geographical contexts have begun to articulate themselves as if they occupied a central structural position within a new kind of inter-state competition and associated economic restructuring.

The materialist reading of the knowledge-based economy: the urban landscapes of technopolization and beyond

The knowledge-based economy may be considered as an active attempt to move from one industrial mode of organization to another (cf. Tremblay

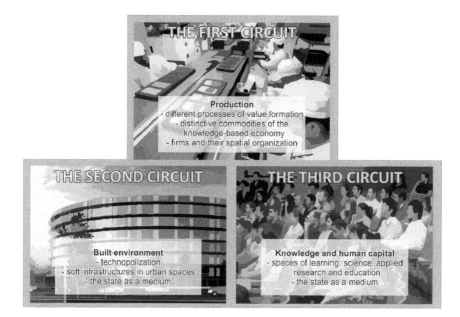

Figure 2.1 The three circuits of the knowledge-based economy.

1995). As a material process, knowledge-based economization hence needs to be elaborated upon in the context of the capitalist mode of production. In such a view, the knowledge-based economy is an economic and political process. It is a more or less coherent and concerted effort to respond to the crisis tendencies of capitalism – over-accumulation and attendant falling rates of profit, most notably – which surfaced on both sides of the northern Atlantic in the 1980s. The materialist ideas concerning the circulation and accumulation of capital seem particularly relevant when parsing together the various elements through which the knowledge-based economy can be understood as an actually existing system of accumulation. This essentially relates to the notion of the three circuits of capital (see Harvey 1978; 1985), each of which can be comprehended as separate yet overlapping and entangled dimensions of the knowledge-based economy. Each of these dimensions will be briefly elucidated in the following pages (Figure 2.1).

The first circuit and knowledge-based economization

Within the capitalist mode of production, the capitalist class operates with money to buy things such as machines, labor force or natural resources in order to produce commodities. These commodities, in turn, are sold in order to generate surplus value or profit. The same process of surplus value creation may take place through a circuit of capital within which a portion of the profits are further invested in commodities (labor power and means of production) with the intention of producing additional profit. What arises from this process is the so-called primary or first circuit of capital (Harvey 1978).

Already in the 1990s, the rise of the knowledge-based economy was associated with (a certain class of) commodities, ranging from cellular phones and computers and related microelectronics devices to advanced materials, bioelectronics and products of the pharmaceutical industry, for instance. In many geographical contexts within the OECD sphere and beyond, the production (including the mechanical assembly of products) of these conceivably "high tech" commodities was understood to signal the rise of a new economic condition. With regard to the production of these commodities, major changes however started to take place in the 1990s when multinational corporations began to relocate their investments in fixed capital. Because of the coercive laws of competition, many multinational firms invested increasingly in geographical contexts where the sufficient skills to assemble high-tech products were available but at much lower costs compared with so-called Western industrial societies. This process brought about an enormous geographical dispersal in the production process of the typical commodities of the knowledge-based economy. At the same time, the knowledge-intensive research and development activities that are linked to these commodities, as well as the related knowledge-intensive business services, began to concentrate geographically.

Within the Western industrial states, the geographical reorganization of production prompted inter-spatial competition over investments in the upper rungs of the production process in which significant portions of surplus value are produced. As a result, this competition has conditioned the location of activities related to research and development, design and marketing, for instance, and has moreover manifested itself in investments in various built environments across a variety of geographical contexts. This connects the knowledge-based economy with the so-called second or secondary circuit of capital.

The second circuit and knowledge-based economization

The second circuit of capital refers to portions of investments that grow out of the first circuit but are channeled into the production of various physical infrastructures. These infrastructures are needed in the processes of production and social reproduction. Thus, new built environments emerge through new investment processes. This makes the second circuit of capital an overlapping or parallel process of the first circuit. Since the classical conceptualizations by both Henri Lefebvre (1970/2003) and David Harvey (1978; 1985), the second circuit of capital, and the related process of real estate and land speculation, has been commonly treated as a process through which surplus value can also be achieved.

Knowledge-intensive capitalism can be comprehended as closely interlinked with particular built environments. This does not represent an unproductive flow of capital which merely facilitates the process in the first circuit; rather, these built environments become sites of the production of surplus value. Accordingly, surplus capital is channeled into various physical infrastructures that are understood as quintessential in the knowledge-intensive form of capitalism. The construction of research and innovation centers, university campuses, technology institutes, technology parks, conference centers, high-quality office spaces, all manner of knowledge-business improvement districts, telecommunications networks, infrastructures of digitalization and various cultural spaces can also be understood as constituents of knowledge-based economization. Many of these built environments, such as the Skolkovo Innovation Center in Moscow, are initiated through a process that brings together the state apparatus and private stakeholders (see, e.g. Kangas 2013).

It is particularly notable that states (and local governments) have taken great pains to finance and guarantee large-scale and long-term projects with respect to establishing the conceivably crucial built environments of the knowledge-based economy. This discloses the fact that states remain vital institutional anchors of political power in the purportedly "global" knowledge-based economy, which is typically construed around urban agglomerations (Brenner 2004; Moisio and Paasi 2013). In the Scandinavian context, for instance, state institutions have played a significant mediating role in underwriting and enhancing flows of capital into the built environments of knowledge-intensive capitalism. As such, the built environments of the knowledge-based economy have bound together actors such as state ministries, multinational companies, local and international construction companies, real estate consultants, investors, accountants, banks and insurance companies in multiple tapestries.

The above-mentioned built environments are arguably infrastructures exemplary of what may be understood to symbolize the ongoing reign of knowledge-based economization. These highlight the ways in which the discourses of the knowledge-based economy also materialize through feedback loops as infrastructures and new technologies. These local environments are construed around broader political discourses touching upon knowledge, skills, innovation, creativity, human capital and learning. The concept of the technopole, which was popularized by Manuel Castells and Peter Hall (1994) in the early 1990s, brings together these physical constructions and wider societal discourses of knowledge-based economization. In using the concept of the technopole, Castells and Hall referred to the "emergence of a new industrial space, defined both by the location of the new industrial sectors and by the use of new technologies by all sectors" and argued that within such restructuring "cities and regions are increasingly becoming critical agents of economic development" (Castells and Hall 1994, 6–7). Accordingly, this is because cities and regions have

> a greater response capacity to generate targeted development projects, negotiate with multinational firms, foster the growth of small and medium endogenous firms, and create conditions that will attract the new sources of wealth, power and prestige.
>
> (Castells and Hall 1994, 7)

The term technopole, in a nutshell, denotes "innovative industrial milieux" which include "various deliberative attempts to plan and promote, within one concentrated area, technologically innovative, industrial-related production: technology parks, science cities and the like" (Castells and Hall 1994, 8). Even though many of the attempts to create such "specific forms of territorial concentrations of technological innovation with a potential to generate scientific synergy and economic productivity" (ibid., 10) have actually failed, the term technopole itself is very telling as a window into the world in the early 1990s. First of all, it discloses the increasing emphasis on the urban and regional in the accumulation processes of knowledge-intensive capitalism; knowledge-based economization and local growth coalitions have become seamlessly entangled over the past two decades. Second, it seems reasonable to understand the concept of the technopole as indicative of a more general process in which capitalism builds physical infrastructures appropriate to its own conditions at a particular moment in time (Harvey 2001, 247). In the widest sense, the notion of technopole can be said to incorporate the technocratic idea of human community in opposition to notions of political community.

The temporal context of the early 1990s was characterized by the local construction of the knowledge-intensive economy of innovations which involved noteworthy investments in new physical infrastructures that would signal a movement away from the resource-based and conceivably "low value" economy firmly construed around the state. The technopolization of the 1990s was thus an essentially urban process of creating new landscapes and broader technology-centered urban forms which were hoped to facilitate economic growth and symbolize new forward-looking political strategies. It is noteworthy that many state governments became thoroughly committed to the process of technopolization. It is not least because of the strong presence of the state orchestrated demand-side interventionism why the early forms of technopolization can be argued to represent Keynesian forms of policymaking and public consumption.

Since early 2000s, technopolization has gradually transformed from its late Keynesian origins toward a more Schumpeterian form. Since the late 1990s, the new urban landscapes of technopolization have been linked with the rise and geographical concentration of the so-called knowledge-intensive business services sector, which became a weighty marker of knowledge-based economization, and more recently with the more subtle forms of start-up urbanism. These services and start-up activities likewise have been construed around new built environments.

In sum, one may argue that since the earliest technopolization, the knowledge-based economy has been intimately connected to the secondary circuit of capital and to the production of concrete urban spaces and the associated urban experience. To recapitulate, knowledge-based economization also refers to materialization through fixed capital: investments in physical infrastructures of science, education and culture, and built environment more generally. These infrastructures range from the re-constructed office spaces of university researchers to large-scale urban formations and even supranational digital networks.

The third circuit and knowledge-based economization

As I argued above, the second circuit of capital brings together urban space and the physical as well as representational aspects of knowledge-based economization. But knowledge-based economization can also be fruitfully discussed with regard to the tertiary or third circuit of capital, which Harvey conceptualizes as comprising

> first, investments in science and technology (the purpose of which is to harness science to production and thereby to contribute to the processes which continuously revolutionize the productive forces in society) and second, a wide range of social expenditures which relate primarily to the processes of reproduction of labour power. The latter can usefully be divided into investments directed towards the qualitative improvement of labour power from the standpoint of capital (investments in education and health by means of which the capacity of the labourers to engage in the work process will be enhanced) and investment in cooptation, integration and repression of the labour force by ideological, military and other means.
>
> (Harvey 1978, 108)

The tertiary circuit of capital hence refers to investments in education, science and technology, research and development and to knowledge production and human capital more broadly. Again, these investments usually take place via the medium of the state. As will be demonstrated in Chapter 6, the state has a particular role with respect to the organization and management of capital flows into the tertiary circuit. The conceivably "global" knowledge-based economy is thus essentially bound to the agency of the state, and to the ways in which investments are channeled into research and development and "into the quantitative and qualitative improvement of labour force" (ibid., 108).

The third circuit discloses how one form of capital can be invested into another type of capital. Of course, the third circuit of capital should not be confined only to knowledge-intensive capitalism, which can be dated back to the 1990s. However, the massive investments in human capital and skills formation and related social experiments during the 2000s illuminate the qualitative characteristics of knowledge-based economization as a process which is predicated on enhancing the productivity of the labor force through new means. It thus seems that the knowledge-based economization of the past two decades has involved what Harvey (1978, 113) calls "sectoral switching": a detectable reallocation of capital from one sphere (fixed forms of capital) to another (e.g. education).

If technopolization, and the related innovative milieus of the "high tech industry", characterized the late Keynesian knowledge-based economization of the late 1980s and early 1990s (Rossi and Di Bella 2017), the more recent developments are manifesting in the increasing investments that seek to produce a new sort of human capital and skills. As an urban process, this gradual extending of the arrangements of knowledge-based economization can be conceptualized in multiple ways. To illustrate, Rossi (2016) argues that one of the key urban planning narratives, the smart city, has been broadened from its technology-centered focus of the 1990s to the more subtle narrative of the start-up city (which is equally technocratic and technological in nature, of course). The start-up city can thus be understood as a peculiar manifestation of the ongoing qualitative transformation of the discursive-cum-material process of knowledge-based economization. The start-up city represents the increasingly self-governing enterprise society whereby urban environments acquire renewed centrality. It discloses a broad constellation of initiatives that bring together the state, local governments, a class of self-organizing entrepreneurial societies, urban environments and multinational high-tech firms as central players. These actors are tied together by the conviction of bringing about a new kind of individualistic and entrepreneurial citizen-subject capable of self-organization, thus resulting in an extended entrepreneurialization of society.

The investments in science, education and "learning" more generally are not only fundamental to governing the processes of the second circuit of capital but are also important in qualitatively re-working the relationship between human subjects and their skills, surplus value and the technologies through which the knowledge-intensive capitalist economy operates. During the past years, significant investments in higher education have been increasingly debated in terms of their potential to contribute either directly or indirectly to the accumulation of capital. These debates, which have taken place intensely across many geographical contexts, reveal that, from the perspective of capital, some types of investments in science and education are potentially unproductive. But the sometimes heated political discussions surrounding the economic potential (nowadays often dubbed somewhat misleadingly as "social relevance") of higher education also disclose how investing in human capital is absolutely central not only in order to facilitate productivity within the primary circuit of capital. These investments in higher education are also being comprehended as pivotal in producing human subjects who are supposedly capable of generating knowledge or skills as new types of commodities that can be commercialized. The inherent challenge here is that, from the perspective of capital, some qualities of the labor can in a relatively short period of time become considered unproductive.

The new capitalist laborers of the knowledge-based economy are often produced with the wish that they would re-think the relationship between their work and wider societal developments also in transnational terms (that is, beyond the nation state) in such a manner that they would embrace a new liberal and conceivably "global" working culture. There are many possibilities to illustrate the scholarly and other debates surrounding this issue. For instance, the term "hacker ethic" (together with many related terms), as it was re-heated in the late 1990s (see Himanen 2001), is illustrative in this context as it defines the working ethics and habits of a successful capitalist laborer in the so-called information age.

Cultural political economy of the knowledge-based economy

The so-called cultural political economy (CPE hereafter) perspective provides us with a coherent way to conceptualize the key processes of knowledge-based economization. As a post-disciplinary approach to capitalist social formations, it draws on ontological realism and epistemological relativism in order to excavate the key materialist and discursive-semiotic aspects of the knowledge-based economy, and their co-evolution and confluence. The CPE thus not only highlights the material processes of the capitalist mode of production and the associated systems of regulation that have been gradually put in place since the 1990s, but it also devotes attention to the semiotic constitution and stabilization of this economy in social practices and institutional forms (see in particular, Sum and Jessop 2013). Within such a frame, much of the impetus for the pervasiveness of knowledge-based economization seems to derive from two interrelated drivers, both of which result from the political context of the early 1990s.

First, the rise of knowledge-based economization stems from the crisis of the so-called Atlantic Fordist accumulation regime which had prevailed, in a more or less coherent form, from the 1950s as the dominant system of regulation. Accordingly, there were a number of material preconditions out of which the knowledge-based economy arose as a partial and potentially unstable semiotic-material solution to the crisis of the existing system of accumulation (Jessop 2004, 160). As a material solution, the knowledge-based economy should be seen as an actually existing economy whereby

> the primary aspect of capital is the valorization of the general intellect in the form of knowledge- and design-intensive commodities (real or fictitious). This involves the production, management, distribution and use of knowledge as a key driver of economic growth, wealth generation and job creation across the private, public and 'third' sectors. In a true KBE, it is suggested, knowledge is applied reflexively to the production of knowledge and most sectors tend to become more knowledge-intensive.
>
> (Sum and Jessop 2013, 284)

This broad definition of the knowledge-based economy underscores the many visions and institutionalized forms through which this economy has manifested itself beyond the world of production, business and firms. These range from e-governance and entrepreneurial universities to intellectual property rights, smart buildings/devices, start-up culture and creative/smart cities.

Within the CPE conceptualization, the knowledge-based economy, as outlined above, sprang up from a series of attempts by state authorities, international organizations and the like to overcome the economic crises of the late 1980s and early 1990s with a fresh economic imaginary. The concept of the economic imaginary is notable in this context. It stands for a wide range of possible strategic visions in a given temporal context dealing with how to achieve political, cultural and economic success in the future. Jessop (2004, 163) points out that "economic imaginaries identify, privilege, and seek to stabilize some economic activities from the totality of economic relations and transform them into objects of observation, calculation, and governance". These imaginaries are discursively constituted and materially produced in corporations, within academia and in numerous political organizations, and constitute an integral part of the process of knowledge-based economization. At a particular rupture, when the prevailing imaginary is challenged because of the obvious crisis developments, a variety of alternative imaginaries are available. Only some of the economic imaginaries nonetheless become embedded in social practices and shape political–economic orders. These involve a particular performative force (the confluence of theoretical and policy paradigms) not least because they also affirm the material interdependencies of the capitalist system. In sum, each imaginary depicts the economic world in its own way, and those that "become hegemonic or sub-hegemonic help to shape economic orders and embed them in wider ensembles of social relations" (Sum and Jessop 2013, 265).

The key point here is that only some of these imaginaries become selected in the process of semiosis, as political forces (be they public or private actors) operate through existing institutional structures, primarily but not exclusively through state structures. The selection of particular imaginaries in turn indicates that these have been disseminated by and to central social forces. Once a given imaginary, or set of imaginaries, takes the form of a dominant imaginary, it begins to re-orient economic, cultural and political strategies and related practices. To make this happen requires that the constitutive theoretical and policy paradigms behind any imaginary are selected and retained to a certain degree. In other words, the theoretical and policy paradigms are entangled when imaginaries are translated into concrete policies, and when they hence become retained and stabilized in various forms, ranging from organizational cultures and state projects to built environments, for example.

What the above highlights is that economic imaginaries are potentially productive in the context of the structuration of social practices. Since the 1990s, knowledge-based economization has been furthered through a somewhat coherent set of political and economic strategies and projects, as well as related visions which guide and reinforce the legitimacy of particular political and economic actions (Jessop 2004, 168). This particular knowledge-based economy imaginary was hence selected over many other possible imaginaries as the fundamental basis of macro political strategies in many geographical contexts. It has been structured in the policies of competitiveness, for instance, and in particular social forms such as legislation, and even in built environments such as university campuses. Since the 1990s, the structuration of the economic imaginary of the knowledge-based economy has in many geographical contexts proceeded to the extent that it can be argued to be a more or less distinguishable accumulation regime and a form of regulation (cf. Jessop 2004). The knowledge-based economy imaginary has thus shaped accumulation strategies, political strategies and policymaking more broadly across many policy fields, and on many geographical scales and sites. This also explains the success of the knowledge-based economy as a strategy for appropriation. In Finland, for instance, universities have been from the 1990s onwards increasingly re-oriented to serve the interests of private capital, and hence to serve the rationality of accumulation through re-appropriating purportedly "ill-used public investments".

One particularly important aspect in the process through which the knowledge-based economy has been selected and stabilized is the centrality of the discourse of competition and competitiveness. Indeed, all definitions of competitiveness and all policy strategies of competitiveness are discursively produced. In particular, the tendency of the knowledge-based economy imaginary to universalize notions of competition and competitiveness (Sum and Jessop 2013) is at the heart of the knowledge-based economization. The hallmark of the economic imaginary of the knowledge-based economy is thus a particular discursive framing on the nature of competition in world markets (more in Chapter 4). This framing not only touches upon competitiveness on the firm level but extends the idea of competitiveness to apply to the context of various social institutions and conditions. It is hence a framing that describes competition as being about the capacities of political communities to dominate the division of labor, commodity chains and financial flows on a world scale. Within such a discourse – which has been constituted largely through theoretical academic work on competition, competitiveness and competitive advantages – the efforts of transnational corporations to position themselves within global division of labor becomes fundamentally entangled with the attempts of territorial political communities to promote their competitiveness through the production of attractive "local, regional, cross-border, national or multi-national economic spaces" (Sum and Jessop 2013, 264–265). This theoretical paradigm is often translated into a wider policy paradigm whereby it is a political imperative to modify social formations and the forms of the state in such a manner that these contribute to wealth creation in the face of international, interregional and intraregional competition. It is worth noting that it is exactly this form of policy paradigm which leads to the "discovery of triad regions, the 'region state', the 'trans-national territory', 'entrepreneurial cities' and so forth, as new phenomena and their naturalization on practical, if not normative, grounds" (ibid., 269).

From the perspective of the CPE, the idea of global competition and competitiveness of political communities is of course a simplifying reference point for orienting economic action. But its significance lies, again, in its constitutive dimension. The typical discourse of competition and competitiveness that is built into the knowledge-based economy imaginary, conditions the ways in which political and economic actors circumnavigate the purportedly global marketplace in their constant attempts to develop competitive advantages. Indeed, as Sum and Jessop (2013, 270) correctly point out:

> official economic strategies – from towns, cities and regions through national states and supranational bodies like the European Union to more encompassing international agencies and global regimes – have increasingly posited the rise of the KBE on a global scale, its centrality to further growth at all scales, and its critical role in long-term competitive advantage and sustained prosperity for new and old industries and services. This has been emphasized even more in the wake of the North Atlantic financial crisis and the Great Recession, with the promotion of knowledge-based, design-intensive or otherwise creative industries and services as the route to growth and full employment.
>
> (Sum and Jessop 2013, 270)

As regards the last quoted sentence, entrepreneurialism and entrepreneurial culture more broadly have increasingly characterized the coming together of the economic imaginary of the knowledge-based economy and the discourses of competitiveness in recent years. At a more general level, there has been an interesting confluence of the discourses of competitiveness and the economic imaginary of the global knowledge-based economy. Whereas global competitiveness in the context of the knowledge-intensive capitalist economy has been framed in various theoretical paradigms through capacities such as innovativeness, creativity and entrepreneurialism, state and other political communities are accorded a key role in implementing wide policy paradigms to promote exactly such "globally relevant capacities" in order to construct a well-functioning economic territory or territory of wealth as "information economy", "learning economy", "creative economy" or the like.

Interim conclusions: the process of knowledge-based economization

The previous three sections have laid a foundation for the concept of knowledge-based economization which highlights the political construction of the contemporary knowledge-intensive capitalist economy. When I use the concept of knowledge-based economization in the ensuing chapters, I refer to its contemporary neoliberalizing form. In this mode, knowledge-based economization represents at least a dominant approach to public policies. It may well be considered as a hegemony project of geopolitical economy (see Agnew and Corbridge 1995) which proceeds in strategic social practices and through expert knowledge claims, takes both intentional and unintentional forms, is manifested in policy-formation and is highly disciplinary by nature. Moreover, knowledge-based economization produces and defines centers and peripheries, and legitimizes certain actions, forms of reasoning and practices over others. Even if the process is partly rooted in national traditions, it also embodies particular universal "explanatory power": it narrates the reasons why the building of territories of wealth and power is in the contemporary political–economic condition more successful in one place compared to the other. Finally, because of the nature of knowledge-based economization, it generates and re-works institutional capacities.

On the basis what I have argued before, one may conceptualize knowledge-based economization as referring to

1 the political rhetoric or argumentation in which knowledge-based economy, knowledge economy, information economy or the like are referred to as societal and economic ideals;
2 the formative role of knowledge-production and related imaginaries and ideas which qualify materialities, objects, substances and devices as constituents of the knowledge-intensive form of capitalism (cf. Çalişkan and Callon 2009);
3 the production of ideas and theories in which certain human capacities, actions, orientations and behaviors are articulated as valuable in the operation of the knowledge-based economy;
4 the ways in which the knowledge-intensive form of capitalism gets constituted in the circuits of capital, and how it proceeds in the spheres of production, built environment and human capital;
5 the role and interplay of public and private organizations, governmental bodies and institutions in the constitution of the knowledge-intensive form of capitalism; and
6 the production of abstract and concrete spaces of spatial planning and development which are legitimized as meeting the demands of the material processes of knowledge-intensive capitalism.

A number of universal discursive features are inherently involved with knowledge-based economization, but which inescapably manifest in variegated ways across a range of national and local contexts. The political significance of knowledge-based economization nonetheless rests upon the effective permeation of the discourses of the knowledge-based economy throughout all policy sectors as well as throughout most fields of economic activity.

Since the 1990s, as a material and discursive process, knowledge-based economization has emerged as a response to particular social and political needs. Accordingly, the knowledge-based economy can be understood as an attempt by Western capitalist states and major international organizations connected to global capitalism to manage the economic and political crisis tendencies which emerged in the late 1980s. As a form of crisis management, knowledge-based economization was about a particular envisioning of the future system of capital accumulation, wealth creation and economic and political success. Its short history and fragmented composition notwithstanding, the knowledge-economy has proven to be a powerful discursive construct which has reshaped practices in both private and public sectors. As Jessop (2004, 168) contended over a decade ago, the knowledge-based economy has become a dominant and even hegemonic discourse

> that can frame broader struggles over political, intellectual and moral leadership on various scales as well as over more concrete fields of technical and economic reform. The basic idea is being articulated on many scales from local to global, in many organizational and institutional sites from firms to states, in many functional systems such as education, science, health, welfare, law, and politics, as well as the economy in its narrow sense, and in the public sphere and in the lifeworld.

The dominance of the knowledge-based economy would not have been possible without the leading role taken by some of the major industrial states, international organizations, such as the International Monetary Fund (IMF), the World Trade Organization (WTO), the OECD, supranational political actors such as the EU and major metropolitan regions in institutionalizing the basic discourses of knowledge-based economization. Needless to say, these political actors will continue to play a focal role as far as the future of the knowledge-intensive capitalist economy is concerned.

Two brief conclusions can be teased from what has been said in this chapter. The first of these deals with the rather ubiquitous or even omnipotent nature of knowledge-based economization. It goes well beyond the narrow economy of knowledge-intensive business practices and the processes of production. Knowledge-based economization is, obviously, about technology and related products, which also provide a sort of symbolic dimension to knowledge intensive capitalism. But it also proceeds through the built environment, which in similar vein symbolically lies at the core of knowledge-based economization. Moreover, knowledge-based economization encapsulates the whole issue of knowledge production and the related scientific and educational practices, to say nothing of the human capital produced in different institutional contexts. The latter also reminds us of the fact that the knowledge-based economy is a governmental technology which seeks to produce a particular type of human subject or capitalist laborer – information and knowledge workers – with specific skills and mindsets. In so doing, the knowledge-based economy can be regarded as a broadly societal phenomenon. Moreover, the state has remained a crucial anchor organization of knowledge-based economization, and it often acts as a medium through which the different projects constitutive of the knowledge-intensive capitalist economy take place.

Second, knowledge-based economization fundamentally re-orientates social and spatial relations and has manifested itself as a great variety of spatial experimentations and related terms such as creative city, smart city, intelligent city, triple helix, technopole, ecosystem of innovations, innovative milieu and global economic integration zone. One of the main reasons why the knowledge-based economization is ultimately about the production of spaces goes back to the fact that contemporary knowledge intensive capitalism re-writes the nature of inter-state competition or, alternatively, it adds a new dimension to it (see Chapter 4). Since 1990s, the knowledge-based economy has provided governments with a new geopolitical vision of world politics as a new sort of global space that is not about clash of civilizations or inter-state wars but rather about existential survival within global networks and associated value chains.

The root logic of this vision can be found in many academic writings in the 1990s. Consider, for instance, the vision which was provided by Manuel Castells in the mid-1990s in his attempt to describe what he identified as the emerging international division of labor. Castells ultimately produced a map in which conventional terms such as North and South would not apply. He went on to divide the world into four megaregions on the basis of the supposed capacities of the states within these regions to operate in the global knowledge-based economy: "producers of high value", "producers of high volume", "producers of raw materials" and "redundant producers" (Castells 1996, 147). This vision nicely demonstrates the wider discourses of inter-spatial competition which are constitutive of knowledge-based economization and which have much to do with the transformation toward the "competition state" (Cerny 1990) or "competitive statehood". Such knowledge-based economization has both discursively and materially affected the state structuration process in many ways, not least through muddling the conceivably domestic and the increasingly integrated transnational political and economic structures. Together with many other visions, the knowledge-based economy provides a modicum of factual solidity that a government may draw on to justify its responses to the perceived threats caused by the purportedly ungovernable global village of messy flows and networks.

3 Geopolitics and knowledge-based economization

On the threshold of the knowledge-based economy and the knowledge-based society

Peters (2007) argues that the terms knowledge-based economy and knowledge-based society come together in policy circles where the master concepts borrowed from the sociology and economics of knowledge have come to help shape and define policy templates for economic and social development and well-being. These twin terms operate like performative ideologies with constitutive effects at the level of public policy, where they come together through a set of dominant and residual ideas that more or less effectively guide the actions of both economic actors and public policymakers. In policymaking, these terms thus not only describe how the world is but also how the world ought to be.

In academic literature, the knowledge-based economy and the knowledge-based society have been widely interrogated in the fields of economics and sociology in particular. Economic geographers, in turn, have been at pains to explain the context specificities of the success and failure of the knowledge-based economy in particular places and regions, resulting in a notable corpus of research on the spatiality of innovation systems, innovations, learning and learning regions. They have also examined the shift from the post-Fordism of the 1990s to a new mode of capitalist economy. To illustrate, Allen Scott (2017, 120) writes about the rise of what he calls a cognitive-cultural capitalism. Even if this concept essentially highlights the qualitative aspects of work in both high-skill economic sectors and some low-skill service sectors, it resonates quite explicitly with the latest developments in the process of knowledge-based economization. Social geographers, in turn, have examined the social stratification of political communities from the 1990s onwards (e.g. Leslie and Rantisi 2012). Political geographers have only relatively recently started to examine the political spatiality of the knowledge-based economy (see Jones 2008; Luukkonen and Moisio 2016). This is regrettable given that knowledge-based economization is ultimately, but of course not exclusively, about the political production of spaces and human subjects.

This chapter sets an agenda for examining knowledge-based economization in a geopolitical framework. The first point here is to rid ourselves of the technological and economic imperative that is built into the concept of the knowledge-based economy, and in so doing restore the importance of politics. Hence, we must not associate knowledge-based economization narrowly with data creation, digitalization, wealth of information or information dissemination (cf. Drucker 1969), or more generally with economic and social processes which result from innovations in the field of information technologies or the so-called creative industries. Rather, and at the risk of repetition, knowledge-based economization can be understood as referring to a dynamic process which embodies certain productive power vis-à-vis political spaces and populace. Such a non-technological reading points to the inherent geopolitical processes of economization wherein the imaginaries and practices of the knowledge-based economy consolidate in spatial form in a particular temporal and geographical context (cf. Jessop 2008, 20).

In such a reading, knowledge-based economization represents a historically contingent phenomenon. One may of course argue that economy has always been knowledge-based characterized by a certain type of human innovativeness and means to maintain and enhance creative human action for various purposes. Similarly, knowledge has undoubtedly been developed and used throughout history for a variety of purposes, such as the mundane practices of governance, economy and business. However, during the past three decades a knowledge-based economization, which is associated with particular geopolitical rationalities and techniques of governance, has gradually emerged as a novel phenomenon.

Indeed, since the 1990s, the OECD sphere in particular has witnessed an unprecedented boom in re-construing cities and regions, states and even supranational polities according to the putative imperatives of the knowledge-intensive capitalist economy. As a political formation, the knowledge-based economy has therefore emerged from the 1990s onwards in tandem with both the circuits of capital and political decision making. Many governments across the globe have re-worked their strategies to meet the supposed requirements of the day. In the preface to the third edition of the *Coming of Post-Industrial Society*, Bell (1999, x) notes revealingly how "the leaders of the Western nations consider their societies to be 'post-industrial' and that the problem facing the rest of the world is how to make the transition to the post-industrial state".

The above-mentioned postulations, I hope, distance the knowledge-based economy not only from its pervasive technological-economic connotation but also from its influential developmental connotation whereby the knowledge-based economy is viewed through a ladders-of-development lens. In the developmental reading, the knowledge-based economy is understood as referring to technologically and economically advanced political units. Within these political units, dynamic firms create extra value by harnessing highly skilled and supposedly "flexible" knowledge-worker-citizen-subjects, public and private infrastructures of research and education and flexible governance structures for purposes of profit making. In such a perspective, the knowledge-based economy appears as the result of a teleological process wherein an industrial nation state takes a perfectly logical step upwards in the imagined ladders of state development and modernization. In the developmental understanding, which is conspicuous in the contemporary public discourse, political communities actually form a hierarchy within the conceived "global" knowledge-based economy in which movement up or down is ultimately based on the performance of corporations that operate within particular jurisdictions. The developmental reading de-politicizes the contemporary condition, and thus the dynamic and complex geopolitical processes involved in such economization.

The state in the polycentric world

Since the 1990s, many OECD states have witnessed an unprecedented boom in re-positioning entire nation states as knowledge-based economies, and in so doing govern economic development, political spaces and populace according to the assumed demands of this economy. Knowledge and political communities, in short, have been coupled in ways that indicate a qualitative political change of the state with respect to the capitalist processes. Innovativeness, new knowledge, learning and human capital are today viewed not only as crucial components for the success of companies but also as key resources for nation states, regions and cities wanting to succeed in the contemporary "globalization". In other words, peculiar geopolitical notions of inter-state and inter-spatial competition are built into knowledge-based economization. A world in which cities, regions, states and supranational polities are competing with everyone else for market share and market access is essentially geopolitical, albeit the logic, terminology and strategic discourses differ compared with the purportedly "earlier era" of military power and territorial conquest.

The latest round of state transformation in the OECD sphere is often studied with regard to the rise and consolidation of neoliberal political practices and related public policies (Brenner 2004; Peck and Tickell 2002). The tendency of neoliberal policymaking to favor the interests of transnational businesses and their local associates at the expense of the interests of local political communities is similarly widely reported. It is proposed in the ensuing chapters that the contemporary discourses and practices of knowledge-based economization resonate with the neoliberal developments. In the OECD sphere, the imaginaries of the knowledge-based economy often articulate critique of spatial Keynesianism and related state formations, and even of some variants of the so-called competition state. In other words, rather than changing the nature of the capitalist mode of production, the discourses and practices of knowledge-based economization have since the 1990s contributed to the gradual spatial consolidation of post-Keynesian national statehood and the associated emergence of new institutional, financial and regulatory landscapes of state power which also extend beyond state borders.

Different labels have been used to define the new geopolitical condition we are presently living through. The arguments furthered in this book may bear a family resemblance to the idea of transnational liberalism as it was discussed by Agnew and Corbridge (1995) already more than 20 years ago. By this they referred to a de-centering and de-territorializing world characterized by overlapping sovereignties and networks of power which is run by the "new ideology of the market (and of market-access)", which according to the authors is "being embedded in and reproduced by a powerful constituency of liberal states, international institutions, and what might be called 'the circuits of capital' themselves". Their focus was on politico-economic practices related to such issues as the globalization of production and finance: they debated the internationalization of the state by arguing that the link between territory and state sovereignty was rapidly unraveling, and amalgamated the rise of transnational liberalism with the then increasingly dominant role of neoliberal ideational elements. But importantly from the perspective of the book at hand, they also went on to discuss the spatiality of the rising hegemony of transnational liberalism as a network of overlapping powers and sovereignties which "define the world of internationalizing state activities" (Agnew and Corbridge 1995, 193). The following quote summarizes one of their key claims about transnational liberalism:

> The new hegemony of transnational liberalism is both polycentric and expansionist, and possibly unstable (in some respects) as a result. It is polycentric because power in the modern geopolitical economy is no longer (if it ever was) monopolized by nation-states. Economic, cultural and geopolitical power is now embedded in a network of dominant but internally divided countries (including the USA, Germany and Japan), regional groupings like the European Community (European Union), city-regions in the so-called Second and Third Worlds, international institutions including the World Bank, the IMF, GATT and the United Nations, and the main circuits and institutions of international production of financial capital. What binds these diverse regions and actors together is a shared commitment to an ideology of market economics and a growing recognition that territoriality alone is not a secure basis for economic or geopolitical power.
>
> (Agnew and Corbridge 1995, 205–207)

During the past two decades, state strategies around the world disclose a number of efforts to create seemingly non-territorial spatial arrangements with the aim of securing the basis for political power through national economic success. These strategies disclose what Demirović (2011) conceptualizes as the transnational network state. This is a state form which "consists of specific transnational state apparatuses, and on the other, it relies on regional and national state apparatuses permeated by transnational priorities and decision-making processes" (ibid., 39). In the ensuing chapters, the polycentric world is thus not understood as a field on which the state is competing for power against "regional groupings", "city regions", "international institutions" or "market players" – actors which would together or separately undermine state sovereignty. Rather, the state is comprehended as a contested terrain through which a range of political actors – be they political parties, social movements, transnational market players or international organizations – seek to extend their agendas and powers. To put it short and sweet: "the power of the state is the power of the forces acting in and through the state" (Jessop 1990, 269–270). In other words, in knowledge-based economization the state remains a key social organization whose power and agency is constituted in the web of influences and struggles of the actors of the polycentric world.

The above-mentioned perspective draws on the strategic-relational theory of the state which highlights that the state as a political and social organization is undergirded by economic processes (see, e.g. Jessop 1990, 2016; see also Kelly 1999). The state – and in some cases even a supranational polity like the EU – occupies a central stage in the socialization of economic orders. Accordingly, the state is a material consolidation of a relationship of forces which at a given time also makes it more responsive to particular strategies than others (Jessop 1990). The contextual nature of the state thus stems from the combination of forces acting in and through the state and the associated historically contingent selection and retention of policies. I argue in the following chapters that the geopolitics of knowledge-based economization signals the emergence of a transnational state apparatus as a particular relation of forces that brings together different "transnational" and "national" as well as public and private actors in the name of knowledge-intensive capitalism. The emergence of this transnational state apparatus epitomizes the ways in which the key forces of knowledge-based economization become central and form new kinds of relationships with and through the state. The power and pervasiveness of knowledge-based economization is thus dependent on the concord between the dominant forces and their accumulation strategies, corresponding state forms and related hegemonic state projects.

The issue of de-geopolitization

A scholarly exploration of the geopolitical in the context of the knowledge-based economy is long overdue. The various spatial articulations of the new technological world of hubs and purportedly slippery "soft" spaces that no longer respects state borders have been tirelessly repeated by business people, management experts, urban developers, innovation specialists, consultants, not to mention political decision makers and scholars, since the 1990s. And the closer we come to the present, the more salient these representations have grown. Analytically, what these representations indicate is that a pervasive conceptual opposition exists between the topological discourses of the knowledge-based economy and the supposedly "outmoded" territorially organized world which is characterized by resource economy, territorial sovereignty and a particular type of national citizenry. The discourses attendant to knowledge-based economization thus possess notable capacity to frame contemporary political–economic conditions and state developments as non-geopolitical. This is perhaps one of the reasons why "global cities", "innovation centers", "special economic zones", "global universities", "high-tech development corridors", "start-up spaces" and the like are rarely examined as geopolitical formations. The de-geopoliticization of the present is obviously entangled with the more general de-politicization of public policies in the OECD world. This phenomenon requires sustained scholarly attention for a number of reasons, not least because it has potential political repercussions for how spatial policy formation across the spectrum of social life takes shape.

An exploration of the phenomenon of knowledge-based economization inescapably touches upon the relationship between the state, cities, populace, the wider world and capitalism. The aim of my geopolitical reading is to disclose and discuss these relationships. Indeed, the societal power of knowledge-based economization derives partly from its capacity to introduce itself as a sort of natural force which brings about a particular type of new world and related spatial order. It is a world in which technological developments with regards to both physical and social spaces produce unforeseen political outcomes. And it is a world in which being visible and attractive, having a reputation for providing something distinctive to offer compared with other locales of the world political map, becomes a crucial component of political success and virtue. And it is a world in which examining the determinants and constituents of successful economic environments, and providing policymakers and political elites with ideational tools to build and facilitate such environments for the sake of both political success and business growth, becomes common practice for scholars of regional development, spatial planning and economic geography.

The transcendence of knowledge-based economization does not diminish but highlights the role of the state in coordinating the construction of more localized competitive advantages. In so doing, the state authorities constantly occupy a central position in coordinating "national attempts" to claim a portion of the global economic market. State authority is in such a world constantly measured and analyzed with regard to the general competitiveness it embodies. This analysis simultaneously reifies the imagery of a particular us-versus-them market-based competition. Failing to play the competitiveness game becomes depicted as nationally irresponsible and economically devastating political behavior – a symbol of government failure.

On the concept of geopolitics

The distinction between geopolitics and geoeconomics is not at the core of my analysis. It suffices, however, to say that the distinction between geoeconomics and geopolitics is problematic from many angles, not least because it implies an analytically flawed and fallacious distinction between economy and politics. In the context of the geopolitics/geoeconomics divide, the distinction between economy and politics is manifested in many ways. To illustrate, it is not untypical to argue that there are geopolitical "tools" or "means" (such as military force) that can be used for geoeconomic ends – whatever these may be. Or, alternatively, that there are economic tools, such as energy, that can be used geopolitically in the foreign policy arsenal of a given state. This latter approach draws its inspiration from the field of strategy, and has little to say about developments in capitalism (cf. Sparke 2017).

Another distinction between geoeconomics and geopolitics can be found in analyses that suggest an epochal transition from a sort of territorial-national geopolitics to (neoliberal) geoeconomics, that is, to globalizing capitalism and its expansionary tendencies. To illustrate, Deborah Cowen and Neil Smith (2009) argue that the contemporary world is characterized by a transition from the geopolitical social to geoeconomics, or, better, that geoeconomics is re-casting rather than replacing geopolitical calculation. In such a perspective, the geopolitical social reverberates with the nation–state building, nationalism and statist practices that were associated with specific governmental techniques such as the extension of social security to all citizens, as well as with the acqui-sition of territory and natural resources with the goal of accumulating national wealth. Cowen and Smith (2009) suggest that geoeconomic social forms and associated calculations are supplanting the geopolitical social in state-related practices. Accordingly, states increasingly seek to accumulate wealth through market control rather than through acquisition and control of territory (Cowen and Smith 2009, 31–32). As a consequence, the territory-resource-wealth nexus is bypassed by "non-territorial" attempts to control markets. In such a view, national territory is no longer aligned with national economic interest. The geoeconomic, in such a view, denotes the privatization of the state itself: "the state becomes an entrepreneur in its own right, a player in the market first and foremost rather than a regulator of the market's 'excesses'" (ibid., 41).

The Cowen and Smith's (2009) argument is important in that it high-lights the historically contingent production of territories of wealth as a crucial geopolitical issue. It is important to stress however that territories of wealth, power, security and belonging are also constantly produced and refashioned in the age of economic expansion, connectivity and global integration (cf. Sparke 2007). Capitalist globalization indicates neither the hollowing out of national state territories and supranational territorial arrangements, nor an epochal shift to a world of geoeconomics. Rather, the contemporary de-nationalized pro-cesses related to the hubs, flows and networks of globalizing capitalism are coupled with efforts to territorialize and nationalize such processes through political action. The materialist conception of geopolitics thus highlights the inherent tension between the social and economic logics in the space econ-omy of capitalism in the context of the state in particular: a contradiction between territorial fixity and spatial expansion which potentially undermines "any structured coherence in a territory" (Harvey 2001, 329). In such a view, geopolitical conflict is characterized less by military confrontation and more by territorial transformation and the related tension between de-territorializing/

de-nationalizing and territorializing/nationalizing processes of capitalism. A geopolitical reading of the knowledge-based economy enables one to re-think in particular the ways in which knowledge-based economization is a spatial process of state transformation.

The materialist conception of geopolitics makes the conceptual distinction between geopolitics and geoeconomics largely untenable. In such a view, capitalism is a dynamic geopolitical process that produces spaces and is re-produced through spatial configurations and human subjects. Furthermore, the restructuring of spatial configurations is motivated by historically contingent ways of comprehending the nature of inter-territorial competition and conflict, the fundamental assets in such competition and the threats a given territorial unit is facing. Geopolitics, therefore, essentially denotes the production of economic value through spatial strategies, and of harnessing this value in the constitution and maintenance of territories of political power. In short, geopolitics refers to the production of territories of wealth, power, security and belonging, as well as to the conflicts and contradictions entailed therein.

At the risk of repetition, I would like to reiterate here that geopolitics of knowledge-based economization refers to a process which produces a spatial organization and related geopolitical subjects. Specific political forces seek to build a "new economy" which is based on innovations, high value, selective state spaces and particular segments of populace. This process is strategic in a dual sense. First, it is strategic in the sense of facilitating the circulation and accumulation of capital in the contemporary historical conjuncture through the creation of certain social, educational and physical infrastructures that allow the generation of surpluses. This re-making of capitalism produces cycles of territorial transformation, which Harvey (2001) associates explicitly with the geopolitics of capitalism. I suggest that this understanding of the concept of the geopolitical also involves crucial issues such as the relationships between states and cities, between political authorities and business firms and between nationalizing and transnationalizing political–economic forces.

Second, the phenomenon of knowledge-based economization is strategic in the sense of producing political territories of competition and subjectivities which can be harnessed to the circulation and accumulation of knowledge-intensive capital. The geopolitics of knowledge-based economization thus refers to the emergence of "economic territories" as fundamental political issues. In knowledge-based economization, the qualities and effectiveness of these economic territories determine the very legitimacy of political power as well as the future of political communities as territories of wealth and power.

The geopolitical constitution of the knowledge-based economy

From the 1990s onwards, the material processes of the knowledge-based economy have been accompanied by political debates and scholarly literature on the development and nature of a new breed of territorial society. This is a telling illustration of the ways in which knowledge-based economization is extended from a world of production to a wider societal phenomenon. Network society, knowledge society, learning society and information society (for a critical interrogation of these terms, see Webster 2006) have in some respects become anchor concepts and terms in academic literature and in policy circles. Ideas on the ways in which society and the knowledge-based economy come together in the present political condition are thus not solely presented in academic literature. Different forces within state apparatus, city governments, regional authorities, diverse international actors such as the OECD, the WTO, the World Intellectual Property Organization and even transnational corporations have produced ideas on the role and meaning of this new society in the age of the knowledge-intensive and globally stretched economy. It has thus become a commonplace over the past two decades that the strategies of cities, regions, states and supranational actors explicitly articulate territorial entities vis-à-vis the knowledge-based economy. This is a peculiar process whereby different kinds of actors seek to locate political communities within the world of business firms, yet at the same time place these corporations within the fabric of political communities. This duality characterizes knowledge-based economization, and it can be easily found in contemporary state strategies across the globe.

The following quotes by the Organization of American States, the EU and the Government of Canada can be considered exemplary, definitely not exceptional, efforts to translate the knowledge-based economy into the language of territorial politics, citizenship and inter-territorial rivalry. All the quotes bring together a set of diverse elements which position a given political community as confronted by purportedly changing political–economic circumstances.

> A knowledge-based society refers to the type of society that is needed to compete and succeed in the changing economic and political dynamics of the modern world. It refers to societies that are well educated, and who therefore rely on the knowledge of their citizens to drive the innovation, entrepreneurship and dynamism of that society's economy.
>
> (Organization of American States 2014)

> The European Union is confronted with a quantum shift resulting from globalization and the challenges of a new knowledge-driven economy. These changes are affecting every aspect of people's lives and require a radical transformation of the European economy. The Union must shape these changes in a manner consistent with its values and concepts of society.
>
> (European Council 2000)

> Our vision for 2017 calls for a Canada that is known as the "Northern Tiger" due to our prowess in productivity and innovation. In the coming

decade, Canada will have seen the largest growth in productivity of any developed economy. By leveraging Canada's advantages as an open economy which supports free trade, a diverse and innovative society, a strong regulatory framework, and capacity for research and development (R&D), Canada will be seen as an attractive country in which to invest. By raising the average skill level of Canadians, we will be better prepared to transition into new jobs and markets that currently do not exist and thereby transform traditional Canadian industries through the uptake of technology. The managerial and entrepreneurial skills of Canadians will be recognized internationally.

(Government of Canada 2016)

As becomes clear in these quotes, knowledge-based economization denotes a number of things in political strategies in different contexts. What these quotes also reveal, however, is that knowledge-based economization is associated with the production of new political spaces and new kinds of political subjectivities. There are also other significant commonalities in these formulations, which bring together seemingly diverse elements such as particular understandings of the contemporary world-political condition, citizens and their skills, the role of technology, human capital and innovation in both economic and political success, as well as the importance of an "attractive society" or state and related "branding" as key factors in international competition. The knowledge-intensive form of economy therefore emerges as a core factor in defining the political ideal type through a diverse set of components. In a scholarly analysis, these need to be identified and examined as interrelated elements that are both connected and constitutive of the phenomenon of knowledge-based economization.

An emphasis on the interrelations and interactions among the different elements of knowledge-based economization obviously resonates with the concept of assemblage, a concept which has recently gained credence in human geography and cognate fields (e.g. Acuto and Curtis 2013a; Anderson and McFarlane 2011; Donovan 2016; for a critical overview, see e.g. Allen 2011) to the degree that "almost everything is today 'assembled' – made up of precarious socio-material relations" (Müller and Schurr 2016, 217). The roots of assemblage thinking are multiple and there are many ways to think with the concept of the assemblage. Rather than engaging in the debate on the nuances of the concept itself, I employ assemblage thinking similarly to Sassen (cit. Acuto and Curtis 2013b, 18–19) as an analytic tactic for singling out and bringing into focus initially disparate but actually co-functioning and co-constituted elements that play a role in knowledge-based economization.

The idea of co-constitution and co-functioning is congruent with many of the key ideas of the cultural political economy insofar as these touch upon issues such as the "discursive" and "non-discursive" as well as efforts to denaturalize economic imaginaries (for the latter, see Sum and Jessop 2013, 147–194). In such a view, knowledge-based economization evolves as a combination of material and social entities that are separable only analytically. In my usage, the geopolitical constitution of the knowledge-based economy refers to interactive "wholes" that consist of heterogeneous components such as institutions, procedures, concepts, analyses, reflections and different kinds of objects and subjects (Moisio 2015).

The geopolitical in the context of knowledge-based economization boils down to three interlinked, constitutive and co-functioning issues (cf. Dittmer 2014; Müller 2015). First, geopolitical discourses articulate the nature and logic of the conceivably knowledge-intensive world within which political communities are located. Second, objectifying calculative practices constitute and reify political communities and their components as units of competition in a global innovation game. These objectifying practices co-function with the geopolitical discourses. Knowledge-based economization thus involves analyses through which a city, region, state, supranational polity or even a university can be understood as a geopolitical unit of competition. Third, geopolitical subjects are produced in educational and other practices to align with the geopolitical discourses and objectifying calculative practices of knowledge-based economization. These three constitutive elements are bound together in the constant efforts to produce territories of wealth, power and spatial belonging, and in the accumulation and circulation of capital (Figure 3.1.). By drawing a distinction between geopolitical discourses, geopolitical subjects and objectifying calculative practices, I seek to demonstrate how ideas, practices

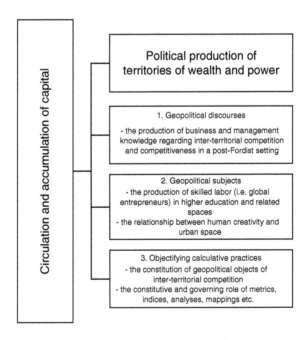

Figure 3.1 Constitutive geopolitical elements of knowledge-based economization.

and populaces come together and constitute the geopolitical in the process of knowledge-based economization.

Brief interim conclusions

What, then, is the benefit of associating knowledge-based economization with the concept of geopolitics? As Anni Kangas and I have argued elsewhere (Moisio and Kangas 2016), geopolitics serves as a necessary antidote to the highly de-politicized representations which portray the knowledge-based economy, and associated social practices ranging from spatial and urban planning to higher education policies, as a mere pragmatic and technocratic enterprise. Tracing the geopolitical in the context of knowledge-based economization accentuates the post-Fordist economy as a site of strategic action where different politi-cal forces and actors, state and non-state institutions alike, pursue their strate-gies and realize their goals. Second, the concept of the geopolitical denotes processes of re-territorialization; it motivates one to focus on the role and composition of various micro- and macro-spaces where ideas, rationalities and technologies intersect in attempts to manage flows of capital (cf. Agnew and Corbridge 1995; Kangas 2013; Moisio and Luukkonen 2015). Third, the geo-political perspective also motivates one to scrutinize the relevance of these spaces with respect to forms of geopolitical subjectivity. In so doing, a geo-political analysis of knowledge-based economization involves an interrogation of the intertwining of the spaces of capitalism with politico-legal spaces which are not necessarily conjoined in the territorial form of the state (Mezzadra and Neilson 2013).

Knowledge-based economization manifests itself as a set of political strat-egies, governmental projects and modes of calculation and analysis which "operate on something called the state" (Jessop 2007, 37). In this capacity, the knowledge-based economy is an instantiation of state power and rep-resents a kind of distributed political authority which is constituted and re-made by private actors, formal state institutions, international organizations and supranational political bodies (Sassen 2008). One may thus argue that the knowledge-based economy represents a particular institutionalization of political power relations around the state, albeit in a manner which does not resonate with national borders exclusively or with public authority solely. Rather, this institutionalization encompasses actors such as manage-ment consultants and scholars, people employed in international organiza-tions such as the OECD, civil servants working at all levels of governance, politicians, urbanists, think-tank debaters, representatives of business firms and lobby organizations. It is therefore difficult to characterize the phe-nomenon of knowledge-based economization in conventional terms such as public/private, domestic/foreign or left/right. Rather, knowledge-based economization epitomizes the ways that state power increasingly mani-fests itself as hybrid formations of private and public authority (Allen and Cochrane 2010) as well as associated spatial formations and practices. Thus policy networks, both domestic and international, are crucial in the context of knowledge-based economization, as ideas and policies as well as policy-makers and advocates travel within these networks.

Finally, knowledge-based economization is characterized by to-and-fro dynamics between the processes of de-territorialization (de-stabilization, often articulated with the concept of the global) and re-territorialization (often artic-ulated with the concept of the nation or local community). In this capacity, knowledge-based economization resonates with the notion of the transnational state apparatus (cf. Demirović 2011). Knowledge-based economization repre-sents a gradual condensation of the relations of political forces that operate on the basis of particular transnational priorities in the context of the state, cities and regions. It proceeds through projects that are predicated upon issues such as innovativeness, creativity, high-value jobs, urbanization, higher education, internationalization, globalization, flexibility and entrepreneurship, as well as through geopolitical discourses of the contemporary capitalist condition.

4 Geopolitical discourses and objects of knowledge-based economization

In 2004, I had an interesting conversation with a prominent Finnish spatial planning officer. He argued that the main goal of state-orchestrated regional planning was rapidly changing. According to the officer, all public governmental interventions were increasingly being tailored in such a manner that they would enhance the development of innovation-driven local and regional economies. This change was, according to him, the result of globalization and the related shift in the ways in which the success of nation states is achieved. This was neither the first nor the last discussion with key state policymakers in which the name of Michael Porter was mentioned, or a more implicit reference made to concepts such as clusters and competitiveness.

This chapter takes stock of the above-mentioned thematic and makes three main arguments. First, I argue that knowledge-based economization is constituted through a set of routinized geopolitical discourses which render the world thinkable and amenable to political programming in a particular manner. These discourses thus describe the spatiality of the contemporary condition in a manner which enables various actors to engage in the proverbial knowledge-intensive capitalism. They are the raw material on the basis of which the knowledge-intensive form of capitalism is practiced in calculations, metrics, indices, mappings, analyses and comparisons which, in turn, define territorial units as geopolitical objects of competition.

Second, I suggest that the popular management knowledge developed by Michael Porter and his colleagues has contributed to the emergence of the geopolitical discourses through which the process of knowledge-based economization proceeds. Given the constitutive power of these management theories, I suggest that an analysis of Porter's theories on the competitiveness of nations in particular uncovers some of the pivotal geopolitical discourses constitutive of the knowledge-intensive capitalist economy. My analysis seeks to demonstrate that these geopolitical discourses are contrived upon a unique type of spatial imaginary which diverges from the "land based" discourses that characterized most of the twentieth century. The geopolitical discourses of the knowledge-based economy portray a new relational yet territorialized spatial drama on a putative global scale. In so doing, these discourses provide a meaningful but highly demanding condition for political leaders to act upon and demonstrate their statesmanship, and for spatial planners to manage regional transformation.

Finally, I suggest that these discourses are fundamental prerequisites which make the governing of the knowledge-intensive economy possible in the first place: they translate the economy into meaningful spatial objects and economic and cultural qualities that can be managed, controlled and manipulated politically. Geopolitical discourses thus both structure and effect the ways in which the contemporary form of knowledge-intensive capitalism is conceived and acted upon in different places.

Geopolitical discourses of knowledge-based economization: production sites and actors

Knowledge-based economization does not entail a shift away from the world of geopolitics, territorial politics and power to a sort of non-spatial postmodern world of "geoeconomy" and related imaginaries (cf. Van Ham 2001, 2, 6). Rather, the knowledge-based economy is constituted within geopolitical discourses which frame territorial politics in a relational manner and which are in a co-constitutive relationship with the other geopolitical elements of knowledge-based economization.

Critical geopolitics typically aims to deconstruct the hegemonic or counterhegemonic geopolitical representations and geopolitical discourses (for a useful critique, see Müller 2008) of security and foreign policies as crafted by political elites or in popular media (ÓTuathail 1996). Perceived through a critical geopolitical lens, the spaces, objects and subjects inherent in the process of knowledge-based economization are produced discursively in representations and social practices. The knowledge-based economy is thus constituted in knowledge production, mapping exercises and strategic planning, and is practiced and acted upon in meetings, conferences and networks of action more generally. In particular, the conceivably uncertain world of knowledge-intensive global capitalism is constantly spatially ordered through analyses and associated concepts and ideas which make a connection between the putatively knowledge-intensive capitalism and territorially defined political communities.

The role of geopolitical discourses in the constitution and co-constitution of geopolitical objects and subjects of the knowledge-based economy is crucial. These discourses connect individuals and populations, along with their capacities and skills, to geopolitical objects of competition such as states, cities and regions. At the same time, the metrics, analyses, mappings, indices and other calculative practices that constitute geopolitical objects as units of global territorial competition (universities, cities, regions, states) reify and contribute to the geopolitical discourses of the knowledge-based economy. These geopolitical discourses thus provide the plot of the spatial drama of the contemporary capitalist condition and a necessary subtext on the ways in which the purported new economy represents a challenge to political communities. The geopolitical discourses and related imaginaries of the knowledge-based economy hence spatialize knowledge-intensive capitalism as a world that is characterized by specific places, populations, events, processes and founding logics (cf. ÓTuathail and Agnew 1992, 192).

A geopolitical analysis of knowledge-based economization examines how and where these geopolitical discourses are produced and how they are disseminated through actors such as scholars and other experts, political leaders, consultants, advocates and advisors, for instance (Moisio 2015; cf. Dalby 1990; ÓTuathail 1992). It hence not only scrutinizes the representations of the spatial specification of politics (Dalby 1991) but also examines the different actors who produce geopolitical knowledge in the context of the knowledge-intensive form of capitalism. A geopolitical analysis also interrogates the ways in which geopolitical discourses are disseminated in wider society through particular infrastructures such as the media. Finally, it examines the mundane enactments of geopolitical discourses in policy circles and various micro-spaces such as universities and schools.

The geopolitical discourses of the knowledge-based economy are produced by and large in certain sites, such as prestigious universities, private and public think tanks and international organizations. These sites have a clear constitutive role with respect to the ways in which the contemporary capitalist condition is understood as a distinctive spatial epoch. They are the command centers of authority which possess notable "socio-economic resources" (Agnew 2013), making their sense-making exercises influential. The actors producing the geopolitical discourses of the knowledge-based economy are thus often connected with well-known academic institutions, and their actions reflect the material structures of contemporary capitalism. In any case, these actors are not mere "mouthpieces" (Müller 2008, 326) but have a constitutive role in the process of knowledge-based economization.

Geopolitical discourses and related spatial imaginaries are produced in particular sites, but in addition there are infrastructures through which this knowledge circulates. Prestigious periodicals with a global reach, such as *Harvard Business Review* and *The Economist*, are influential because of the reputation they enjoy in the fields of business, leadership, management and policymaking. They contribute to the consolidation and routinization of the geopolitical discourses of the knowledge-based economy. These magazines form part of the intellectual infrastructure through which the geopolitical discourses of the knowledge-based economy are disseminated among various professionals, managers, business elites, officials, political decision makers and policy pundits. Since the 1990s, the geopolitical discourses of the knowledge-based economy have been circulated also in several of the classical geopolitical "airport periodicals" such as *Foreign Affairs*.

The consumption of the geopolitical discourses of the knowledge-intensive capitalist economy in turn indicates the ways in which academic and quasi-academic theories not only shape policymaking in a given locale but also how these are transformed in the context of political decision making and planning (see. e.g. Kuus 2007). This moves the point of focus away from the representationalism of the geopolitical discourse and toward "the work of discourse"

(Thrift 2000, 385), that is, toward analyzing the place-bound social practices of translation and learning of geopolitical discourses.

Geopolitical discourses of the knowledge-based economy: the role of management knowledge

Drawing on Thrift's (2005) arguments, one may propose that from the 1990s onwards, knowledge-based economization has been intimately entangled with what had been dubbed the first "concerted global discursive operation of the cultural circuit of capital" and its efforts to engender "fast thought" among policymakers and political leaders (cf. Thrift 2005, 12, 13). In such a view, the geopolitics of the knowledge-based economy does not refer primarily to the interaction between business and academia. Perhaps more importantly, knowledge-based economization has been characterized by the interaction between public authorities, the management academe and management consultants.

Arguably, a particular type of management knowledge production or management theorizing has played an essential role in ordering, reproducing and transforming capitalist social formations in the age of putative knowledge-intensive capitalism (Jessop 2004, 159). I suggest here that the geopolitical discourses of knowledge-based economization can be examined and hence brought to light through an analysis of popular management theories. Since the late 1980s, the management literature has grown in tandem with the rise of the imaginaries of the knowledge-intensive economy and has been embraced by many state and city governments, as well as agencies and political institutions such as the OECD, IMF, EU and WTO. The management literature has also extended the political and normative understanding of knowledge-intensive capitalism to the rest of the economy and across geographical and social spaces (cf. Thrift 2005). I suggest below that a particular type of management knowledge has contributed to the geopolitical discourses which re-frame territorial competition.

The geopolitical discourses of the knowledge-based economy are produced within epistemic communities which do not operate in the traditional seats of geopolitical reasoning such as military academies, security policy think tanks, international relations departments and ministries of defense. Rather, these communities operate in business and management schools and various public and private think tanks and other related organizations such as consultant companies. The geopolitical discourses of the knowledge-based economy are thus archetypically produced in elite business schools such as Stanford, INSEAD and Harvard (cf. du Gay 1996), international consultant companies with a focus on management and through the efforts of management gurus. These elite business and management schools, management consultancies and gurus produce the bulk of management knowledge central to the progression of knowledge-based economization. Within this idea industry, management professionals produce the rudimentary ideas which are effectively developed and packaged by both universities and management consultancies.

The packaged management knowledge represents lucrative business opportunities and is disseminated in periodicals, general and special media outlets, blogs, reports, books, videos and seminars, and is consumed not only by business leaders but also, and perhaps more interestingly, by politicians, policymakers and government officials. This also discloses how knowledge-based economization is constituted in the processes of production and communication of ideas.

Infrastructure such as management seminars, within which particular management knowledge and related fads are disseminated and consumed, represent a fundamental link that bridges business and government in the process of knowledge-based economization. Thrift (2005, 90) correctly argues that these seminars are a fundamental part of business life. But it is not only business leaders who use these seminars to make sense of the supposedly chaotic and confusing operational environment of contemporary knowledge-intensive "global" capitalism. Policymakers and political leaders, too, utilize seminars and conferences to cope with the purportedly fast, uncertain, complex and tumultuous political–economic condition.

Indeed, if knowledge-based economization is marked by the rise of a new breed of business leader as a "cultural diplomat" (Thrift 2005, 43), it may not be overly bold to suggest that it is similarly characterized by the emergence of management politicians and management officials who comprehend knowledge as the ultimate source of competitive advantage for political units in the age of global competition. Through seminars and other media, politicians, policymakers, administrators and officials become trained geopolitical agents who are converted to the fundamental importance of spatial and societal change in the age of knowledge-intensive capitalism. For these geopolitical agents, "accumulation becomes the very stuff of life, through persuading the population to become its own prime asset" (ibid., 94).

Management knowledge is not geopolitically neutral, and policy practices which are premised on such knowledge produce, reproduce and transform states, cities and regions. Management knowledge does not of course represent a singular body of thought. Nonetheless this knowledge is geopolitical in nature and highly subjectivating (for the formation of "economic" subjects, see Larner 2012). The management theories I refer to below constitute and legitimate some spatial policy practices and policies of citizenship while marginalizing others (cf. Clegg and Palmer 1996, 3) and are arguably central to the emerging transnational "consciousness" which characterizes contemporary policymaking communities (see Peck and Theodore 2015, xv).

Porterian geopolitical reasoning: nationalizing inter-local competition

Knowledge-based economization has proceeded concomitantly with the rise of particular management theories. Theories concerned with the management of globalizing business organizations in particular have been broadly utilized in managing political communities since the 1990s. At the same time, knowledge production that treats states, cities and regions as if these were quasi-business organizations has become salient and influential. Employing different management vocabularies in the context of political communities likewise contributes to knowledge-based economization and raises the prominence of managerial professionals and other experts of management in the governmental attempts to stabilize the conceived uncertainty of contemporary global knowledge capitalism.

Geopolitical management theories constitutive of the process of knowledge-based economization meld together innovation, entrepreneurialism, technology, information, flexibility (as opposed to bureaucracy), learning, growth and the politics of space. These theories serve as ideational frameworks which articulate the way the world works, how it ought to work and how the success of not only firms but also political communities is created and sustained in the age of knowledge-intensive capitalism.

Since influential management theories are productive in the context of knowledge-based economization, an analysis of these theories offers the potential to uncover the geopolitical discourses which are embedded in these theories. Indeed, there has been only very scant interest in a geopolitical reading of the management literature. This is regrettable given that these management theories effectively spatialize the global knowledge-based economy and articulate it as a world of its own logic and specificities. These management theories thus involve a geopolitical reasoning which rationalizes certain forms of policymaking.

The rest of the chapter elaborates the work of Harvard University Professor Michael Porter. My claim is that a Porterian form of geopolitical reasoning is an essential discursive constituent of knowledge-based economization. Porter began to articulate political communities in relation to their capacity to produce economic value in specific settings in the late 1980s, and an analysis of his work discloses the ways in which political success in this political context increasingly came to be understood as occurring through the capability of firms to produce high value and the capacities of governments to support their activities in specific locales.

Michael Porter is one of the best-known management gurus, public intellectuals and academic policy advisors of the post-Fordist capitalist condition. His work signals the coming together of notable business schools (with their skillfully commodified products), management consultancies and management gurus (as people who invent and distribute ideas, concepts and insights). The intellectual figure of Porter thus uncovers some imbricated aspects which are worth mentioning in the era of academic management gurus.

First, the work of Porter signals how effective management knowledge is grounded on a certain academic quality label. Management gurus often work as educators in prominent universities and business schools, where their students are inculcated with new ideas and insights. The prestigious university brand increases the symbolic status of particular management theories and related packaged knowledge commodities. Indeed, one may consider the 2001-founded Institute for Strategy and Competitiveness (ISC) at the Harvard Business School as the foundry of the process of commodifying, marketing and circulating the key ideas of Michael Porter and his colleagues in the worlds of business and policy. This Porter-chaired institute belongs to a continuum of development at the Harvard Business School, which already in the 1980s began to organize symposiums to promote particular strategic business planning approaches to urban government.

Magretta's (2012, 7–8) claims that "Porter occupies a unique position", that "his frameworks have become the foundation of the strategy field" and that Porter's key theories are being taught "in every serious business program around the world" may not be terrible exaggerations. Porter has been awarded, for instance, the Global Management Guru Award, the Thinkers50 Lifetime Achievement Award, and has been ranked twice on the top of the Thinkers50 biannual ranking list of the "world's most influential management thinkers" (Thinkers50 2015). In mid-2017, Google Scholar records c. 340,000 hits for Porter's publications, which makes him undoubtedly one of the most cited business and economics scholars in the world.

Second, Porter's key concepts form the backbone of a packaged management knowledge that is rather user friendly and which can be sold, circulated and consumed not only by firms but also political communities. His theory on the competitive advantage of nations, for instance, is tailored in such a manner that it "can be applied to any particular nation" (Porter 1998a, xv). Porter's key concepts and related ideas are widely accepted, adopted and applied in policy circles. One of his basic intellectual questions – "why are some countries or regions more successful than others" (Magretta 2012, 1) in innovation-driven economic development – has been particularly appealing to governments in the OECD sphere and beyond after the crisis of Atlantic Fordism.

Porter's ideas on innovation-driven growth have been widely disseminated in policymaking. Together they comprise a seemingly non-political and compact toolkit which state and local governments can use to nurture their competitiveness, productivity and economic efficiency. To illustrate, Porterian national competitiveness and cluster ideas have been discussed and analyzed in the context of Korea, Italy, Sweden, Japan, Switzerland, Germany, Britain, the US, Denmark, Germany, India, Mexico, Bolivia, Peru and Rwanda. Furthermore, Porter's team has undertaken competitiveness assessment and national studies in Armenia, Bermuda, Botswana, Bulgaria, Canada, Colombia, El Salvador, Estonia, Finland, Britain, Hong Kong, Ireland, the Netherlands, Nicaragua, Norway, Kazakhstan, Portugal, Russia, Saudi Arabia, Singapore, South Africa, Taiwan, Tartarstan, the UK and Venezuela. Moreover, Porter has conducted extensive studies of economic strategy for the governments of Canada, India, Kazakhstan, Libya, New Zealand, Portugal and Thailand (Porter 1998a, xxiv–xxv). In 2000, Porter lists economic development initiatives, based on the cluster concept, that include 29 nation states, 14 major regions, states or provinces and 11 cities or large metropolitan areas (Porter 2000, 31). The list has become more extensive since year 2000, of course.

The World Bank embraced cluster work as its core strategy in late 1990s, and numerous chambers of commerce, regional banks and city governments have circulated Porterian concepts and underlying reasonings. In 1988, Porter was recruited to President Ronald Reagan's Commission on Industrial Competitiveness, which sought to examine the national competitiveness of the US. Porter's more recent contributions to the actions of the World Economic Forum (WEF) and its national competitiveness indicators further illustrate the historically contingent and profound policy influence of his work. Since the 1990s, Porter's conceptualizations of the nature of the contemporary capitalist condition have been normalized and routinized through conferences, consultancies, books, seminars, appearances, the WEF and the like. The latter in particular has significantly contributed to the normalization and routinization of the concept of competitiveness in the context of nation states.

In sum, Michael Porter has acted as a policy advisor to tens of governments, ranging from local to supranational, and played a key role in policy networks which bring together consultants, policymakers, political leaders and the executives of international organizations and businesses. Many of the Porterian ideas on productivity, value creation, competitive strategy and clusters have become axiomatic for nation–state governments across the globe since the 1990s and particularly in the aftermath of the 2008 economic crisis. The multitude of state projects which can be connected to Porter's concepts demonstrates the applicative and flexible nature of these management fashions or "knowledge-brands" (Sum and Jessop 2013). These may function as neoliberal therapy in the context of nation states, cities and city-regions, and the same concepts can also be used to justify attempts by state governments to internationalize and de-border nation states.

The point here is not to interrogate whether the adoption of Porterian frameworks have had positive or negative economic and social impacts in different geographical contexts or whether the adoption of such expert knowledge has led to the annihilation of democratic policymaking and to the related emergence of consultocracy (see, e.g. Kantola and Seeck 2011). The nature of Porter's work is discussed in this book by virtue of the fact that it constitutes more generally many discursive elements of knowledge-based economization. His work also signals how innovation-driven management ideas cross and stretch the border between the world of business firms and political communities, and in so doing bring business and management effectively into the realm of politics and government. This is, of course, also a fundamental element in the process of knowledge-based economization.

Porter's work on the competitive advantage of nations can be considered as a sort of big bang which was followed by a mushrooming of academic scholarly literature on territorial competition and competitiveness. The conceptual frameworks and the related indices Porter and his colleagues at Harvard University and elsewhere have developed in books, articles, talks and conferences from the 1980s onwards are characterized by a notable endurance which cannot be explained without understanding the historical milieu within which these frameworks have been invented. The Porterian theories of territorial competition must therefore be comprehended as a historically contingent phenomenon.

Porter's work, which is at least loosely Schumpeterian, found a fertile ground in the context of the crisis of Atlantic Fordism and contributed to the rise of the putative knowledge-intensive form of capitalism. In other words, the Porterian geopolitical discourses provided a destination point in the new post-Fordist spatial condition to strive for at exactly the moment when the Western industrial states were experiencing low growth, high inflation and rising unemployment. Porter's work ultimately highlights the growing prominence of innovation, learning and human capital for the purposes of firms in such a manner that facilitates the production of nation states but also cities and "regions" as innovation-driven economic territories or territories of wealth.

Porterian geopolitical reasoning and knowledge-based economization

The geopolitical discourses inherent in knowledge-based economization are premised on diverse forms of idea-work and analysis which touch upon issues such as innovation, networking, learning, creativity, entrepreneurship and competitiveness in the context of territorial entities. These discourses frame the relationship between political community and political strategy in a spatial manner, and they furnish the ideational and symbolic capital that enable the political elites to act in the name of the state, city and region.

Michael Porter's work in the 1990s on the nature of territorial competition and related ideas such as the diamond model and cluster concept presumes a particular relationship between the state and global knowledge-intensive capitalism. An analysis of Porter's theories on strategy, competition and the competitive advantage of nations in particular brings to light some of the geopolitical discourses through which knowledge-based economization proceeds.

The rest of this chapter provides a geopolitical reading of a selected set of Porter's work in the 1990s and early 2000s. The focus is on texts on competition, competitiveness and the competitive advantage of nations. These works mark a transition in Porter's work from firm strategies and competitive advantages of industries and companies to the competition between nations (the so-called nation states), regions and cities. This corpus of work also marks a qualitatively new kind of Schumpeterian emphasis which places innovations and technological change at the core of the geopolitical strategy of nation states.

This shift in interest from companies to the relationship between business firms and states is most explicitly articulated in *The Competitive Advantage of Nations* (first published in 1990), one of the most influential management texts of our time. In this book, Porter extends his earlier firm-level approach to competition (in particular Porter 1980; 1985) to nation states, and in so doing places the issue of national economic competitiveness at the heart of national interest. Porter's work particularly aims at those states which are trying "to move away from dependence on cheap labor and natural resources" (Porter 1998a, xxviii). This is one of the reasons why Porter's work on territorial competition and competitiveness entails some of the geopolitical discourses that are crucial constituents of knowledge-based economization. In order to uncover these discourses, I single out five overlapping imaginaries central in the Porterian geopolitical reasoning.

Epochal shift to the era of innovations: the new age of territorial competition

First, the Porterian concept of national competitiveness is tightly connected to the purported knowledge-intensive phase of capitalism. Articulating an epochal shift to a new form of inter-territorial competition is not only a fundamental discursive characteristic of Porter's work but also reveals one of the central discursive constituents of knowledge-based economization as a spatial phenomenon. Porter suggests that

> although location remains fundamental to competition, its role today differs vastly from a generation ago. In an era when competition was driven heavily by input costs, locations with some important endowment – a natural harbor, for example, or a supply of cheap labor – often enjoyed a comparative advantage that was both competitively decisive and persistent over time. Competition in today's economy is far more dynamic. Companies can mitigate many input-cost disadvantages through global sourcing, rendering the old notion of comparative advantage less relevant. Instead, competitive advantage rests on making more productive use of inputs, which requires continual innovation.
>
> (Porter 1998b, 78)

Within the process of knowledge-based economization the new world is thus constituted as a vast field of innovations, profit and success or failure of entire nations. It is a field on which nation states compete through their strategies and through the performance of "their" firms. In this inter-state competition, nation states are not in danger of being conquered militarily by other states, nor are they in danger of disappearing from world political map entirely. Rather, nation states are in danger of losing their political–economic basis and related status, prestige and reputation among states. Furthermore, this articulation of inter-state competition includes the promise that less "developed" nation states may climb the ladders of the political–economic development hierarchy of states and in so doing change their status entirely. In such a view, the recent restructuring of world affairs is premised on competition between firms and political communities as "economic territories" (Brenner and Wachsmuth 2017, 86). This kind of reasoning not only draws on Joseph Schumpeter's ideas on the role of innovations in competition and strategy but also represents a form of geopolitical realism descendent from the strategic management school of thought – and to a lesser extent from international economics. Echoing the geoeconomic reading of world affairs that appeared in the early 1990s (see, e.g. Thurow 1992), for Porter the state represents a strong self-interest and a clearly defined national interest. Within such a frame, states seek to maximize outcomes within their borders, regardless of how other nation states are affected (Moisio 2017).

The Porterian geopolitical reasoning can be comprehended as a form of geostrategy which discusses the capacity of the state to act strategically in order to strengthen its place and region-specific economic potentials. In this capacity, the Porterian geopolitical reasoning is premised on an idea of inter-state rivalry over the capacity to produce economic value. This capacity, in turn, determines the overall success of a nation among its competitor nations if rated on the basis of prosperity, affluence and "development" (Moisio 2008). In sum, this inter-state rivalry is not about mastering strategic locations in physical geographical terms but rather touches upon the active strategic locating of the state in the spaces of a global economy of innovations and the associated hierarchy of states.

Global inter-state competition, or a contest of local business environments

Knowledge-based economization is constituted through an imaginary of the global. Porter's work articulates inter-state competition on the global scale as being the core dimension of the contemporary capitalist condition. Because "global competition nullifies traditional comparative advantages and exposes companies to the best rivals from around the world" (Porter 1998, 87), inter-state competition is inescapably global in nature. Porter fabricates a world in which the relationship between corporations and governments is a key issue for nations' competitiveness and hence for their fate in the global setting. Accordingly,

> factor inputs themselves have become less and less valuable in an increasingly global economy. Neither is competitiveness secured by size or military might, because neither is decisive for productivity. Instead, prosperity depends on creating a business environment, along with supporting institutions, that enable the nation to productively *use* and *upgrade* its inputs .... Failure to understand the distinction between comparative advantage and the new competitive advantage of nations is one of the root causes of problems in economic development. Merely using the resources available, or assembling more resources, is not enough for prosperity .... In the modern global economy, prosperity is a nation's *choice*. Nations choose prosperity if they organize their policies, laws, and institutions based on productivity.
>
> (Porter 1998a, xxi–xxii)

An analysis of Porter's work discloses another important discursive component of knowledge-based economization: inter-state competition is not portrayed as a zero-sum race to the bottom, for "many nations can simultaneously improve their productivity, and with it their health" (Porter 1998a, xxii).

Porter's work is premised on the idea that the contemporary world is marked by "a broader struggle over profits, a tug-of-war over who will capture the value an industry creates" (Magretta 2012, 9). The basic concern in Porter's theory of national competitiveness and inter-state competition is hence why firms and industries which are located in one particular nation state territory innovate and thus create more value than firms and industries which are located in another state territory. Comprehending how some industries are more successful, productive and competitive in some states rather than in others ultimately informs the notion of territorial competition. The same logic of comprehending forms the basis for state-based Porterian competitiveness indexing, comparisons and related benchmarking, which similarly constitute knowledge-based economization. Inter-territorial competition in knowledge-based economization is premised on an imaginary of "winning" states which attract a particular type of investments and companies and provide them with a putative unique environment that differs from those offered by territorial rivals. The declaration of winners and losers in comparative practices like "competitive indexing" indeed normalizes the concept of competitiveness at the scale of the nation state (Fougner 2006).

The concept of cluster conveys a number of the qualities of the geopolitical discourses that in part constitute the process of knowledge-based economization. Cluster refers to "a geographic concentration of competing and cooperating companies, suppliers, service providers, and associated institutions", and often include governmental or other institutions such as universities (Porter 1998b, 78). The concept highlights not only the role of geographical concentrations of firms but also the need of nation states to attract companies to locate within their borders. Porter (2000, 16) argues explicitly that "new influences of clusters of competition have taken on growing importance in an increasingly complex, knowledge-based economy". Because the "basis of competition has shifted more and more to the creation and assimilation of knowledge", Porter (2008, 171) goes on, "the role of the nation has grown".

The geopolitical discourses constitutive of the process of knowledge-based economization portray the nation state as a set of localities which either have or do not have the potential to thrive in global competition. Indeed, a constant local-global-national interplay is a fundamental feature of knowledge-based economization. Porter argues how "the enduring competitive advantages in a global economy lie increasingly in local things – knowledge, relationships, and motivation – that distant rivals cannot match" (Porter 1998b, 78). It is in this context that the concept of cluster contributes significantly to the geopolitical concept of national competitiveness which, in turn, challenges the traditional idea of comparative advantages and related territorial specialization.

Porter (1998b, 78) argues that clusters are a "striking feature of virtually every national, regional, state, and even metropolitan economy, especially in more economically advanced nations". The concept of cluster therefore discloses a world of knowledge-based economization, a world of absolute advantages and related competition over investments, income levels and profits. It is a quality of "advanced nations" in particular to be capable of enhancing value production in local milieux. The concept of cluster and the associated notion of advanced nations, together produce one of the central geopolitical discourses of the knowledge-based economy: the understanding of the world as if it were characterized solely by firm-based economic growth and micro-economic business environments and associated critical masses (Porter 1998b, 78).

In the Porterian geopolitical reasoning, firms, their interaction and the political support they get, emerge as key political issues through which inter-state competition plays out. The keys to national competitiveness are functional geographical micro-spaces which have a particular political–economic anatomy. Clusters facilitate the productivity of companies and bring them into interaction. This kind of Porterian understanding of agglomeration economies is constitutive of the process of knowledge-based economization. Accordingly, geographical concentrations are fundamental elements of national competitiveness because they include multiform innovation potential that can be harnessed by business firms. They increase the productivity of companies based in these locales and stimulate the birth of new businesses.

The role of the state in governing global competition in the world of innovations

The concept of cluster is a key element of knowledge-based economization. The concept produces a world of national micro-spaces – the strategic magnets of economic activity that provide the necessary social bases and economic as well as cultural incentives (a will to compete but also cooperate) not only for innovation and related utilization of knowledge but also for inter-territorial competition – which determine the nation's fate as a territory of wealth and power. In the Porterian state-centered geopolitical reasoning, if the state government is successful in providing politically stable and economically motivating framework conditions (e.g. through taxation and public investments) through both micro- and macro-economic means, the success of these micro-spaces translates into national wealth (Porter 2000).

Rather than downplaying the role of government and politics, knowledge-based economization highlights the role of public institutions in governing a nation's fate as a territory of wealth. According to Porter (1998a, xxiii), this implies "a minimalist government role in some areas (e.g., trade barriers, pricing) and an activist role in others (e.g., ensuring vigorous competition, providing high-quality education and training)". One might actually argue that in knowledge-based economization wealth generation is placed at the core of "national interest" and understood as governed by productivity.

The Porterian reasoning highlights the need for political coordination and action in the generation of political success. The geopolitical discourses of knowledge-based economization actually responsibilitize governments in two noteworthy respects: governments are compelled to both invest public money in innovation-driven growth and coordinate productivity in all sectors of human life and economic activity. Political actors need to understand that "productivity, not exports or national resources, determines the prosperity of any state or nation ... Recognizing this, governments should strive to create an environment that supports rising productivity" (Porter 1998b, 89).

The cluster concept expresses the spatiality of the constitutive discourses of knowledge-based economization. Porter's "diamond model", in turn, further highlights the role of the state. The four factors of the diamond – factor (input) conditions, demand conditions, context for firm strategy and rivalry and related and supporting industries – also become key factors in inter-state competition (Porter 2000, 20). The co-evolution of the supply-side factors, in turn, creates the micro-economic foundations of national success that enable "national" firms to gain and sustain competitive advantages. This is where the diamond model and the cluster concept come together: the micro-foundations of prosperity are strongest when they form a cluster. Geographical concentration enhances interaction among the four factors in the diamond model and boosts productivity, growth, employment and, hence, national competitiveness. The diamond model and cluster concept not only allow Porter to argue for enhancing competitiveness vis-à-vis competitor states but also disclose an important discursive dimension of knowledge-based economization: namely, an understanding that states can contribute to their competitiveness through political interventions which motivate firms to take risks. Moreover, it is the responsibility of the state and other public authorities to construct a business environment which enables increases in firm productivity, profits and, thus, national wealth.

In this context, one important qualitative dimension of the geopolitical discourses of knowledge-based economization is worth highlighting: the responsibilization of governments to invest in innovation-driven growth. Indeed, public policies in the OECD states have been characterized by attempts to increase support for industries through public research-and-development funding and to enhance the development of Porterian clusters since the early 1990s in particular (Sum and Jessop 2013). The geopolitical discourses which highlight global inter-territorial competition thus seem to have effected what Mazzucato (2013) calls the entrepreneurial state.

Mazzucato (2013) discloses the fact that states have effectively accelerated innovation and associated technological developments since the 1980s. Governments have played a pivotal role in creating businesses based on innovations. Accordingly, governments have created framework conditions which have been effectively utilized by business corporations in high tech and beyond. Even though this fact is almost invariably neglected by neoliberal protagonists of knowledge-based economization, various supply and demand-side governmental interventions and associated national projects have been crucial to furthering the development of the knowledge-intensive form of capitalism during the past three decades.

One may argue that the process of knowledge-based economization has largely advanced through states which have acted as risk-takers at times of political–economic uncertainty. These governments have provided "patient" strategic funding for corporations, universities and the like but have also tailored policies in order to create markets. In so doing, such governments have fundamentally furthered innovation-driven societal development in the age of putative global inter-territorial competition. Within the past two decades or so, this has brought about a sort of innovation state that channels notable public investments into various intangibles, and provides opportunities for business firms to tap into public coffers.

The spatial flexibility of territorial competitiveness, and the global value chain as a geopolitical space

The economic imaginaries of territorial competition and competitiveness related to knowledge-intensive capitalism are spatially flexible. They may highlight the role of cities, city-regions, metropolitan areas or regions. The Porterian clusters may even "cross national borders" (Porter 1998b, 79). Linking the performance of a business firm to its location and eventually nationalizing this location nonetheless expresses one of the basic tenets of not only Porterian geopolitical reasoning but also the process of knowledge-based economization more broadly. Accordingly, governments should think of their entire territories as business environments within which particular potentials of innovation can be harnessed for effective use (Porter 1998a, xxiii). In other words, even if the contemporary world requires thinking beyond national frameworks and innovating for an increasingly global market, knowledge-based economization is produced in geopolitical discourses that highlight the role of the nation state as a strategic space of action in the context of global competition. The subordination of cities and regions to the "national" objectives of the innovation state has manifested itself in a number of ways. One may for instance argue that state governments which embrace knowledge-based economization constantly responsibilitize cities and regions to develop innovation-driven local economies and associated projects or risk being ineligible for the public money available through various state-orchestrated funding schemes.

Within the process of knowledge-based economization, cities and regions are often constituted as facilitators of national competitive advantages and units of competition which are subordinated to the state. Their legitimacy, performance and very existence is defined and measured on the basis on their economic competitiveness. This kind of geopolitical reasoning fuses the idea of the competitiveness of political communities and firms so that different factors ranging from the price and cost competitiveness of a business firm to the role of public authorities in engendering and enhancing the role of economic micro-spaces become crucial issues in public policymaking. Accordingly, virtually all public policymaking should contribute to national competitiveness.

The Porterian geopolitical reasoning highlights that the success or failure of the state and related political forces can be measured on the basis of their efforts to enhance the competitiveness of firms. In the geopolitical discourses of the knowledge-based economy, the nation state is constituted ultimately as a facilitator of the profitability of capital and labor. The primary goal of the nation state is to act strategically in order to facilitate the accumulation of capital within its territorial jurisdictions. This can be done through creating a supportive and attractive political–economic environment for business activities, and through maximizing the availability of a highly skilled and flexible workforce. In addition, the state needs to ensure that there are no major politically created obstacles to innovation-driven growth. Within such a frame, the national interest is basically a moving object: a constant attempt to achieve the status of the knowledge and innovation-driven "economic state", a sort of highest category of states which have successfully situated themselves within global value chains.

In the process of knowledge-based economization, the global value chain – another central concept in the contemporary management literature – appears as a pivotal strategic space to which states are compelled to position themselves. In other words, the global receives its meaning through the seemingly firm-centered and stateless global value chains as well as the related value hierarchy of such chains. Indeed, the ubiquitous policy debate on the need to attract a particular kind of "high value" foreign direct investment is a perfect illustration of the emergence of the global value chain as a state-centric strategic space. It is a space in which a variety of governance functions have been delegated to private actors (see also Mayer and Phillips 2017). Similarly, relaxing taxation regimes and implementing policies of competitiveness, lowering investment costs, creating exceptional business spaces and using subsidies to boost the attractiveness of territorial economies to multinational corporations are today widely promoted as fundamental means to re-position a "nation" with regard to the global value chains. These strategic acts receive their justification from the geopolitical discourses constitutive of knowledge-based economization. Accordingly, entire territorial states can be re-positioned relative to their competitor states (Granas and Nyseth 2007). For instance, the recent efforts to brand states or nations can be understood as one of the manifestations of the emergence of the global value chain as a geopolitically meaningful strategic space.

Productivity and the fate of nations

Finally, internalizing the elements of competitiveness in a particular manner contributes to the process of knowledge-based economization. The pivotal question in Porter's conceptualization of national competitiveness is how to increase productivity. He singles out various factors of national competitiveness, and lists diverse infrastructure issues such as housing stock, health care, cultural institutions, transportation systems and resources such as a nation's human capital resources and the availability of investment capital. Porter proposes that every nation should analyze its competitiveness and ensure that all national institutions contribute to nurturing national competitiveness through enhancing processes that seek to increase productivity (Porter 1998b, 74–91). Low productivity thus signals that a nation's political institutions are not working properly in the face of global competition. Accordingly, the political institutions have not been able to facilitate the movement toward the innovation-driven economy both in terms of technological change and compelling individuals and populations to act more productively. The generation and maintenance of jobs in high tech, health care, marketing, finance, consulting, biotechnology, telecommunications, digital networks, electronics, automation, energy and aeronautics thus requires political forces to develop particular business environments and a related culture of competition in order to increase productivity.

In sum, knowledge-based economization is constituted through imaginaries that couple the issue of productivity with national fate. Accordingly, it is the role of every government to elevate "the national priority placed on competition" (Porter 1998b, 681) through creating incentives for its populace. Nation states and their populaces are hence connected to the global competition for prosperity through the idea of productivity, which, in turn, is a decisive factor of political success. Productivity is an issue which requires national governmental action because a nation which loses its ability to compete in a range of high-productivity and high-wage knowledge-based industries is in a constant danger of losing its standard of living and its status as a territory of wealth. Porter (2008, 177) hence argues that "it's the type of jobs, not just the ability to employ citizens at low wages, that is decisive for economic prosperity".

Some implications of Porterian geopolitical reasoning

To summarize what has been said on the previous pages, the competitive advantage of nations refers to the national attributes that foster competitive advantage in particular industries and to the implications both for firms and for governments (Porter 1998a). I have suggested that such a theory contributes to the process of knowledge-based economization.

But Porter's theory has also sparked serious academic criticism. Krugman (1996, 18), for instance, laments that

> while influential people have used the word "competitiveness" to mean that countries compete just like companies, professional economists know very well that this is a poor metaphor. In fact, it is a view of the world so much in conflict with what even the most basic international trade theory tells us that economists have by and large simply failed to comprehend that this is what the seemingly sophisticated people who talk about competitiveness have in mind.

Krugman proclaims that under conditions of relatively open trade, nation states are never in a fundamental win-lose competition against each other.

Accordingly, states should not be understood as wealth-creating social organizations either in policymaking or in research. For Krugman, national competitiveness is a "dangerous obsession" and, at best, only a "poetic way of saying productivity" (Krugman 1994).

Scholars have also pointed to the contradictory nature of the Porterian idea of substantial inter-state competition in the post-Fordist world. They have argued that the new capitalist condition is characterized by specialization through local or regional concentration of economic and business activities in the high-tech sector, for instance. Agnew (2003, 78) argues that in such a context "national economies (as opposed to more localized ones) are even less likely to be in 'competition' than they were in the past when industries were more organized on a national rather than a transnational basis". Bristow (2005) proposes that regional competitiveness – a variant of the Porterian concept of competitiveness – is a chaotic concept and much overvalued in policymaking. Kitson *et al.* (2004) observe that the concept of regional competitiveness is elusive and has, harmfully, become almost naturalized as one of the core phenomena of modern capitalism. Brenner and Wachsmuth (2017, 86), in turn, criticize the concept of territorial competitiveness both in academic research and in policymaking. Accordingly, they argue, it leads to a kind of "competitiveness trap". For them, territorial competitiveness is premised on "flawed intellectual assumptions"; it serves largely as "a means of ideological mystification in the sphere of local policy development" and results in "socially polarizing policies".

Irrespective of the many relevant critiques, Porter's conceptualizations of the ways in which territorial nation states compete through their internal spaces in the post-Fordist context have had major implications with respect to how policy goals and contents, policy instruments and policy programs have both been articulated and taken shape in different geographical contexts during the past 20 years.

The geopolitical discourses of the knowledge-based economy highlight the idea that coming to terms with the fundamental uncertainties of contemporary capitalism requires effective national strategy work. The policy relevance of the Porterian geopolitical reasoning is hence at least partially based on the effective nationalization of local and regional concentration of economic activities, related assets and profitable human behavior. The geopolitical discourses of the knowledge-based economy touch upon the issue of how the economic success of a nation determines its political success as a territory of wealth and how economic success is ultimately based on local economic milieus. This renders world affairs understandable in such a manner that political leaders become increasingly prone to define their states as entrepreneurial business actors and to articulate their national interest on the basis of inter-state economic rivalry (Moisio 2008; Browning and de Oliveira 2017).

The idea that more or less coherent territorial nation states are involved in economic competition was somewhat paradoxically placed on the agenda by the crisis of the Keynesian-Fordist mode of capital accumulation. It thus found its momentum in the context of the fear of the unraveling of the "national" mode of accumulation. In the 1998 version of *The Competitive Advantage of Nations*, Porter (1998a, xxvi) revealingly looks back on the early 1990s and explains the success of the book:

> The book appeared at a time of growing competition in virtually every nation …. Whether prosperous or mired in poverty, nations, states, and regions all over the world were searching for ways of coping.

That the theory of the competitive advantage of nations provided a seemingly actionable framework for how to improve the state's competitiveness is one of the reasons why it has been so welcomed by practitioners of government.

But an analysis of Porter's theory on the competitive advantage of nations also exposes a duality which characterizes the process of knowledge-based economization more generally. It underscores the increasingly localized and regionalized basis of economic performance within industrialized states. Simultaneously, it highlights the fundamental need to politically advance such localization and regionalization as a state-centered strategy. Knowledge-based economization is indeed constituted through geopolitical discourses that nationalize the inter-city or inter-urban competition which many argue is the fundamental characteristic of post-Fordism (see, e.g. Scott 2001).

Indeed, the geopolitical discourses of national competitiveness clearly have particular affective qualities, as they address "national" anxieties, pride, threats and social tensions, linked to growth or decline, as well as related pressures of the economic restructuring of states "in a globalized information age" (Sum and Jessop 2013, 305). Porter's work on the competitive advantage of nations is not only impregnated with affective and highly contextual qualities but also evinces an understanding that the nation state can and should be articulated through concepts which were previously used predominantly in the context of business firms.

It would be hence an understatement to argue that national competitiveness is merely a contemporary buzzword, or that it is a mere ideological fantasy or conceptual fallacy (Brenner and Wachsmuth 2017, 100). It should rather be treated as a combination of economic imaginaries that contribute to the formation of the essential geopolitical discourses of the contemporary capitalist condition. The concept territorializes the economic processes inherent in the knowledge-intensive form of capitalism. It also motivates governments to imagine that sub-national territories, cities and city-regions "must compete with one another for economic survival through the attraction of transnationally mobile capital investment" (ibid., 85).

The geopolitical discourses of the knowledge-based economy produce the state discursively as an active and coherent agent – even if the state is inescapably characterized by many different objectives, agendas and agents. Competitiveness has nonetheless become a nationalizing and territorializing policy object in itself, and it can be connected to many different policy fields and articulated in many situations. Even though ideas and practices related to territorial competition date back centuries, the Porterian geopolitical reasoning that emerged in the 1990s has played a critically constitutive role in the process of knowledge-based economization during the past three decades.

Geopolitical discourses which highlight territorial competition and competitiveness and the role of local clusters in engendering the competitiveness of nation states have had implications in spatial planning, too. In policymaking, the Porterian ideas of competitiveness – which are premised on the interplay between nationalization, localization and urbanization of national interest – were in the early 1990s still related to late managerial Keynesian state interventionism. The Porterian geopolitical reasoning materialized in different geographical contexts in the form of technopoles, industrial parks, innovation parks and the like. This late Keynesian knowledge-based economization was already spurred by the idea of national territorial competition in the purportedly new kind of innovation-driven global capitalism. It manifested itself as efforts to build spaces of competition through state-orchestrated but locally manifested planning initiatives that often focused on built environments and related land use.

The role of land use planning in the building of national competitive advantages through local geographical concentrations has not altogether diminished. It has nonetheless been increasingly coupled with centrally and locally orchestrated (soft) strategic planning which is premised on the goal of constructing a diverse set of economic potentials through urban space. This has resulted, it must be stressed, in the production and imagining of various "soft spaces" and ubiquitous geographical nodes or spots of innovation. In other words, the Porterian imaginaries of territorial competition and competitiveness are still to be found at the core of state policies and local development policies, albeit nowadays in a qualitatively different fashion compared with the situation in the 1990s.

The concepts of national competitiveness and the state's international competitiveness remain axiomatic notions in policy circles across the globe, but the emphasis on industrial clusters has been increasingly accompanied by new strategic planning and related vision work concerning start-up ecosystems, commodified urban spaces, spaces of experiments and stratified techniques of increasing the innovative potentials of the nation state populace. There is an ongoing shift therefore from built environments to the putatively deeper spaces of economy which the term ecosystem of innovations is often used to depict. This shift is manifesting itself in a number of states and cities as the increasingly prominent role of a kind of "economic potential planning". One may thus argue that during the past 10 to 15 years new wine has been mixed in the old bottles of competitiveness.

Time, space, location and interaction in geopolitical discourses of the knowledge-based economy

I have suggested in this chapter that the geopolitical discourses of knowledge-based economization, easy to find in mainstream academic writings, highlight that the ways in which state success and the sought-after system of capital accumulation come together in a particular historical conjuncture is a matter of politics, policy and geography. These discourses are essentially structured around particular notions of time, space and "strategic interaction". I provide a brief summary of these below.

The first of these elements, time, highlights the rupture within the organization of the economy in general and the "national economy" in particular. Accordingly, the knowledge economy can be placed within the long development of the market economy within which

> the main source of wealth in market economies has switched from natural assets (notably land and relatively unskilled labour), through tangible created assets (notably buildings, machinery and equipment, and finance), to intangible created assets (notably knowledge and information of all kinds) which may be embodied in human beings, in organizations, or in physical assets.
>
> (Dunning 2000, 8)

The temporal component of knowledge-based economization effectively highlights the knowledge economy of intangible assets as a sign of progress and as the main source of wealth augmentation. This is then juxtaposed with the perceived economy of the past which was construed through natural resources or created tangible assets. The transition from, say, a hydrocarbon-based national economy to an economy which uses and produces technology effectively through knowledge and highly educated workforce is a significant and positively loaded aspect of the discourse. In other words, knowledge-based economization creates and is premised on peculiar ladders of development among states, cities and regions with the knowledge-intensive "learning economy" representing the most advanced driver of societal development.

The stark contrast between the old economy and the advanced new economy portrayed in the geopolitical discourses of knowledge-based economization adds a new element to the ways in which inter-state competition has from the 1990s onwards been conceived among policymakers and other actors. The fundaments of knowledge-based economization are predicated on a particular Schumpeterian idea on the centrality of technology and technological innovations in producing economic growth, overall societal progress and, thus, territories of wealth and prestige. It does not come as a revelation therefore that the inter-state competition within the geopolitical discourses of the knowledge economy is often articulated as if it were highly technology based. It is nonetheless evident that this comprehension of inter-state competition is a continuation of older logics of inter-state rivalries: technological advancements in industry were particularly in twentieth-century geopolitical thought taken up as signs of "national strength" (for instance the role of the automobile industry was enormous for the symbolic status of a state). Knowledge-based economization, however, qualitatively alters the relationship between state success and technology. It emphasizes the centrality of political regula-tion which encourages the private (and public) sector to embrace cutting-edge technological developments and to abandon old technologies and associated modes of behavior and thought.

Second, the geopolitical discourses of the knowledge-based economy add a significant political-geographical element to complement the above-men-tioned temporal dimension. The geopolitical discourses of the knowledge-based economy thus not only divide spaces as old and new but also touch upon the spatial organization of the knowledge-intensive capitalist economy. Almost invariably, the geopolitical discourses of the knowledge-based economy denote the mirror image of a "fully territorialized" economic activity characterized by comparative advantages whereby "economic viability is rooted in assets (including human practices and relations) that are not available in many other places and cannot easily or rapidly be created or imitated in places that lack them" (Storper 2000, 43). The ubiquitous emphasis on mobility and related spatial relationality, which is often articulated as a departure from the nation-state-centered territorialized economic activity of the past toward the present economic activity of relational spaces which are characterized by created com-petitive advantages, is one of the central features of the geopolitical discourses of the knowledge-based economy. Accordingly, "assets, far from being largely fixed and immobile as in bygone days, are now eminently increasable and mobile" (Dunning 2000, 9).

It is particularly for this reason that the geopolitical discourses of the knowl-edge-based economy are seductive. They hint that success in the knowledge-driven economy can in principle be attained by anyone and that such economy can flourish almost everywhere where certain human, institutional and admin-istrative capacities come together in particular combinations. The geopolitical discourses of the knowledge-based economy are thus enormously concrete and tempting for elites in states, cities and regions who vigorously reject "that they are condemned to live within the old logic of spatial division of labor that locks them into particular functions determined by events long time ago" (Castells and Hall 1994, 8). This quality of knowledge-based economization is more generally one of the reasons why many places have during the past two dec-ades worked hard to become first "technopoles" and later "start-up capitals" of their host nation or even of the wider world.

The third crucial aspect of the geopolitical discourses of the knowledge-based economy is that they not only articulate a distinction between the past and present, and between the territorial and relational nature of this new econ-omy, but also re-define the nature of a kind of "strategic interaction" between a firm and political communities. One of the constitutive undercurrents of the phenomenon of knowledge-based economization is an understanding that the success of a political community, be it a nation, city or region, can be measured through its economic prosperity with respect to performance in the economy of intangible assets. The basic dimension of the interaction between a firm and society is thus bound to the dynamics of asset-seeking foreign direct investment (FDI). In such a discourse, society appears as an active competitive unit which seeks, for instance, to minimize the dynamic transaction costs of firms (those related to learning and the coordination of innovation-related tasks, for instance).

In the geopolitical discourses of the knowledge-based economy, multinational companies (MNE) in particular try to match their strategic needs for profit making with political communities such as states and cities. As a consequence, such communities appear in these discourses as apolitical investment landscapes or sites for investments which embody a particular type of naturalized behavior and related "economic" actorness. Accordingly, communities of various kinds inevitably seek to "respond" to the purportedly increasingly important locational strategies of the MNEs (i.e. quest for desired intangible assets) by offering the "most congenial complementary immobile assets" (Dunning 2000, 29). Even if firm and society both appear as strategic economic agents within the mechanisms of knowledge-based economization, the geopolitical discourses of the knowledge-based economy disclose a somewhat uneven interaction between firm and society in such an economy. It is the firm whose strategic decision-making dealings with investments and locations make visible the success or failure of policies tailored within given political communities.

The geopolitical discourses of the knowledge-based economy also touch upon the "hubization" of the territorial state. This is a pivotal component of these discourses given that it portrays the world ultimately as a field of competing locations which seek to offer specific resources and innovation capabilities within their borders. This is exactly how knowledge-based economization, even if at first glance it may look like a firm-centered one, is ultimately about political communities and their decision-making. Given that the geopolitical discourses of the knowledge-based economy represent the position of a state in global value chains as the central aspect which determines the social and political future of states, cities and regions, state and local governments are forced to refashion themselves as anchorages that can meet the needs of the mobile knowledge-intensive firms

> as the core competencies of firms become more knowledge-intensive, yet more mobile across space, so the choice of location in the production, organization and the use of those assets is becoming a more critical competitive advantage. To the national and regional policy-makers the challenge is to offer, both to indigenous and foreign-owned firms, the spatially anchored resources and capabilities within their jurisdiction, which are perceived by these firms to be at least as attractive complements to their own ownership-specific advantages as those offered by other countries or regions.
>
> (Dunning 2000, 7)

Finally, one dimension in the geopolitical discourses of the knowledge-based economy is what may be called the responsibilization of public authorities at different institutional contexts. Accordingly, it is exactly the heightening mobility of firm-specific core competencies which requires that various micro-regional authorities take increasing responsibility to ensure the availability and quality of the requisite location-bound complementary assets to attract the right kind of mobile investments. Competitive advantage appears within such an understanding as dependent on both the provision of basic infrastructures in places and regions, and on the "identification and promotion of a set of the specific unique advantages which cannot be easily imitated by other regions" (Dunning 2000, 29).

Through channeling particular responsibilities to public authorities with regard to the conceived qualities of "mobile firms" and "mobile assets", the geopolitical discourses of the knowledge-based economy lay the fundamental rationale for place marketing and country branding, for instance. These have emerged as significant features of knowledge-based economization during the past decades. The responsibilizing quality of the discourses of the knowledge-based economy is crucial. It seduces, motivates and forces the national, supranational or local policymakers and authorities to localize the mobile knowledge economy through finding and developing putative "unique advantages" which stem from their places and regions, advantages which the local actors strive to define as ones that cannot easily be created in other locales.

The production of political communities as geopolitical objects of competition in virtual spaces of comparison

In this section I call for drawing greater attention to the production of geopolitical objects and the related practices of measuring, modeling and indexing which constitute the knowledge-intensive economy as a distinguished field of action and competition. I highlight such issues because knowledge-based economization involves the production and consolidation of political communities as if they were geopolitical objects of competition in global knowledge economy.

The production of these objects of competition occurs in calculative social practices, and such production enables, restricts, disables and potentially transforms knowledge-intensive capitalism. It is nonetheless clear that the geopolitical discourses of the knowledge-based economy and the production of geopolitical objects of competition are two sides of the same coin. One may argue that the production of geopolitical objects of competition sparks geopolitical discourses of territorial competition and competitiveness into life. Without such production, inter-territorial competition in global knowledge-intensive capitalism would lose a critical part of its epistemic base. The geopolitical object of competition is thus "force-full"; it does things (Meehan *et al.* 2013, 3) in the process of knowledge-based economization. In short, the production of geopolitical objects of competition provides the necessary base for discussing cities, regions and states as actors of the knowledge-based economy (also Kitchin *et al.* 2015).

Public and academic debates of the global knowledge-intensive form of capitalism are often connected to political communities, with this or that political unit succeeding or failing in global competition. This kind of articulation and analysis thus reveals a pivotal element of knowledge-based economization: the calculative practices that initially enable political actors to compare and act upon political communities as if they were meaningful units of the global knowledge-based economy. In the ensuing pages, I discuss the role of indices, graphs and related things in the production of geopolitical objects of knowledge-based economization. These objects are thus connected to and generated in significant social practices that play a central role in the territorialization of knowledge-intensive capitalism.

The social practices which produce the geopolitical objects of competition visualize the geopolitical discourses of the knowledge-based economy by means of calculation. In these practices, the knowledge-based economy is translated into metrics, indices, graphs, figures, maps of all sorts and tables. Furthermore, these practices of measurement locate cities, regions and states in the purportedly fierce international competition for affluence, political prestige and vitality. Inasmuch as the socio-technical practices also measure "strengths" of political communities in terms of human capital/resources, these practices form a direct link between the geopolitical subjects and geopolitical discourses of the knowledge-based economy.

The practices which assemble the knowledge-based economy as a reality through a set of measurable geopolitical objects collectively embody what some authors call virtual spaces of comparison (Larner and Le Heron 2002) or a global space of competition and emulation (McCann 2008, 896). These are, ultimately, peculiar spaces of inter-spatial learning in which relations proliferate not only between policy worlds but also between places (Prince 2015): states, cities and regions are positioned with reference to one another with respect to the various prerequisites and associated variables of the knowledge-based economy. These issues and variables are, in turn, firmly predicated on what Castells and Hall (1994, 7) dub "comparative international experience". Already in the early 1990s they revealed the pivotal logic of these virtual spaces of comparison in early knowledge-based economization by arguing that

> Those areas that remain rooted in declining activities – be they manufacturing, agriculture, or services of the old, non-competitive kind – become industrial ruins, inhabited by disconsolate, unemployed workers, and ridden by social discontents and environmental hazards. New countries and regions emerge as successful locales of the new wave of innovation and investment, sometimes emerging from deep agricultural torpor, sometimes in idyllic corners of the world that acquire sudden dynamism. Thus, Silicon Valley and Orange County in California; Arizona, Texas, Colorado, in the western United States; Bavaria in Germany; The French Midi, from Sophia-Antipolis via Montpellier to Toulouse; Silicon Glen in Scotland; the electronics agglomeration in Ireland; the new developments

in Southern Europe, from Bari to Malaga and Seville; and, above all, the newly industrializing countries of Asia (South Korea, Taiwan, Hong Kong, Singapore, Malaysia) that in two decades have leapt straight from traditional agricultural societies – albeit with high levels of literacy and education – to being highly competitive economies based on strong electronics sectors.

(Castells and Hall 1994, 7)

It would be interesting to interrogate the development paths of the states, regions and places mentioned in this quote. But I believe that the geopolitical message of the quote is more pertinent. The virtual spaces of comparison are based on construing the global knowledge-based economy as a particular hierarchy of places. In such a hierarchy, some places and regions become what Castells and Hall (1994, 7) call "role models". This is not a politically innocent hierarchy but rather one with a sort of compelling normative and affective function. These role models, they go on to argue, "have a dramatic influence on the collective consciousness of countries, regions, and localities, as well as on the development projects of their respective governments" (ibid., 7). In the context of knowledge-based economization, these role models therefore have constitutive effects on how different actors perceive the deep spatial logics of the knowledge-based economy. The virtual spaces of comparison are thus not only descriptive but also, and more importantly, highly affectual, productive and even disciplinary with respect to other social and governmental practices.

To be fair, different kinds of virtual spaces of comparison existed before the 1990s. To illustrate, during the Cold War the strength of the state was measured in terms of natural resources, the size of population, army size, "national homogeneity" and the size of particular industries such as machinery and steel production. These state resources were also represented through various media. It should be also noted that the OECD first started producing state-based statistics, indicators and comparisons on gross domestic expenditure on R&D (the so-called GERD index) already in the 1960s. However, the logic, intensity and role of the virtual spaces of comparison have changed drastically since the 1990s. The miscellaneous competitiveness, creativity, innovativeness and productivity indices and related reports have not only gradually replaced the Cold War territorial and militarist league tables in public debates. In their capacity to uncover and visualize "false policies" in various representations these indices and reports have also become highly influential in the context of public policymaking. In other words, these indices seem to offer a sort of universal set of tools with which "responsible" governments may manage a political organization as a knowledge-intensive territory of wealth.

The new virtual spaces of comparison have been produced by scholars, global consultant companies, international organizations and foundations with the help of new computational techniques and data-collecting procedures. These virtual spaces of comparison fundamentally render knowledge-based economization possible, and often reify the Porterian geopolitical rationality which I analyzed earlier in this chapter. These spaces are bound to techniques and practices of measuring and calculating and, importantly, have the capacity to translate complex processes of knowledge-intensive capitalism into succinct numerical figures. This "elegance of the single figure" (Miller 2001, 382) enables both business circles, policymakers and politicians to monitor, debate, praise, criticize or justify policymaking in the context of cities, regions and states.

The different indices and metrics constitute the knowledge-based economy as a set of territorial objects in numerous ways. Many of these are produced through advanced methodologies for gathering, analyzing, sorting, quantifying and distributing data. The indices and metrics may arrange individual researchers, faculties, entire universities or even states in order of ranking. Or they may rank cities and states on the basis of their "overall competitiveness". Some of these indices mix economic and political indicators, thus effectively pairing economic performance with particular political conditions. And then there are the world-known and widely distributed annual reports which contain an extensive set of state-based analysis on the different facets of the competitive advantage. Consider, for instance, the *Global Competitiveness Report* which is published annually since 1979 by the WEF. It evaluates and compares productivity, prosperity and economic growth prospects in 140 states through various indices and circulates its findings in the form of infographics, interactive "heatmaps" and basic datasets through seminars, videos, publications and blogs (World Economic Forum 2016). These indices are widely reported in the media across the globe, and have particular appeal among policy circles (Bristow 2010). The WEF annual report thus epitomizes the ways in which international actors assemble the knowledge-based economy in charts and tables, or scoreboards (cf. Barry 1993), as consisting of territorial objects of competition. Many of the related reports, such as the one developed by the Swiss-based World Competitiveness Center of the Institute for Management Development in early 2000s, unfold the same way of objectifying the territorial units of competition in knowledge-intensive capitalism.

What characterizes these different indices and reports is that most have emerged since the 1990s in tandem with the discourses and material processes of what Thrift (2005) calls "soft capitalism". Consider, for instance, the well-known *Industry and Technology Scoreboard of Indicators* which was first published in 1995. It is a booklet that includes economic and science and technology indicators which rank countries on different dimensions. Today, there are more than 100 similar kinds of indices which, in one way or another, assemble the knowledge-based economy in territorial terms. Some of these indices – such as the *Knowledge-based Economy Index*, the *Knowledge Economy Index*, the *Knowledge Index*, the *World Knowledge Competitiveness Index* and the *Global Innovation Index* – are indicative of the growing field of indexing, the relevance of which is based on their comparative and manipulative content. Beyond the commercial activity, different kinds of international organizations contribute to the virtual spaces of comparison, and thus, to the formation of the knowledge-based economy as a set of competing territorial objects. In 2006 alone, the OECD measured and analyzed the effectiveness of the territorialized knowledge economy through nearly 60 different indicators (Godin 2006). In sum, international consultant companies, international organizations, public and private think tanks and rating agencies and different kinds of social movements that are structured around famous public intellectuals (such as the Creative City Movement) or individual consultants (see Prince 2012) all contribute to the production of the virtual spaces of comparison. In this capacity, they are notable contributors to knowledge-based economization.

The virtual spaces of comparison and emulation exemplify relational spatiality. But at the same time these relational spaces function territorially. They provide a relational space of comparison within which the knowledge-based economy appears as a set of objects that can be acted upon. These spaces re-work the territorial state with an emphasis on institutions, places and spatial exceptions as strategic sites through which the political and economic success of the state is possible to generate (cf. Sassen 2013, 28).

5 On geopolitical subjects of knowledge-based economization

This chapter interrogates the geopolitical subjects of knowledge-based economization in which the skill problem appears like a society-wide "we concern" (Jones 2008, 391). The process of knowledge-based economization thus involves re-working people's conduct, perceptions, actions, motivations, skills and weaknesses vis-à-vis the purported requirements of "global competition". This process proceeds through governmental interventions which bring together the regulation of population and space (cf. Legg 2005; Moisio and Paasi 2013). One may thus argue that the production of these self-managerial subjects belongs to the sphere of economic subjectification. In these governmental interventions particular images are invoked of the profitable/useful self/ citizen who potentially fits not only contemporary but also future mechanisms of capital accumulation. What ensues is an attempt to engender a population with particular capacities, and to structure the behavior and performance of particular segments of population through certain educational and other techniques. A geopolitical analysis of knowledge-based economization analyzes the ways in which such economization involves manipulating and guiding bodies and lives spatially in the age of conceived war over talent.

Theories on the information society, post-industrial society and network society are premised on the notion of an increasingly fluid transnational space of knowledge-intensive capitalism, but these are often articulated and analyzed through discreet spatial entities such as states, cities, regions and megaregions. For any analysis of the phenomenon of knowledge-based economization, these theories are highly interesting as they effectively bring together the knowledge-intensive economy and a particular geopolitical subject.

By using the concept of the geopolitical subject, I refer to an organized set of human figures, understood to be equipped with particular desired skills, behaviors and orientations which can be harnessed in the production of territories of wealth, competition, status, power, security and belonging in the context of the knowledge-intensive form of capitalism. These figures together represent a kind of collective geopolitical subject of the knowledge-based economy. They are ideal figures which encapsulate the spatial tenets of knowledge-based economization and related territorial identities and citizenships. In the following pages, rather than inquiring into how a human subject develops an understanding of herself/himself as a political subject of the knowledge-based economy, I examine the ways in which a particular collective geopolitical subject is envisioned, defined and assembled in influential academic writings that arose in the 1990s.

I approach the above-mentioned thematic through the well-known academic theories of Manuel Castells on the nature of the networked world in the age of knowledge-intensive capitalism and concomitant technological advances. Before entering the thematic of the geopolitical subject, it is necessary to examine some of the spatial foundations of Castells' theory, as well as to discuss the role of territories and the state in his writings on "informational capitalism". I seek to show that the ways in which the network society is argued to bring together de-territorializing and re-territorializing dynamics, perfectly portrays some of the geopolitical discourses out of which a particular geopolitical subject has gradually emerged as a socially and politically meaningful phenomenon.

Rather than considering the impressive work of Manuel Castells as simply describing the nature of contemporary societies, I treat his work also as prescriptive. The academic theories of Castells and other distinguished academic gurus of the new economy and society thus are seen to exert a productive power over societal dynamics. In so doing, these academic contributions not only greatly influence the thinking of contemporary social scientists and policymakers but also throw into relief the ways in which the knowledge-based economy is geopolitically constituted. These academic theories therefore embody both productive and analytical power. They illuminate how academic theories which appeared in the 1990s make some of the recent developments on the society-economy-technology-business-citizenship interface meaningful in spatial terms and provide a basis for imagining and tailoring policy tools to cope with the new world which these theories portray as emerging or already in place.

The social theories tailored by the illustrious voices of social science such as Castells disclose how particular ideals about the future are brought into the present, and how these theoretical projections also potentially re-work the present when they are acted upon in policy circles. And yet, these theories are not produced by autonomously acting individuals who "have manipulative control over the structural conditions for their action" (Müller 2008, 325). Rather, geopolitical discourses speak through these individuals (and their theories), who have been arguably implicated in the rise of knowledge-intensive capitalism since the 1990s (cf. Thrift 2005, 21).

Spatial foundations of the new geopolitical subject

Knowledge-based economization is almost invariably clustered around the concept of the network. Network is a historically contingent projection of the world, one which seems to exist in a co-constitutive relationship with knowledge-based economization which took a geopolitical form in the 1990s. One must thus discompose the idea that the world is really made up of networks and succumb to the notion that geopolitics is embedded in such an assumption (see Walters 2012). In other words, network is not only a catchword of contemporary management texts, regional development literature and political speeches more generally, but also a geopolitical narrative which re-works political communities spatially vis-à-vis the supposed relational spatiality of markets. I claim that the geopolitical subjects of knowledge-intensive capitalism are co-constituted with geopolitical discourses which highlight the fluid surface of mobile, unstable, loose and informal linkages extending beyond the purportedly rigid hierarchies of the territorially fixed nation state, and which are premised on ideas of flexibility, spatial selectivity, fierce competition and related extreme vulnerability.

In order to illustrate this point more thoroughly, I inquire into the realm of recent social theory. Since the 1990s, the nature of the new economy and society has been widely debated and theorized in scholarly circles, both explicitly and implicitly in parallel concepts. These conceptualizations can be comprehended as serious attempts to describe the changes of the post-Second World War Fordist-Keynesian-national industrial society and accompanying territorial political order. Concepts such as information society, post-industrial society (Bell 1973/1999) and network society (Castells 1996) have been used to depict the purportedly unprecedented political–economic changes that started to take place in the 1990s in particular. These concepts both de-territorialize and re-territorialize the global knowledge-based economy in a particular manner.

One of the most notable scholarly debates has surrounded the idea of the information or network society. Both of these stand for the rapid development of information and communications technologies over the past decades, and the role of these technologies in storing, disseminating and processing information in particular. The various roles of information in the formation of knowledge that can be exploited economically in production or in the wider field of human activities is similarly located at the heart of these academic theories. Daniel Bell's (1973/1999) ideas on the rise of the information economy can be considered as an early attempt to scrutinize the processes wherein a kind of novel information hegemony transforms classical industrial society. Bell envisioned a post-industrial society in which the societal dynamics of the industrial society would be forged anew.

The vision of Bell and his followers on the nature of this imagined post-industrial society is premised on the importance of knowledge and information in economic activities, which they see as capable of transforming entire social fabrics. Bell's (1973/1999) ideas on the nature of socio-economic change were also premised on a view that knowledge would become the most important factor of production and business competitiveness. Knowledge, according to Bell, is also the basis of the exercise of power. In similar vein, Manuel Castells (1996, 17) employs the term informationalism to point out how the application of knowledge upon knowledge itself had by the 1990s become the primary source of productivity and a backbone of both a new economy and society. Here, the term informationalism refers to a pervasive process wherein the societal and cultural forms of industrial capitalism are replaced by new social formations:

> The generalization of knowledge-based production and management to the whole realm of economic processes on a global scale requires fundamental social, cultural, and institutional transformations that, if the other technological revolutions are considered, will take some time. This is why the economy is informational, not just-information-based, because the cultural-institutional attributes of the whole social system must be included in the diffusion and implementation of the new technological paradigm, as the industrial economy was not merely based on the use of new sources of energy for manufacturing but on the emergence of an industrial culture, characterized by a new social and technical division of labor.
>
> (Castells 1996, 91)

Since the 1990s, Manual Castells has undeniably been one of the most influential academic writers and commentators on the knowledge-intensive form of capitalism. His concept of the network society (Castells 1996) is particularly revealing in this context, and his later insistence in arguing that the contemporary world is already a network society (see, e.g. Castells 2005) has been politically influential in many geographical contexts. Accordingly, the information age is built on networks which link states, institutions and individuals in different tapestries. But rather than producing a flat world, differentiation between those who are and those who are not part of the networks of informational capitalism characterizes the contemporary condition. The network society thus consists of new network enterprises, states, places, regions and subjects, and is both integrating and fragmenting.

The network society is highly spatial in nature. Castells (2005) uses the spatial term "global" to define the contemporary condition. In Castells' words:

> because the network society is based on networks, and communication networks transcend boundaries, the network society is global, it is based on global networks. So, it is pervasive throughout the planet, its logic extends to every country in the planet.
>
> (Castells 2005, 4)

Even if the network society diffuses throughout the entire world, it does not include all people: it is characterized by a growing gap between winners and losers. Castells in fact argues that the network society "excludes most of humankind, although all of humankind is affected by its logic, and by the power relationships that interact in the global networks of social organization" (Castells 2005, 5). The network society hence represents a sort of non-territorial imperialism, a world in which highly uneven processes are predicated on a division of those who are interacting in global networks and those who are interacted with or affected through these networks (Castells 1996). The network society has no clearly identifiable center of power; rather, it is characterized by links that connect nodes (metropolises) with each other and with hinterlands. The spatiality of the network society is, therefore, ultimately shaped by processes that potentially marginalize places within the highly developed countries as well.

The key features of the geopolitical subject of the knowledge-based economy are conditioned by a set of key ideas about the fiercely competitive spatial and urban nature of the network society. Castells (1996) highlights that an actor's capacity to connect him/herself to networks is a fundamental resource in the network society. The different capabilities of actors to secure connectedness leads to fierce competition and deleterious uneven development within the network society. This competition is not based on the classical understanding of inter-state competition among bounded territorial units. The new race to the top is based on a fear of being marginalized outside of networks, "the widespread fear of a jobless society" (ibid., 201). The complexion of the network society is thus not only characterized by fierce competition. It is also marked by an understanding that business firms, cities and states are all equally vulnerable in the face of the ubiquitous networks and the related space of flows.

Castells' (1996) concept of the space of flows ultimately depicts a world in which nobody is completely secured; unpredictability characterizes the new geopolitical condition. Essentially every corporation, state and city is constantly threatened by the deep processes of the space of flows, to the extent that both private and public organizations and even individuals need to constantly develop their adaptive capacities and be ready for different kinds of shocks. Castells thus conceives of the world as "constantly rolling over, continually on the brink" (cf. Thrift 2005, 97). Cities, for instance, are brought onto an "urban roller coaster" which "illustrates both the dependence and vulnerability of any locale, including major cities, to changing global flows" (Castells 1996, 384). Strategic political action in the network society is about re-organizing and managing circulation within the global network: diminishing the bad and maximizing the good circulation in the context of a given political community. Failure to take this kind of strategic action with regard to the global flows and circulations invites the risk that things will fall apart, bringing about misery and poverty.

Irrespective of the "global" emphasis on networks, Castells' (1996) ideas on the network society in fact territorialize the global knowledge-based economy. Some passages of his three-volume study, *The Information Age*, translate the key tenets of the knowledge-based economy into a kind of territory talk. Castells (1996) articulates re-territorialization mainly through cities and states. Given that Castells is a notable urban theorist, it is no surprise that the concept of the space of flows denotes primarily a system of interconnected cities – or rather their business districts and innovation centers – which forms a hierarchy and is characterized by "fierce inter-city competition" (ibid., 382). Major cities are nodal points (ibid., 378–387) of networks through which information

flows and capital accumulates. The most important cities are portrayed as globally connected "development engines" (ibid., 409) or "command and control
centers" of informational capitalism. By way of interacting with each other
these cities possess relative autonomy from state territories. The ways in which
Castells both territorializes and de-territorializes the state vis-à-vis the network
society in this context is particularly telling and characterizes the process of
knowledge-based economization more generally:

> The global city phenomenon cannot be reduced to a few urban cores at
> the top of the hierarchy. It is a process that connects advanced services,
> producer centres, and markets in a global network, with different inten-
> sity and at a different scale depending upon the relative importance of the
> activities located in each area vis-à-vis the global network. Inside each
> country, the networking architecture reproduces itself into regional and
> local centers, so that the whole system becomes interconnected at the
> global level. Territories surrounding these nodes play an increasingly sub-
> ordinate function, sometimes becoming irrelevant or even dysfunctional.
>
> (Castells 1996, 380)

The emphasis on the dysfunctionality of the territorial state has significant family resemblance with Kenichi Ohmae's (1993) critique of the "equalizing"
political management of state spaces. By following at least implicitly this form
of reasoning, Castells argues that certain "new industrial spaces" or "milieus of
innovation" indeed determine the success and failure of political communities
in the network society (ibid., 386–393). These new kinds of territories, which
essentially "deborder territoriality" (Sassen 2013), are integral ingredients in
the geopolitical assembling of the knowledge-based economy.

Even though the state is portrayed as massively challenged by all sorts of de-
territorializing flows and global mobilities as well as by new territorializations
around cities and semi-autonomous "regions", the state appears in Castells
theory as a notable anchor institution of the network society. The statization of informational capitalism thus stands out as an important feature of this
theory. The ways in which Castells (1996; 1997) articulates the role of the
state in the network society are hence particularly interesting (many of the
statistics Castells provides are indeed state based). He describes the welfare state
as badly challenged and threatened not only by the forces of global competition and associated uncertainties – some of which emanate from the nature of
networked informational capitalism and the related volatility and mobility of
money capital – but also by the networked spaces of "informational politics"
which challenge the very ideas of territorially delineated democratic politics.

Irrespective of all these pressures, the state nonetheless plays a role in the
network society. It is an institution that is both explicitly and implicitly, and
sometimes ambiguously, articulated throughout Castells' (1996; 1997) treatment of the network society. Castells (1996) however destabilizes the coherent
understanding of the modern nation state, which must now operate in new

circumstances. Already in the first edition of the *Rise of the Network Society*, Castells (1996) portrays the network society as involving a peculiar reorganization of the international division of labor around "geographical concentrations", the borders of which "do not coincide with countries" (ibid., 147). Accordingly,

> What I call the newest international division of labor is constructed around four different positions in the informational/global economy: the producers of high value, based on informational labor; the producers of high volume, based on lower-cost labor; the producers of raw materials, based on natural endowments; and the redundant producers, reduced to devalued labor. The differential location of such different types of labor also determines the affluence of markets, since income generation will dependent upon the capacity to create value incorporated in each segment of the global economy.
>
> (Castells 1996, 147)

This seemingly de-statist perspective on the international division of labor becomes nevertheless politically meaningful through statization. Castells argues that all states are "penetrated by the four positions indicated because all networks are global in their reality or in their target" (ibid., 147). What this means in policy terms is that state governments should develop a sort of variable geography which maximizes the share of the production of high value within their jurisdictions.

The new division of labor also indicates that for Castells the state is not spatially what it used to be. He argues that as a political institution the territorial state faces a significant de-territorializing and de-nationalizing geopolitical transformation, and that it is in the process of taking the form of a "network state" (Castells 2005). This is a state which is marked by both heightening domestic divisions and increasing integration with what Castells calls "global affairs". The key geopolitical logic of this transformation is explicitly articulated in the following lengthy quote:

> The rise of a new form of the state gradually replaces the nation-states of the industrial era. This is related to globalization, that is, the formation of a network of global networks that link selectively across the planet all functional dimensions of societies. Because the network society is global, the state of the network society cannot operate only or primarily in the national context. It has to engage in a process of global governance but without a global government ... Furthermore, to connect the global and the local, nation-states have asserted or fostered a process of decentralization that reaches out to regional and local governments, and even to NGOs, often associated to political management. Thus, the actual system of governance in our world is not centered around the nation-state, although nation-states are not disappearing by any means. Governance is

operated in a network of political institutions that shares sovereignty in various degrees and reconfigurates itself in a variable geopolitical geometry. This is what I have conceptualized as the network state.

(ibid., 15)

This "statization" of knowledge-intensive capitalism discloses the more general ways in which the fluidities inherent in knowledge-based economization are territorialized to take the form of separate, territorially re-shuffled and competing states whose governments are rendered responsible for certain tasks.

Bringing labor into space

The knowledge-based economy is constituted in efforts to bring into being new and useful kinds of "productive subjects" that suit the conceived contemporary and future spaces of the knowledge-intensive economy. In the process of knowledge-based economization both managers and workers are reconfigured as subjects of accumulation as well as useful citizens. The new spatiality of the network society and the new division of labor in particular, brings into the picture a new geopolitical subject: the "informational labor" (Castells 1996) which holds together the processes of informational capitalism. Castells suggests that the position of a state within the new international division of labor is not based on the "characteristics of the country" but on the "characteristics of its labor" and "its insertion into the global economy" (Castells 1996, 147). What thus characterizes the geopolitics of the knowledge-based economy is the mode of government which seeks to seize opportunities through policy experimentation on select segments of its populace. Skill formation in particular is at the core of these experiments. Governments which are at pains to reconfigure political communities as knowledge-based economies thus pay particular attention to certain social practices related to human engineering through education and research. Within the past 20 years, the knowledge-based economy has indeed been actualized in policy initiatives and state strategies that focus precisely on the institutional design and strategic re-orientation of education, skill formation and higher education more generally (Jessop 2008).

The geopolitical subject of the knowledge-based economy refers to a particular collective agency. This agency, I believe, has emerged as a crucial geopolitical resource for states which seek to manage global circulation and to connect themselves with the conceived global networks and related value chains. Accordingly, the future of the state or any other political unit can be controlled by manipulating the characteristics of labor, including its spatial orientations and capacities. Indeed, the production of the new "informational labor" (Castells 1997) involves the dissemination of what Sue Roberts (2003) calls "global strategic visions". These visions, which often refer to the network as a new way of conceiving political space, are essential in the making of the global as an actually existing sphere of action in the process of knowledge-based economization. Again, these visions are produced and mobilized by prestigious (and also less prestigious) universities and business schools, think tanks, lobbying organizations, consultants and management gurus, who reflexively circulate ideas and ideologies on this new phase of capitalism (see also Jones 2008, 382).

The geopolitical subject of the knowledge-based economy is embodied by what Castells (1996, 196) terms the "spirit of informationalism". It refers to how the collective of information workers who are effectively networked and loaded with a creative and adventurous ethos as well as unabashed personal drive. They are "producers of informational capitalism" or "knowledge generators and information processors" whose contribution is most valuable to the economy (Castells 1997, 345). These figures are thus characterized by their expertise and skills in the fields of technology, communication and strategy, and are anxious to engage in different kinds of knowledge-intensive businesses and activities. Alternatively, they may dedicate themselves to ensuring the success of a large corporation or take personal risks to found a start-up company. They nonetheless embody both the ability and eagerness to produce innovations in the domains in which they happen to work (Stalder 2006). Qualities such as excitability, adaptability, openness to relocation and appreciativeness of a sort of "global hustle" or "global chisel" characterize these producers of informational capitalism. The following quote from Castells (2005, 18, emphasis in original) depicts some of these qualities:

> At the source of the entire process of social change there is a new kind of worker, the self-programmable worker, and a new type of personality, the values-rooted, flexible personality able to adapt to changing cultural models along the life cycle because of her/his ability to bend without breaking, to remain inner-directed while evolving with the surrounding society. This innovative production of human beings ... requires *a total overhauling of the school system*, in all its levels and domains. This refers certainly to new forms of technology and pedagogy, but also to the content and organization of the learning process. As difficult as it sounds, societies [states] that will not be able to deal with this issue will encounter major economic and social problems in the current process of structural change.

Particular skills and more general qualities together constitute the geopolitical subject inherent in knowledge-based economization. This subject is composed of professionals who are capable of connecting themselves to different kinds of global networks and of utilizing information networks to conduct all manner of global affairs. These skills and qualities are also important, for they empower the "informational labor" to cope in the network society, within which "the notion of a stable, predictable, professional career is eroded" (Castells 2005, 9) and "flexibility" emerges as a notable personal and collective property. The geopolitical subject of the knowledge-based economy is thus familiar with the "individualization of work" and the "fragmentation of societies" (Castells 1996, 201).

Well-educated and project-oriented informational labor runs the key functions of the knowledge-based economy. This class of labor is a carrier of a new geopolitical rationality and initiative. In this capacity, this labor becomes the key societal force within political communities, and also a central governmental concern. Over the past two decades, the sheer strategic emphasis on the informational labor issue is one of the reasons why knowledge-based economization is characterized by a polarizing social structure. The rise of this new geopolitical subject thus makes the generic industrial labor of the "industrial state" disposable, or at least strategically less important than during high Fordism (Castells 1996). This is irrespective of the fact that manufacturing activity is not disappearing, and that the generic workforce remains the actual majority.

At the pinnacle of the knowledge-based economy are the "dominant managerial elites" who share cosmopolitan mindsets and particular lifestyles, possess extensive local and global connections and congregate in major cities (Castells 1996, 415). One author suggested revealingly in the *Harvard Business Review* in 1993 that in an age in which knowledge is the key competitive resource and information "the new raw material", and in which "knowledge workers" and the organizations they inhabit form an infrastructure for such resources, the "manager's job is to create an environment that allows knowledge workers to learn – from their own experience, from each other, and from customers, suppliers, and business partners" (Webber 1993).

In sum, the new geopolitical subject of the knowledge-based economy, the informational labor or "knowledge workers", brings together the relational and the territorial political spaces. This subject embodies capabilities to operate effectively in global networks, and occupies a central position in wealth creation and in generating the political success of the state, city or region. The new geopolitical subject of the knowledge-based economy is a collective which brings together managers and skilled workers, as well as firms and political communities. It is composed of what Castells (1996, 244) calls the commanders (strategic decision-makers), researchers (innovators), designers (packagers of innovation), integrators (particular amalgamators) and operators of the knowledge-based economy. Even though the strategic position of these figures differs within the production process, as widely articulated ideal types they all represent a kind of individualized economic nomadism indicative of the new managerial, technical and professional occupations which overcome the contained spaces of the industrial era and associated nationalized state spaces and mindsets. This type of a "Silicon Valley subject" thus fundamentally differs from the place-bound and thus fixed generic labor of nation-state-centered capitalism. It discloses political efforts to produce "standardized forms of individuality" (Alvesson and Willmott 2007, 2) characterized by certain desired personalities, beliefs, preferences and tastes that are understood to fit to the needs of contemporary capitalism.

The geopolitical subject of the knowledge-based economy is territorially disruptive in its nature. It represents a sort of revolutionary (but not necessarily progressive) agency which was considered potentially de-stabilizing and thus dangerous during the Cold War rivalries between capitalism and communism. The consolidation of the state around the figure of the loyal national citizen capable of contributing to industrialization and related state modernization has of course not been entirely replaced in the new territorial consolidation process or by the rise of the new ideal subject.

Rather, the new globalizing citizen figures of the knowledge-based economy signify the rise of social engineering or human resources and human potential management in the age of knowledge-intensive capitalism. This kind of management has the potential to bring about the fragmentation of citizenship and the further destabilization of national homogeneity.

6 Higher education, geopolitical subject formation and knowledge-based economization

Since the late nineteenth century, political strategies have often highlighted the role of education as being at the forefront of societal change. Education has been an integral part of nation-building, state-building and economic development. Similarly, the role of education as one of the central practices of constructing the state as a territory of wealth and belonging is undisputed.

Education and higher education were essential elements in the genesis of the Keynesian national welfare state as a particular geopolitical unit (cf. Nordin and Sundberg 2014). If anything, the construction of the Keynesian welfare state was characterized by a remarkable expansion of education, both spatially and across social classes. Provision of education became a form of universal social engineering and one of the key mechanisms through which what is customarily known as the welfare statehood unfolded. Primary and secondary school systems were homogenized, spatial networks of higher education institutions expanded and curricula developed on the basis of particular national needs. This was the case in the OECD sphere in particular. One may thus argue that the spatial modernization of the state and the constitution of educational systems took place concomitantly. The state was simultaneously constituted as a compartment of space and educational systems.

The bond between the geopolitical construction of the state as a territory of wealth and education as a particular type of social engineering has not unraveled despite the gradual evaporation of Keynesian national welfare statehood. This link has rather qualitatively transformed from the 1990s onwards. The goal of the rest of this chapter is to discuss the ways in which the geopolitical can be understood in the context of universities. The starting point in such a perspective is that universities are complex societal organizations whose purposes and actions extend well beyond producing pure scientific progress. Moreover, universities change qualitatively in the course of time. I suggest in this chapter that the knowledge production, educational practices and societal interaction of universities are still understood as a key source of national success and national prosperity (also Kerr 2001). Simultaneously, however, universities increasingly contribute to the construction of a de-territorializing, transnational societal and political order, thus "globalizing" or "internationalizing" the state.

As a testament to the above-proposed notion, there is a vast consensus today that universities play a significant role in knowledge-intensive capitalism. They are widely presumed to produce scientific excellence that can be harnessed and commercialized by business firms. Universities, in such a view, are increasingly approached as active agents in the knowledge-based economy. Simultaneously, universities form a decisive strategic-political infrastructure of competitiveness for political communities which strive for competitive advantages. Universities are thus not only considered engines of economic growth, competitiveness and employment, but also strategic political spaces. The discourses of the knowledge-based economy have therefore fundamentally structured, but not entirely determined, higher education policy formulations in different geographical contexts. As cities, states and regions seek to position themselves within the global value chains and in the upper tiers of all manner of rankings, universities have been fundamentally re-worked as political and, as I will suggest, geopolitical sites.

My experience in the Finnish and in some other European contexts is that major societal re-structuring is today at work in universities. Indeed, within the increasingly axiomatic discourses of the global knowledge-based economy universities are no longer given a merely supporting role as "national" organizations of such economy. Rather, universities are increasingly conceived of as pivotal actors of the global knowledge-based economy. They inculcate global geopolitical subjects with "skills and vision", and perform as partners to business firms. Moreover, they may even become lucrative "national" businesses themselves.

Universities as geopolitical sites

Globally, there are more than 17,000 institutions of higher education, and many of these call themselves universities. Some are state institutions, others more or less autonomous organizations which are nonetheless funded primarily from public coffers. Then there are private universities which are funded from many different sources and which enjoy significant organizational autonomy. Only a relatively small portion of universities operate in more than one country. Moreover, only a relatively tiny portion of the universities in the OECD sphere have founded large-scale external campuses abroad.

Irrespective of their organizational form or funding basis, universities have been gradually re-worked since the 1990s, at least in the OECD sphere. Universities have undergone a significant administrative and institutional restructuring during this period. Simultaneously, various political forces have sought to internationalize universities and even entire national university systems. And yet, most universities still operate in a characteristically national context, under the control and tutelage of state ministries.

In the ensuing pages, I conceptualize universities as key contributors to knowledge-based economization. First, these institutions are political technologies through which the geopolitical subjects of the knowledge-based economy are educated. Universities operate within and through particular geopolitical discourses and their functions are tightly tied up with particular types of knowledge formation. Second, universities appear as political objects in a number of calculative socio-technical practices such as university rankings. In my reading, universities are geopolitical sites of knowledge-based economization, the dimensions of which can be charted in a number of ways. I scrutinize three overlapping dimensions below: universities as learning environments, universities as scaled sites and universities as geopolitical objects.

Learning environments

Universities are a particular type of discursive and material learning environment. The learning environments of universities are constantly re-negotiated and contested, and, accordingly, an inquiry into these environments offers a useful lens for understanding the changing societal and wider geopolitical agency of universities, as well as their endeavors to bring about societal change. A university, in short, has many uses (Kerr 2001).

Since the 1990s, the discourses and practices of the knowledge-based economy have arguably had fundamental implications for higher education in diverse geographical settings. The uses of the university have become tightly aligned with the political practices and business trends of knowledge-intensive capitalism. The links between the knowledge-based economy and higher education have gradually become more active, pervasive and salient. During recent years in particular, institutions of higher education have hence been increasingly re-imagined and harnessed as growth-facilitating political institutions but also as resources in the profit-seeking strategies of private companies. This has happened in an age of political economy which is undergirded with terms such as human capital, triple helix, human creativity, talent, intangible assets, entrepreneurialism and the state's international competitiveness.

There is very little research at present on the ways in which the imperatives of knowledge-intensive capitalism have manifested themselves in the learning environments of universities. This is regrettable given that the reconstructing of universities in the name of the "new economy", "globalization" and "national competitiveness" has involved notable efforts to construct new learning environments for higher education.

The notion of learning environment refers here to the material, physical, symbolic, intellectual and political spaces within which both the substance of higher education as well as the more informal extracurricular activities are situated. Technology, pedagogy and space are taken together within the learning environments of universities. The learning environments of universities are important as they function as a central component in the efforts to re-work the capacities and orientations of students and staff through different kinds of physical environments, technologies and spatial arrangements. The learning environments are thus explicitly germane to the content and organization of the learning process itself (cf. Castells 2005). In such a view, a learning environment is a political technology through which education, by ordering not only knowledge but also the experience of learning, can be said to control human beings (Müller 2011, 2).

Learning environments can also be considered as mediums through which universities communicate with different societal, political and economic actors and seek to create favorable external images or brands. Indeed, within the past few years, universities have actively transformed their physical environments and visual images in order to develop "connectivity" with different actors of the knowledge-based economy – including other universities. New innovation centers, business accelerators, start-up spaces, nontraditional learning spaces for students (with new affectual elements) and a class of post-industrial lecture halls have recently been constructed in many universities across the globe. As a vice-rector of a university I once interviewed stated (2016), the new physical environments of universities should "breathe" creativity and embody the university as a physical and spiritual "ecosystem". According to this individual, this new ecosystem signals the departure from the old factory or school type of university that belongs to the industrial era and should be forgotten. This distinction between the environments of the "industrial university" and the "new university" is revealing and by no means exceptional. At the heart of this distinction is the axiom that universities should educate a new class of laborers by estranging them from the purported practices, orientations and manners of the Fordist industrial era. Indeed, the ethos of these learning environments is actively promoted in the official marketing materials of universities across the globe. As a result, the visual, textual and symbolic features of universities have taken an increasingly transnational and entrepreneurial form.

However, a university as a learning environment is not a monolithic commonplace but rather a contested political space. Different public and private forces constantly seek to operate through these environments, which also contain a particular type of historically contingent epistemic goals. Historically speaking, these environments have thus been intimately connected to what Castells (2005, 18) calls the "innovative production of human beings". This connects the learning environments of universities to the issue of the geopolitical subject of the knowledge-based economy, that is, the informational laborer. Indeed, the gradual consolidation of the university-industrial complex in the name of the state's international competitiveness is a picture of the times. In other words, the knowledge-based economy has become a powerful policy paradigm not only for the institutional re-working of universities and the wholesale re-designing of their learning environments, but also in terms of skill formation (also Jessop 2008).

Stimulating creativity and innovation in new ways, so as to foster these in virtually all domains of social life, has in fact become one of the central epistemic elements of the learning environments of universities. Considering the contemporary university as a geopolitical site brings us therefore to the central ideas of the so-called creative economy. The well-known debater and adviser on creative economy and creative business, John Howkins, for example, is explicit in making a distinction between what he labels "the ordinary economy" and the "creative economy". The former operates with scarce material resources and competition is based on prices. Within the latter form of economy, in turn, individuals and firms use intangible resources which are purportedly infinite, and yet the actors still compete also via price. At the heart of the creative economy is an understanding that we have moved to a world of increasing returns based on the infinity of possible ideas and, accordingly, the individual's faculty to (ingeniously) use these ideas to generate new products and transactions (Howkins 2001, 130–131).

The ways in which the learning environments of universities have been re-designed in many geographical contexts are explicitly structured by the above-mentioned understanding of a shift in the logics of returns, and the role of resources vis-à-vis these returns. Moreover, the widespread acceptance of the colossal significance of this economic shift enhances the value of particular management knowledge on managing and guiding the creativity process of both individuals and collectives with respect to the administration of universi-ties but also individual academic programs. But the supposed shift in the global economy also highlights the role of universities as physical-spiritual test sites within which the creative mindset can be manufactured. The perennial rise of the culture of teamwork (shared office spaces, etc.), "deals and hits" and busi-ness clusters, as well as the emphasis on the creative entrepreneur in higher education practices must be situated within the rise of the imaginaries of the knowledge-based economy and the creative economy as one of its impor-tant components.

Universities as scaled geopolitical sites

Universities can be regarded as scaled geopolitical sites. Universities are scaled in political decision making, policymaking and in scientific and educational practices by different actors. Higher education was central in the building of the Keynesian national welfare state as a geopolitical object. Indeed, the nationalization of higher education in post-Second World War Europe and beyond created a strong cultural understanding according to which institutions of higher education are important factors in competition with other states or "nations" (Välimaa 2004). The construction of the Keynesian welfare state was thus characterized by a remarkable expansion of higher education, both spatially and across social classes. Provision of higher education became not only one of the markers of national strength but also a particular form of social engineering. Higher education thus became one of the mechanisms through which welfare statehood evolved both domestically and internationally.

In post-Second World War Europe, universities were "nationalized" through state funding and regulation, university networks expanded in many of the OECD states and curricula developed on the basis of conceived national needs. National industries, national societal orders and the health problems of national populace were closely connected with universities as geopolitical sites. During so-called high Keynesianism, the notion of the "national university system" came to symbolize the link between the nation, the territorial state and higher education in a number of countries.

There already exists a raft of insightful research analyzing the recent "neoliberalization" (Pike 2012), "corporatization", "privatization", "marketization" and "internationalization" (Knight 2006) of universities as well as the birth of the "entrepreneurial university" (Clark 1998). However, the manner in which universities have become scaled in the face of the dictates of knowledge-intensive capitalism has only recently come under systematic scrutiny (Koch 2014; Moisio and Kangas 2016). This is regrettable given that the scientific, educational and administrative practices of the Fordist-Keynesian national university constitute the substrate through which the essentially "Schumpeterian" and "internationalizing" educational and scientific practices are currently being introduced (see Belina *et al.* 2013).

At the level of both symbols and epistemic contents, the contemporary university is a peculiar combination of nationalizing and transnationalizing elements. Even state universities have nonetheless increasingly rid themselves of nation-centrism and selected more globally oriented strategies in terms of their stated values and the priorities of their actions, as well as their organizational compositions. But at the same time a strong cultural understanding according to which institutions of higher education are important for competition with other nations has remained strikingly strong. In any case, as geopolitical sites of the knowledge-based economy, universities are being de-nationalized in part through logics that ostensibly reflect a particular transnational consensus. In such a view, transnationalization takes place within the micro-spaces and small practices of universities and is hence both institutional and locally embedded. This resonates with Sassen's (2005) argument according to which de-nationalization takes place within supposedly national contexts and thus does not entail the demise of the territorial state. Universities can therefore be understood as both drivers and outcomes of the processes of the knowledge-based economy and the capitalist globalization more broadly (see, e.g. Olds 2007).

The relationship between universities – as nodes or sites of globalization – and the territorial state (and also the city) has changed over the course of time. The empirical part of the chapter at hand highlights the fact that the Finnish state has been active in setting up new frameworks for higher education in order to further globalization and enhance territorial competitiveness (cf. Wahlström 2014). Universities have become pivotal sites of negotiation between the state government and various transnational actors and organizations, including global business firms. This has manifested itself in a gradual re-working of universities regarding existing national regulations and associated constraints. As part of such re-working, the various constituents of universities have been positioned within extensive webs of interdependencies through which the university is expanded beyond its immediate environment (cf. Addie *et al.* 2015).

Although the process varies from university to university, and from country to country, universities in the OECD sphere are today expected to contribute to national success and prosperity in the purportedly borderless knowledge-based economy. Richard Florida (2007, 251) argues revealingly how universities are today perceived as "undeniably powerful talent magnets, attracting ... the best and brightest to our shores. They are the Ellis Islands of the Creative Age". In other words, academic knowledge production and associated educational practices of universities have gradually become integral parts of the internationalization strategies of the state itself (cf. Harland 2009). As a result, universities have been spatially re-constituted in policy discourses and practices related to teaching and research in such a manner that has implications for student, teacher and researcher alike.

Universities as geopolitical objects of competition

I have earlier discussed the role and importance of objectifying calculative practices and related systems of comparison in the process of knowledge-based economization. I argued that cities, states and regions are produced as geopolitical objects of competition in such calculative practices. Nonetheless, the formation of cities, regions or states as geopolitical objects is effected through measurements, analyses and comparisons of other objects as well. Indeed, a university can be comprehended as one of the geopolitical objects through which the performance of states, cities and regions can be measured.

For decades, the OECD has produced detailed country comparisons of national systems of higher education. Similarly, governments have produced their own national university comparisons throughout the twentieth century. However, since the 1990s, university ranking has emerged as a potential market for private consultancies, which have been active in tailoring different kinds of university rankings, league tables and indices. These rankings, which often aim to identify the world's leading (and also poorly performing) universities through different types of ranking criteria, typically measure scientific output and excellence but also reputation, level of internationalization and other elements of the learning environments and governance of universities. These rating organizations have thus become peculiar geopolitical actors of the knowledge-based economy, and are arguably closely related to the commodification of knowledge and even the commodification of universities.

Rankings such as *World University Rankings* (The Times Higher Education Ranking), the *Academic Ranking of World Universities* (the so-called Shanghai list) and the *THE-QS Ranking* are today widely followed in the higher education sectors and their indices are widely circulated in the media. These rankings contribute to the emerging "international standards" of higher education and direct the focus toward individual universities and therefore divert attention away from national comparisons of entire "national systems of higher education". Importantly, these rankings produce universities as objects of global geopolitical competition, and thus connect these institutions to "national interest" in a new manner.

Today, university rankings play a notable role in the internal management processes of universities in terms of their efforts to develop and secure reputation in the global higher education market. The role of university rankings in building particular "reputational geographies" (Jöns and Hoyler 2013, 45) is thus a significant geopolitical phenomenon of the knowledge-based economy. Reputation is important not only from the perspective of the attractiveness of a university in the markets of higher education but also from the perspective of public funding and accountability. It is similarly striking to notice the ways in which universities use or misuse these rankings in their various efforts to represent themselves as exceptional learning environments. International ranking schemes thus have a direct impact on the institutional decision-making of universities – irrespective of the methodological limitations of these schemes, and regardless of the difficulty of climbing up the ranks of the various rankings, which use disparate criteria.

As many of the rankings and league tables include discipline-based comparisons, these rankings are also increasingly used by university managers to distinguish between valuable and less valuable fields of research and tuition. The role of ranking schemes in the practices of running universities has thus become increasingly visible. It is exactly through these practices that the contemporary geopolitical condition is directly experienced by university teachers and researchers, who are supposed to be increasingly aware of their role as contributors to the international excellence – often dubbed "world class" science and education – and reputation of the university within which they happen to work. The more international excellence is defined and understood as a capacity to participate in global economic processes, the more individual researchers and research groups become hedged in by the geopolitical discourses of the knowledge-based economy, and the related imaginaries of nation's competitive advantages.

Important for the treatise at hand is to realize that the ranking schemes and associated bibliometrics are objectifying social practices that constitute universities as geopolitical objects of competition. Universities are objectified as units of the knowledge-intensive global economy that can be compared, disciplined and thus placed under the eye of governmental power. Rather than providing useful information for universities themselves, university ranking schemes and related metrics represent governance by comparison that becomes a constitutive element of the transnational state apparatus. Within such an apparatus, universities appear as objects of competition and are entangled with other objects through which the international competiveness of political communities is measured, analyzed and acted upon.

Some further contours of the geopolitics of higher education

The previous arguments already hint at some of the ways higher education and geopolitics come together. In the geopolitical perspective, higher education is much more than a purely pragmatic and technocratic enterprise. It is a site of strategic action for different political forces and actors, including state and non-state institutions alike, to pursue their strategies and to realize their goals. Second, geopolitics of higher education concerns the processes of re-territorialization and de-territorialization, and takes into account the various micro- and macro-spaces where ideas, rationalities and technologies of government intersect. A geopolitical perspective on higher education thus highlights an "investigation of the intertwining of the economic space of capitalism with political and legal spaces, which are no longer fully conjoined in the territorial form of the state" (Mezzadra and Neilson 2013, 66). The geopolitical perspective on higher education also highlights the relevance of these spaces with respect to forms of political subjectivity. Finally, on theorizations of the world as becoming, the geopolitical perspective on higher education highlights that institutions of higher education are productive of ideas that shape future geopolitical action (also Dittmer 2014).

In this perspective, the geopolitics of higher education does not refer to "geopolitical education" or associated geopolitical knowledge which circulates in select institutional environments, diplomacy schools, military academies, universities or the like, or which is embodied in various educational materials. It rather designates the envisioned and materialized higher education learning environments which function as apparatuses of governance, that is, those which constitute, normalize and naturalize certain representations of the knowledge-based economy (see also Koch 2014).

As mentioned above, a key aspect in the geopolitics of higher education is subject formation. An inquiry into subjectification within universities must therefore be situated within the epistemic and material structures of the knowledge-based economy, and within the relationship between the state and capitalist economy (Mitchell 2003). This also implies that efforts to instill loyalty to the state and a particular type of patriotic thinking (e.g. Müller 2011) are only one geopolitical aspect of higher education. Rather, the geopolitics of higher education takes note of a wider attempt to enhance such qualities in human subjects that conform to the prevailing and, importantly, also envisioned future systems of capital accumulation (also Thrift and Olds 2004).

Universities are not passive agents of knowledge-intensive capitalism but rather contribute to the creation of a social and political reality that the key actors of such economy suggest already exists. Given this, it would be possible to approach and analyze the geopolitics of higher education from two partly overlapping angles, as illustrated in Figure 6.1. First, an ethnographic form of

Figure 6.1 The two paths of analyzing the geopolitics of learning environments of universities.

inquiry would investigate the assemblage – its discourses, governing techniques and subjectivities – through various everyday practices or experienced spaces of subjectivity, for example, students, professors, administrators and planners. It would also inquire into whether this project being orchestrated by the knowledge-intensive capitalism is succeeding and whether (and how) it is being resisted. The second line of research would examine higher education as a strategic space linked to the desire to generate new types of professional subjects. This latter form of analysis is the focus of the rest of the present chapter. It is primarily text and policy based, and does not seek to address the ways in which individuals work with particular discourses of the knowledge-based economy.

As I have already suggested, knowledge-based economization proceeds though spatial-institutional experimentations that territorialize the knowledge-intensive "global" economy as distinct political units. These experiments of the knowledge-based economy are often predicated on an understanding that the world of the (global) knowledge-based economy actually already exists and that there is no other alternative than to come to terms with its internal dynamics through behavior change.

Not least because of the temporal quality of the geopolitical discourses of the knowledge-based economy to orient toward the future, the state in knowledge economization becomes ever more experimental and entrepreneurial in its delivery of policy. This does not of course indicate that entrepreneurship somehow replaces production in state strategies but rather that entrepreneurship and production become entangled in new ways with regard to skills and subjectivities. The state which operates within the discourse of the knowledge-based economy is motivated to generate productive subjectivities within particular sites. As production is increasingly seen to take place in social relationships, subjectivity itself becomes productive, not just skills (Read 2009, 33).

The coming together of the modern state and (state) university marks the complex relations between particular segments of population and the territorially institutionalized state apparatus. In short, this coming together illuminates how the state seeks to control bodies, souls and associated skills, capacities and orientations (Lemke 2007, 44; also Elden 2013; Hannah 2001; Jones 2012) in the constant re-production of the state as a territory of wealth and power. The central question of the rest of the chapter is how the capacities and spatial orientations of individuals and populations are being reshaped in knowledge-based economization. This chapter argues that one of the characterizing aspects of the knowledge-based economization is a determination to responsibilize universities in order to forge innovative, devoted, resilient and entrepreneurial state citizens who are capable of generating national success in a purportedly competitive and urbanized "spiky world" (Florida 2008).

In the process of knowledge-based economization portions of citizen-subjects are produced as "globally capable" through spatially and institutionally selective arrangements. These subjects are envisioned to become capable of connecting themselves with all sorts of networks characterized by the highest surplus value. Knowledge-based economization requires engendering a certain type of entrepreneurial life, a life which is oriented toward individualization of both success and responsibility. It is only the current emphasis on individualization and liberalism that distinguishes this type of entrepreneurial geopolitical subject from the German ordoliberal (the so-called social market economy) ideal subject: the innovative, energetic, enterprising, competitive, risk-taking, self-reliant and self-responsible state citizen (see Bonefeld 2012).

In terms of subjectivity crafting, knowledge-based economization is unique in that it unfolds in a peculiar duality. The subjects of the knowledge-based economy should be equipped so that they understand the nature of business in the global market "beyond the state". But at the same time these subjects should also remain loyal (territorialized) in their spatial orientation and political belonging; they should be globally oriented but simultaneously committed to generating success in a given state or polity.

The changing figure of an engineer from the 1950s to the present: the case of Finland

In this section, I suggest that an investigation of the ways in which the state has sought to bring into existence an engineer as a geopolitical subject in different conjunctures may shed light on the operation of state power in the context of knowledge-based economization. The rest of this chapter is based on empirical material on engineer education in Finland as well as documentary material dealing with how the Finnish state apparatus has sought to regulate the capacities, mentalities and orientations of engineers since the 1950s. My analysis thus calls for a close inquiry into particular segments of "strategic populations" within the state and how the changing state strategies and attempts to govern their skills, "talent" and indeed their very being disclose the changing geopolitical strategies within a given state.

In order to undertake such analysis, I first provide some contextual notes on the political economic context in which the university reforms in Finland took shape. This contextualization is crucial given that the constitution of geopolitical subjects of the knowledge-based economy – and the whole process of knowledge-based economization – must be firmly grounded in real-world events and related experiences. These experiences are circulated through infrastructures of affect (Dittmer 2014, 389) such as the media. It can be argued that ideas regarding the need for the new geopolitical subject have emerged concomitantly with a particular experiencing of knowledge-intensive capitalism both at the scale of everyday life and among experts, politicians and policymakers.

I am tempted to argue that the political need for the production of new geopolitical subjects is grounded in the geographically specific circumstances regarding the changing dynamics of labor markets. Most OECD states have witnessed a shift from goods to services, the rise of information and communications technology (ICT)-related jobs and the relatively rapid disappearance of manufacturing and agricultural jobs. This change in economic structure, together with the more general volatility of labor markets as well as the actions of large and even smaller companies in outsourcing manual jobs, has been the source of the conviction that the contemporary global condition is turbulent and that nobody is entirely secure. This experience has thus been grounded upon the demise and outsourcing of industrial jobs, a more general vanishing of middle-class work and the changing structure of employment within some OECD states.

The Finnish case is illustrative of such development and not exceptional (Figures 6.2. and 6.3.). During the past 40 years, the share of industrial manual jobs has declined from 25.5 percent to 14.9 percent. In absolute terms this means a loss of nearly 300,000 industrial jobs in a country of slightly more than five million inhabitants. During the same period, the total number of jobs in the ICT sector (electrical and electronics industry, telecommunication, information technology services) has increased from 56,000 in 1975 to 113,000 in 2015. The decline of industrial jobs has been particularly striking in the field of forest industry – historically a major contributor to livelihoods in Finland, and still accounting for approximately 20 percent of the country's revenue – which has lost more than two-thirds of its workforce in four decades. Since 2007, the decline of industrial jobs has hastened. In some regions in Finland, industrial jobs have vanished with striking rapidity: Central Finland, for instance, lost 30 percent of its industrial jobs between 2007 and 2014.

During the past ten years or so, reactions to the decline of traditional manufacturing employment in some corners of Western Europe and elsewhere has been accompanied by an increasing loss of some of the knowledge-intensive

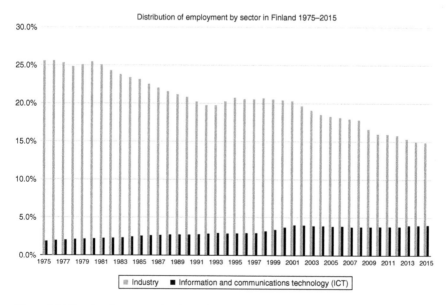

Figure 6.2 The development of industrial and ICT jobs in Finland 1975–2015 (Statistics Finland 2016). Note that "industry" includes manual labor in ICT.

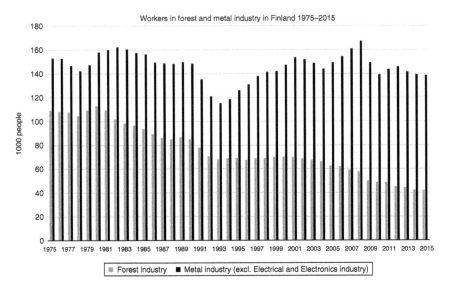

Figure 6.3 The development of jobs in the two basic industrial sectors in Finland 1975–
2015 (Statistics Finland 2016).

jobs that were established in the 1990s. Since 2005 in particular, multinational corporations have not only outsourced their production and services,
thus causing predicaments for local subcontractors, but also cut and relocated
engineering jobs. This development has prompted severe economic and
social problems as well as related epiphenomena in many localities. From
2007 onwards, the decline of ICT-related manual jobs has also included jobs
in research, development and design. Nokia, the multinational corporation
which came to symbolize the ICT boom and related information society discourse in the 1990s in Finland, alone has downsized its workforce in this
geographical context from 24,000 (in 2007) to around 5,600 (in 2016); this
significant drop has also been marked by a notable loss of jobs which require
highly skilled labor.

The "double destruction" of jobs, covering both traditional industrial jobs
and the advanced science-based work, has effected a widely articulated sense of
political powerlessness which is generally argued by governmental agencies and
trade unions alike as being brought about by the inevitable nature of "globalization" (sometimes dubbed globalization 2.0). The picture is now very different
compared with the era of spatial Keynesianism. During those days, centralized
systems of wage negotiations and devaluations of the "national" currency (the
Finnish *markka*) functioned as a political mechanism to address business cycles
that jeopardized the competitiveness of national industries (see, e.g. Vartiainen
2011). The government was also able to use unemployment and, thus, surplus
labor power as a means to discipline workers about the negative implications of
their wage claims for the national success (Pekkarinen 1990, 37).

Today, the widely reported political weakness in the face of "global forces" has been, interestingly enough, accompanied by a series of demands to completely end the public subvention of the "mature sectors" of industry (such as wood-processing industry, see Laukkanen 2016) and to fundamentally redevelop the skills and orientations of the national population to better cope with the purportedly unavoidable events that mark the contemporary global condition. For instance, the recent emphasis on the importance of start-ups for national economic success, and the related plans to include more entrepreneurial content in primary school tuition, must be understood against this backdrop. Familiarity with the processes of knowledge-based economization has thus convinced Finnish political circles to highlight the importance of small- and medium-size knowledge-intensive firms and the associated entrepreneurial "strive for growth" attitude (which is understood to characterize a particular start-up culture/citizenship) as the new source of economic and political success.

The rest of the chapter is based on research into the higher education reforms in Finland, which culminated in 2010 with the founding of Aalto University (also called an "innovation university", hereafter AU) and the passing of a new law on universities (see also Kangas and Moisio 2012). The idea is to focus on the ways in which the reform has targeted professional citizens, engineer education in particular. This is in part because the engineer is a figure that has occupied a central position in the state strategies of Finland since the country's independence (1917). S/he has been an integral part of state-led and nationally scaled modernization, industrialization, military and national defense systems, as well as processes of urbanization, planning and economic growth. The engineer has therefore occupied a central position in all sorts of state strategies within this state since the 1950s; it can thus be understood to mark the rise of the technology oriented, modernizing and indeed nationalizing state strategies which were played out in the Western capitalist states after the Second World War. The engineer with particular orientations, capacities and skills was arguably located at the core of state strategies which sought to construct the "national" since the 1950s. This figure thus came to epitomize an interesting geopolitical being during the Cold War. Arguably, this is now changing.

The following analysis of AU epitomizes the knowledge-based economization of the university. It highlights changes that critical human geographers often discuss in terms of neoliberal corporatization of the university (e.g. Castree and Spark 2000; Belina *et al.* 2013). Three aspects in particular are highlighted below. First, AU is located right at the heart of transnational policy flows that revolve around the ideas and practices of an entrepreneurial university (e.g. OECD 2012) and it provides a mechanism through which such ideas are re-spatialized in a locale. Second, the genesis of AU demonstrates that higher education, as a mostly publicly funded enterprise, plays a central role in the strategies of private actors to extend their power toward the state. Third, AU is an outcome of the ways in which public and private educational interests entangle in efforts to qualitatively re-equip and transnationalize "professional citizens" for a new system of knowledge-intensive accumulation. It thus belongs among the historically specific ways of negotiating the instability and persistent crises of capitalism by way of producing new forms of the subject.

In addition to a body of various kinds of publicly available documents, semi-structured extended interviews were recorded in 2014 with six key political actors, civil servants and university rectors, including the former prime minister of Finland (2003–2010), the permanent secretary of the Ministry of Education and Culture and key representatives of the Confederation of Finnish Industries. In addition, two more interviews were conducted in 2016 with the presidents of two Finnish universities. The interviewees have been closely involved in the recent university reforms in Finland and in the founding of AU. The interviewees were posed questions that mainly had to do with the rationale behind the contemporary university reforms and the founding of AU. I also attended the main start-up event in Finland in 2014, known as Slush, which is considered to form part of the learning environment of AU. In addition, notes were gathered at an international higher education seminar that was organized by AU as an informal part of the Slush event.

The geopolitical discourse of the university reform in Finland

In this section, I inquire into the geopolitical discourses of the knowledge-based economy upon which university reform in Finland is predicated. These discourses position the state in a particular way within knowledge-intensive capitalism and prompt it to adopt particular types of strategies – higher education reform being one of them.

As noted in Chapter 4, the geopolitical discourses of the knowledge-based economy foreground the link between the state and the world in a distinctive way, enabling different actors to act upon the state. These discourses posit that there is a major transformation taking place in world politics and redefines the place of nation states in a specific way. In Finland, these discourses have significantly contributed to the re-orientation of the strategies of the state across policy fields, particularly since the early 2000s.

My conversations with the interviewees normally started with a set of questions that sought to discern how the interviewees viewed the conditions prevailing in Finland and beyond and how the present, in their assessment, differs from the epoch of the welfare state. There was a tendency on the part of the interviewees to narrate a fundamental historical break or a rupture, a transition from an epoch characterized by states as "unified wholes" or "closed societies" to an increasingly complex and challenging contemporary condition. They touched upon the de-territorialization of the state by making references to the fluidity of the social world and argued that ubiquitous risks and challenges are inherent in the rise of the global competition. This transition was also argued to mean that the main source of wealth had switched from natural resources and tangible assets to such intangible assets as knowledge and information.

A related aspect of the geopolitical discourses of the knowledge-based economy is their emphasis on spatial relationality and mobility. This is often articulated as a move away from the territorialized economy and immobile assets of the past to the present economic arrangement where assets are increasable and mobile, and unfold in relational space. My interviewees indirectly referred to the instability and persistent crises of capitalism by painting a picture of the present global economic turmoil as a situation in which the notions of relative political fixity, division of labor, stability and predictability have become unraveled. The present was described as hard to govern precisely for the reason that instead of simple national conflicts and oppositions, it is characterized by a fluidity of all social relations. The idea of the increasingly difficult world played an outsized role in their efforts to characterize the context for higher education reforms.

The interviewees articulated the relationship between the state/nation, the present and the world in terms of economic vulnerability and risk. As one of my interviewees stated in our discussion: "we adopted a very positive attitude toward globalization and we knew that the selected knowledge-based strategy was very risky, but we thought it was the only strategy that was available" (Author's interview 2014). Basically, all interviewees relied on a very similar logic of reasoning. The prevailing conditions were argued to warrant new survival strategies. This was said to be the case in particular for Finland, a small state fragile as a result of the way it is exposed to the world economy. The interviewees also identified certain critical failures in dealing with the situation. They made reference to a gradual loss of industrial jobs, the difficulties of attracting foreign direct investments (FDI) and the unique structure of the Finnish economy, which relies on "large economic players". There has, indeed, been a decline of 19 percent in the number of industrial jobs in Finland over the period 2007–2012, a considerable drop in FDI after the 2008–2009 economic crisis, and over 60 percent of the country's exports are produced by the 20 largest enterprises (Statistics Finland 2015). Due to the conceived "smallness" of the state, its exposed posture and the landscape of large corporations, Finland was portrayed as particularly vulnerable to the volatile nature of the world market, and fostering specific capacities and qualities in its population was portrayed as the way out of this dilemma. The demands of the de-territorializing global economy were thus re-spatialized with reference to the discourse of necessity. The same logic is repeated in countless official documents:

> Large multinational companies have been the cornerstone of Finland's economy, but are now undergoing continuous operational regeneration, in reaction to changes in the global market situation. These companies will find it easiest to fragment and transfer their operations anywhere, while managing their value networks. In Finland, determined efforts must be made to grasp opportunities for retaining production operations that increase added value and generate new development .... Large multinational companies capable of seizing control of global value networks will be the success stories of the future. The prerequisites for this must be

monitored and strengthened. An obvious prerequisite is a high level of competence [of population] that meets the needs of enterprises, as well as a sufficient labor supply.

(Prime Minister's Office 2013, 39)

Re-spatialization of the global economy here occurs through the idea that the state can and must strategically re-situate itself vis-à-vis multinational businesses that have organized their production in global value chains. As it can do little to strengthen the ostensibly national firms which are constantly under assault from their OECD-country based rivals and the so-called emerging-world upstarts, the state is faced with the task of coming up with strategies through which it can relocate its territorial economy vis-à-vis global value chains. While value chains were discussed by the interviewees as being governed by economic imperatives and/or the multinationals, there was seen to be some room for state agency, though this was an adaptive form of agency. While the world was described as the playing field of multinationals, it was seen as the task of the state to create such spaces that would attract the multinationals to place some of their operations within the state's territory. This logic of thinking is re-produced in the following excerpt which discusses state strategies in an increasingly digitalized economy.

In a digital economy, it is increasingly easy for a growing number of businesses to transfer their operations anywhere in the world. Competition between providers of the best locations is stepping up …. The state could contribute to the creation of marketplaces within the digital economy, attracting knowledge-intensive industries to invest in Finland.

(Prime Minister's Office 2013, 26, 35, 37)

The portrayal of the world as a playing field of globally oriented businesses develops logically into a doomsday scenario. It suggests that the nations and "regions" that harness ideas, upgrade skills and generate knowledge-intensive jobs will simply be the most successful polities in avoiding unemployment, the development of bad jobs and thus, national disaster. Accordingly, any nation which loses its ability to compete in the range of high-productivity/high-wage knowledge-based industries characterized by innovation, high technology and talent is said to be in danger of losing its standard of living and will be doomed to a future in the periphery (Porter 2008, 177). All the interviewees were very responsive to the logic of this scenario, thus echoing what the *Economist* reported a few years ago: Finland has been "updating" its version of capitalism by way of moving on to "brainwork in global networks" (The *Economist* 2013, 8).

The new learning environment

One of the ways in which the state has responded to the demands of the knowledge-based economy is by way of producing new learning environments of higher education. In the ensuing pages, I turn my attention from the geopolitical discourses of the knowledge-based economy to the components of a particular learning environment as specific condensation of material, symbolic, intellectual and political elements constitutive of knowledge-based economization. I suggest that the new learning environment is being built with the expectation that it will nurture such competencies and characteristics in the population that meet the requirements of the global economy (multinationals, venture capitalists etc.) and thus connect the state space of Finland to the global value chains. I analyze what kinds of physical and immaterial settings of learning and education are being designed to advance a shift from the iconic national worker-citizen of the post-Second World War period to the globally attuned citizen-subject.

The creative entrepreneur and the culture of start-ups

AU was originally and very tellingly developed under the rubric of University of Innovations and constitutes one of the core substances of the Finnish higher education reform that culminated in 2010. The founding of AU, with the help of supplemental funding of 700 million Euros (of which 500 million was public money), was instigated by a handful of export-based business representatives – key industrialists with the support of the highest political elite and central state officials. The promise of the leading industrial sectors to contribute at least 200 million Euros to the foundation of AU not only fundamentally enticed the willingness of the state government to launch general university reform but also committed the government to the substantial public financing of AU.

The founding of AU illustrates a particular heterogenization of space; it evidences how the state became a key agent in the establishing of a "globally competitive university" which, in terms of re-spatialization, meant turning the Helsinki capital city-region into an educational node, a hub for domestic and global talent, or a high-tech city-region (Ministry of Education 2007). In addition, the initiative for AU discloses a bid to transform work subjectivity, to broaden the capacities and skills of individuals toward new transnational substances and spaces. Such an expectation is also expressed by the professor of entrepreneurship education at AU, who argues that the institution's tuition aims to further the birth of an entrepreneurial identity and that entrepreneurial identity is not limited to the mundane matter of running of a business: "rather it is a world-view according to which your own attitude is key and that there are no safe havens in this world" (Kalska 2013). In the first Aalto Academic Summit this view was also shared by a notable Finnish science policymaker who argued that entrepreneurialism is a mindscape, a kind of novel culture that can be partly engendered by public intervention.

My interviewees also argued that AU had to be founded because a new kind of learning environment was needed, for engineers in particular. This was in response to the fact that the fundaments of higher education in engineering – the hard core of natural sciences that can be utilized in industrial processes – had remained relatively untouched by the previous reforms of higher education. Interestingly, this attempt is not so much visible in the formal curricula as it is manifested in the ways in which AU has sought to function as a novel type of an environment for learning. The genesis of AU was based on the issues of technology and innovations; it was to bring together knowledge on business, technology and design innovations in a way which would create a breeding ground for new kinds of globally oriented economic players.

My discussions with the interviewees about AU invariably revolved around the idea that the contemporary world requires not so much new science skills but new forms of professional attitude, which were articulated in terms of individuality and creativity. Fostering such entrepreneurial culture among a new generation of Finns was referred to as a key justification for the founding of AU. The fact that emphasis was put on these kinds of attitudes rather than concrete skills resonates with the way in which the knowledge-based economization involves constituting individuals as human capital and how this transforms notions of labor and workers. As Read (2009, 33) observes, "capital no longer simply exploits labor, understood as the physical capacity to transform objects, but puts to work the capacities to create and communicate that traverse social relations". As production is seen to take place in social relationships, subjectivity itself becomes productive, not just skills (ibid.) This is the context within which the interviewees' call for new knowledgeable and enterprising subjects (cf. Thrift and Olds 2004) capable of modifying their relationship to business and work in a purportedly rapidly changing world makes sense and must be understood.

The stakeholders of AU thus envisaged the new university as an effective strategy of subjectification which, by way of fostering a start-up culture not only among its students and staff but also wider society, encourages individuals to see themselves as "companies of one" (Read 2009, 30). This has a notable social political relevance, as it resonates with the contemporary trend away from careers built on long-term labor contracts toward temporality of jobs. Key elements and the logic of this way of thinking are re-produced in an article published in the *Aalto Magazine:*

> The startup movement is like the rock scene," say business students Miki Kuusi and Antti Ylimutka. People want to be like successful rockstars, so more and more start playing the guitar, but only a few can become world famous. This is why it is important that there's a lot of beginners. The phenomenon spawns new bands – and, analogously, new enterprises …. Kuusi and Ylimutka say that startup entrepreneurs share common traits like ambition and a drive for accomplishment. These people won't start a hardware store or a hair salon to provide them with a steady income for the rest of their lives. Instead, they employ venture capital to build products or services for the international market at a dizzying pace.
>
> (Kalska 2013)

Perceiving themselves as rockstars or companies of one, individuals are less inclined to think that they would have something to gain from collective organization and solidarity. Rather, they are encouraged to make investments in human capital which transforms desire for independence into a business spirit. There is a striking distance between this way of thinking of professional life and the previous state-centered professional life (of engineers).

This transformation also entails a shift in the way in which individuals are made subjects. The interviewees envisioned the learning environment of AU as a specific kind of governmental apparatus expected to foster such qualities in individuals that suit the new landscape of charismatic entrepreneurialism. It is interesting to note that this new culture of learning was expected to be engendered if, in addition to physical settings of education (e.g. buildings and classrooms), the bodies and affective energies of students and scholars representing different disciplinary backgrounds were brought together. Moreover, the AU case illuminates how the current form knowledge-based economization is marked by a particularly intense affective rhetoric of neoliberal governmentality (cf. Read 2009, 29). Indeed, AU and special projects clustered around it are almost invariably characterized with notions such as "enthusiasm", "full steam", "hustle", "drive", "ambition" and so on.

The interviewees as well as the analyzed documents referred to the new combination of material objects, bodies and the invisible infrastructure of learning with the notions of "start-up culture" or "ecosystem". Various kinds of events, institutional structures, principles, professorships and student activism – *Entrepreneurship Society* being today the largest form of student activity at AU – were cited as its constituent elements. What purposes are they expected to serve? In its promotional materials, AU often refers to these ostensibly creative spaces as platforms that enable students, professors, researchers and developers to meet, interact and collaborate. Moreover, interdisciplinary "factories" have been designed to "facilitate new forms of collaboration in an environment where academic teams, researchers and students work together with companies and communities" (Aalto University 2014). In addition, the stated task of the Aalto Center for Entrepreneurship is to create successful business out of the interactions and innovations taking place within this culture and its spaces, that is, to make the participants part of the processes of innovation.

From the point of view of the dynamics of re-spatialization it is also interesting to note that the key principles of the new learning environment of AU echo what Saxenian (1994) originally associated with Silicon Valley and Boston's Route 128 region. This spatial connection – which effectively discloses some of the ways in which the transnational citizenship is built in the functioning of AU – is not at all insignificant as there are also attempts to build actual connections between AU and Silicon Valley. The company incubator Startup Sauna, for instance, regularly takes students to Silicon Valley in order to embed and familiarize them with what the chairman of this organization markets as a local culture that promotes entrepreneurship through "moral support", encourages risk-taking and experimentation and provides suitable role models. The practice of making study trips to the US and its expected impact on the societal atmosphere has also been recognized by *The Economist*

(2013, 10). In 2010, it published a story about a group of students from Aalto University on a study trip to the Massachusetts Institute of Technology. Upon their return to Finland, they embarked on what the publication calls "the most constructive piece of student activism in the history of the genre". During their visit, the students had been

> converted to the power of entrepreneurialism" and "organized a 'summer of start-ups' to spread the word that Finland's future lay with new companies, not old giants. The summer of start-ups turned into a season of innovation. The student revolution was part of a wider reconsideration of the proper relationship between government and business.
>
> (*The Economist* 2013, 10)

This provides yet another innocent but at the same time revealing example of the kind of back-and-forth re-working of spatial arrangements and associated subjectivities that characterize contemporary geopolitics of knowledge-based economization in the context of higher education.

Linking entrepreneurial culture with internationalization

Within the learning environment of AU both student and staff are surrounded by the ideals of excellence, economic productivity, profitability and risk-taking (on these ideas more generally, see Brown 2006, 694). This learning environment, which brings together such material elements as lecture halls, buildings, innovation labs and their interiors and also spaces of business incubation, to name but a few, is structured around the dogma of internationalization. This re-spatializes the idea of entrepreneurialism in a very specific way, suggesting that a nationally scaled learning environment is unlikely to be entrepreneurial:

> It is not possible for a university to be entrepreneurial without being international but the university can be international without being entrepreneurial. Internationalization is the process of integrating an international, intercultural or global dimension into the purposes, functions or delivery of education.
>
> (OECD 2012, 14)

The internationalization of the learning environment of AU has taken both conventional and novel forms. The conventional forms of student and staff mobility schemes and the associated international science collaborations have been accompanied by new types of practices of internationalization that take place both within and beyond the campuses of AU.

The OECD also urges universities to integrate education activities "with enterprise-related activities to ensure entrepreneurs are adequately prepared for creating start-ups through their education and that they have the support to put what they have learned into practice" (OECD 2012, 10). This evidences a desire to turn state-orchestrated and state-sponsored public spaces into a mechanism that re-spatializes the dictates of knowledge-intensive capitalism. AU, as a whole, forms part of the state's attempt to respond to this challenge. Its learning environment also comprises components that have been even more clearly designed for this purpose. For example, the Aalto Ventures Program seeks to teach entrepreneurship by way of providing students with the "skills, tools and global networks" (Aalto University 2015) needed in the creation of new business, and, for this purpose, extends beyond the actual physical facilities of AU into new spaces of action. AU has also founded the Aalto Center for Entrepreneurship, which is tasked to commercialize research originating at AU and thus to connect the university with the de-territorializing flows of global capital.

The above-mentioned developments represent efforts to interlink and create a productive match between the formal educational programs and research conducted at AU and the global flows of capital. The constitution of individuals as specific types of internationalized entrepreneurial subjects, transnational citizens, lies at the crux of these efforts; it is a process which is assumed to take place within such learning environments where "the students understand the benefits of developing an entrepreneurial mindset" (OECD 2012, 10). It would be possible to cite a number of examples of how the AU learning environment is geared toward these goals but a particularly salient example is the start-up mentoring in which a nascent start-up company is mentored by a "person with an entrepreneurial mindset … familiar with the key players and market mechanisms" (Aalto University 2015).

Another component of the geopolitical co-constitution and co-functioning of AU is the Slush event, the single largest start-up event in northern Europe, supported and eagerly promoted by AU in its marketing efforts. In 2014, Slush brought together almost 14,000 students, professionals, investors and high-tech executives from almost 3,500 companies from all over the world. The event is particularly interesting from the point of view of knowledge-based economization as it epitomizes not only how things are "made to happen" by concentrating bodies – that is, young professionals, students and representatives of footloose capital (the so-called angel investors in particular) – in a particular location, but also how the affective experience of participation contributes to the formation of transnational citizenship (cf. Dittmer 2014). Commentators frequently made use of notions such as excitement, enthusiasm, ambition and energy to characterize the atmosphere of the event. Taking part in it, I also sensed such affective energy – to an almost exhausting degree.

Curiously, although the very logic of the event bypasses official structures and systems as well as territorial borders, states played a central role in Slush. The prime minister of Finland, accompanied by the vice-premier of China and the Estonian prime minister, officially declared the event opened. Through the bodies and performances of these political figures, the entrepreneurial enthusiasm of the event was re-spatialized within an international framework of the state system. In their talks, these political leaders spoke the language of country promotion, inter-state competition, national competitiveness and state investment landscapes. This illustrates how re-spatialization – understood as back-and-forth re-working of spatial arrangements – informs the conceptualization of the world as constantly becoming (cf. Mitchell 2003, 8; Dittmer 2014, 495).

Even if the learning environment of AU is expected to be a globally connected node, the project as a whole remains firmly attached to a state-centric framework. For the state, AU forms part of an attempt to "activate Finns to participate widely in various competence and knowledge networks" (Ministry of Employment and the Economy 2008, 4). In essence, this represents a nationally scaled, state-centric topography which is articulated in terms of the learning environment of AU being one element in the re-working of the entire fabric of Finnish society. It is expected to transform the purportedly introverted national culture and narrow-minded mentalities of the Finns – sometimes discussed in terms of the "culture of envy" and the "culture of shame" – and replace the purportedly old values of the agrarian past or the "industrial" welfare statehood with such attitudes and orientations that are not in conflict with new forms of "connectedness".

The global engineer

The developments in AU, a key institution for the education of engineers, are particularly interesting given that the figure of the engineer has occupied a central position in the state strategies of Finland since independence (1917). Particularly since the 1950s, the engineer was an integral part of state-modernization, industrialization, military and national defense systems, urbanization, planning and economic growth. What is referred to as the construction of the national Keynesian welfare state would not have been possible without a pool of engineers with skills in mathematics, physics, chemistry and data processing. These skills were pivotal in constructing national industries in the export-oriented sectors of machinery and forestry, but they were also central in state planning more generally. Engineer education in technical universities and faculties was developed and maintained during high Fordism not only for purposes of sustaining capitalist systems of accumulation tied to national systems of production (Liesto 1988) but also for the purposes of securing national strength in a security and foreign policy environment which was perceived as challenging. Higher education in engineering has thus played a critical role in the genesis of such modernizing state strategies that constructed the national as a meaningful and pivotal geopolitical category. In Finland, purportedly "talented", "cheap" and "politically loyal" engineers became part of the national narrative of constructing the welfare state, and their subjectivity was tied to the national polity.

Systematic training in engineering has been offered in Finland for over 100 years. For much of this time, it has been tied to the project of national development and has thus assumed a broad homology of territory and economy. Recently, however, the coupling of the national territory of wealth and engineer has become less stable, as illustrated by the reform rhetoric according to which engineer education should be increasingly geared toward the production of "global engineers". This de-coupling forms part of efforts to reform engineer education to better meet the demands of the purportedly new international division of labor and the dictates of global commodity and value chains. As argued by a professor of engineering at Aalto University: "The highly analytical, technically-focused engineering 'geek' is a person of the past" … "engineering education worldwide is not providing an adequate supply of globally prepared engineers" (Pellinen 2013). The subjectivity of the new generation of engineers as transnational citizens thus becomes produced at the intersection of the discourses of globalism and entrepreneurialism, and partially detaches itself from the discourses of the nation and patriotism.

The new learning environment of AU is expected to foster the subjectivity of global engineer among its students and staff. The genealogy of the term global engineer can be traced back to the debate on higher education and public policy that started over a decade ago, mostly in the OECD sphere. Originally, the expression was coined to highlight social responsibility in the face of various "global (i.e. shared) problems" ranging from poverty and underdevelopment to global warming. But the concept has since been "coopted" for alternative uses and is increasingly employed within an exclusively economistic perspective, that is, geared toward the production of economic growth in knowledge-intensive capitalism. The globalization discourse plays an important role in naturalizing and depoliticizing economic subjectivities in the discussions over engineer education. The production of globally attuned engineers is argued to be a purely pragmatic and technocratic enterprise, a response to the demands that the changing economy sets:

> Globalization is linking national economies in new ways. Nations are transitioning from distinct economic entities to essential segments of one global economy. Likewise, business competition comes from everywhere, requiring engineers to develop a global perspective. The international competition for talent is intense. In today's world, no country can remain isolated or impose barriers to international talent and trade. To be successful in this global environment, you must develop personal, social, business and cultural global literacies.
>
> (Malkinson 2003)

The global engineer thus illustrates the way in which knowledge-based economization *re-positions* the engineer with regard to the state-society nexus through the idea of entrepreneurialism; *re-equips* him or her with interdisciplinary skills that cross the border between technological, business and design innovations; *re-calibrates* the engineer from a technical "geek" to someone who has internalized creativity as a way of life; and *re-locates* him or her within "the global", understood as a culturally differentiated marketplace in which states seek to locate themselves with regard to transnational corporations and their value chains.

The global engineer provides an archetype of the kind of globally attuned subject that the learning environment of AU is expected to produce. Both the interviewees and the written documents make explicit reference to such a character. This shows that in geopolitics of higher education an engineer is not just a human being with technical capacities. She or he is rather a geopolitical figure, a subject who is constantly being re-made by the "discipline" of engineering and its learning environments. This is highlighted by the fact that engineers have historically been located at the intersection of transformations in the relationship between the state and market as well as the national and global, as the following quotation illustrates.

> If things are allowed to develop as they have to this point, and our land educates only administrators, soldiers and civilian servants, you don't need a crystal ball to see that such a country is destined to be forsaken.
>
> – Agathon Meurman (1826–1909)
> cited in *On the Education of Engineers*

The global engineer that the AU learning environment seeks to produce is a character that shares much of what Mitchell (2003, 387–388) refers to as the "outward-looking cosmopolitanism" of "globally oriented state subjects", that is, actors who are able to adapt to rapidly shifting personal and national contexts and whose characteristics are thus in tune with the demands of capitalist globalization. The global engineer is similarly envisaged as an ideal type of a managerial self (Orta 2013) that can be produced through high-quality teaching, research training and extra-curricular activities. A global engineer thus embodies transformations of higher education policies, spatial transformations and the larger accumulation strategies of contemporary capitalism.

Similarly to how Fordism involved a reshaping of the entire fabric of society, including a determination "to elaborate a new type of man", the production of global engineers must be seen as part and parcel of contemporary efforts to produce forms of the subject through which the instability and persistent crises of capitalism can be negotiated. Arguably, the figure of the global engineer forms part of a post-Fordist strategy whereby the state seeks to relocate itself vis-à-vis production increasingly organized in global value chains as well as to engender new business to compensate the potential failures in attracting and retaining foreign direct investments. Paradoxically, it is a statist figure which "reduces citizenship to a notion of market entrepreneurship" (Giroux 2012, 253).

It is clear that since the early 2000s such a vision has gradually come to steer Finnish engineering education. Already in the late 1970s there were calls to increase entrepreneur training in the Technical University of Helsinki (Liesto 1988). The idea, however, remained firmly anchored in a national setting. Nowadays, however, engineers are being prepared for a world which is at once "borderless" (as implied by the proverbial world market) and uncertain but at the same time lucrative, that is, characterized by limitless opportunities that can be harnessed through skills and creative agency.

However, although the global engineer is characterized as a competitive, creative and globally oriented character – a de-territorialized figure of the knowledge-based economy to a great degree – his or her existence and purpose nonetheless continues to be promoted or legitimated within national parameters. Paradoxically, the geopolitical discourses of the knowledge-based economy continue to actualize the almost mythical idea of a nation's citizenry sharing a common economic fate (Kangas 2013, 574). These suggest that the "skill problem" targeted by reforms of higher education is a "nation-wide 'we' concern" (Jones 2008, 391). This is an example of the way in which the geopolitical assemblage re-territorializes the knowledge-based economy by way of nationalizing it. It also serves as a reminder of the fact that a straightforwardly de-territorialized reading of the figure of the global engineer as a form of transnational citizenship would easily overlook how narratives that remain bound to national territorial frameworks also work to sure up the de-territorialized post-Keynesian regime of accumulation (see also Koch 2014).

Coping with knowledge-intensive form of capitalism: reforming higher education in Finland

The previous sections have shown how the geopolitical assemblage of higher education functions as a mechanism through which the developments of global capitalism are realized and acquire place-specific manifestations. I have hoped to demonstrate that it is through re-imagining universities that the state responds to calls suggesting that its key task is to create societal conditions that facilitate innovations (e.g. Aalto University). "An essential task for government", as the Confederation of Finnish Industries sees it, "is to create a climate and an infrastructure where innovations are possible" (Confederation of Finnish Industries 2007: 7).

Although a largely publicly funded institution within the fabric of the state, AU is imagined as a novel learning environment where subjectivities of capitalist laborers are re-forged and the entrepreneurial strategies of private industries extended to the social spaces of professionals and young adults in particular. My inquiry into AU has also demonstrated the willingness of the higher education elite to respond to the strategies of the state by pushing universities to the center of knowledge-intensive capitalism. University managers have therefore acted as docile bodies when confronted with political leaders who constantly underscore the contemporary "competitive environment" within which the Finnish nation and the Finnish state need to cope. This willingness to act geopolitically occurs in particular through a strategic exploitation of the discursive structures of the knowledge-based economy on the part of the top management of universities. From this angle, the institutions of higher education are not passive victims of corporatization or marketization of universities but active agents in generating particular Schumpeterian political economies of the state.

This represents a significant change. Since the 1960s, higher education in Finland was elementarily bound to what is commonly referred to as social government. It operated within the nation state format and was premised on investing in state-owned industries, maintaining private enterprise as well as transforming the subjects of government into useful social citizens with particular rights and responsibilities. Since the early 2000s, this system has been increasingly questioned, mainly due to a perceived danger of declining industrial competitiveness.

The general role of higher education in the spread of the discourses and practices of the knowledge-based economy has been insightfully documented in numerous contexts. Thrift and Olds (2004, 286), for example, suggest that these "cultural circuits of capital" have "been aligned with the state" and have thereby become involved in global geopolitical interventions. Attempts to re-make Finland and re-code its citizens also fall within state strategies to bring the state and the cultural circuit of capital together through higher education. Yet there are certain peculiarities as to how this has unfolded in Finland.

In certain contexts, globally well-known elite institutions of higher education have been assigned an important role in re-structuring and re-orienting national economies and molding the subjectivities of national citizenries. These elite universities have not opened branch campuses or pursued partnerships with local institutions in Finland. One of the interviewees argued that "the Finnish political circles considered that the Finnish education market would be too small and too unattractive for global elite universities" (Author's interview 2014). The Finnish context rather, is characterized by an attempt to qualitatively re-engineer the existing "national" university system, as well as by the establishment of one state university (AU) as a particularly "innovative" learning environment. The cultural circuits of capitalism have thus penetrated Finnish society primarily by engendering the adoption of transnational models of higher education within ostensibly national institutions.

Business circles and individuals representing technology industries in particular were central forces in mobilizing the state to undertake the higher education reforms and to establish Aalto University. In the context of AU, the activism evidenced in the actions of the leading business institutions demonstrates the ways in which different non-state institutions act vis-à-vis the state through the discourse of the knowledge-based economy. As a consequence, one of the trends in Finnish higher education policies since the "little recession" in 2002 has been an increasingly transparent attempt to make university education more connected and "relevant" to business through commercialization of ideas as well as skills. The state has therefore actively sought to find the means to act at the interface of the public and private. The Government Program in 2011 explicitly states as its core message that "common forms of research cooperation will be created for higher education institutions for the purpose of collaboration with companies" (Prime Minister's Office 2011, 57).

The most common way of legitimizing such collaboration is to refer to the need to "strengthen the role of universities within the system of innovation" (Ministry of Education and Culture 2014).

The founding of AU was also motivated by a particular kind of spatio-temporal reasoning in which the national appears interestingly as a problem. Echoing the statement of the ex-minister of education and culture (Virkkunen 2010), the interviewees invariably argued that the Finnish system of higher education was outdated, ineffective and too "national". The existing system was cast as overly geared toward domestic competition rather than oriented toward "global competition".

One of the goals of the university reforms was not only to increase competitive behavior within academia but also, and perhaps even more importantly, to qualitatively modify the logic of competition by extending the spaces of competition beyond the national borders. In this context, global university ranking charts were often referenced by the interviewees as a testament of the need to qualitatively re-engineer the idea of competition. The Ministry of Education and Culture has justified the reforms as a "reaction to the changes in the operational environment". Accordingly, the Finnish universities have been facilitated to operate in an "international environment" through affording these institutions the capacity to compete and cooperate in the international arena (Ministry of Education and Culture 2014).

The premise of global competition was the guiding principle with respect to how the central actors comprehended and legitimized the need to undertake the Finnish university reforms and to found AU. They shared an understanding that the present condition was characterized by a phenomenon which one of the interviewees labeled as the "global market" of higher education. It was the lack of global orientation which was argued to be the cause of the mediocre performance of the Finnish university system in the global education market.

The Finnish state appears here as a facilitator whose primary task is to establish an intellectual connection between the citizenry and global spaces of action:

> The prerequisite for sustainable growth is intellectual closeness to the rest of the world. Intellectual closeness manifests itself as common international conduct, whose international aspect no longer seems to require separate emphasis. We are already closely involved with members of global value networks.
>
> (Prime Minister's Office 2013, 35)

The reasoning of the representatives of the interviewed business and state agents clearly did not epitomize any form of laissez-fare political culture according to which government should limit its power to intervene in the (higher education) market. Rather, the state was seen to be forced to undertake the reforms in order to intervene in and tinker with the spaces of competition. The Finnish state thus appears as the agency required to inject and re-spatialize the "global" market principles into the Finnish university sector and, through it, into society at large.

The recent *Government Report on the Future* – together with a whole gamut of other reports – is similarly premised on the idea that the state is faced with a critical situation whereby the growth that "financially underpins its citizens' and inhabitants' wellbeing" must be created by "special measures" (Prime Minister's Office 2013, 7). The report portrays an image of a state whose future is determined essentially by the entrepreneurial spirit of its population. It laments that the Finns "should create a bold culture of entrepreneurship in Finland, encouraging entrepreneurial activity of all kinds" (Prime Minister's Office 2013, 43). The founding of AU represents precisely the need to qualitatively re-engineer spaces of higher education because of the conceived substances of the global market.

Interim conclusions

In this chapter, I have focused in particular on the construction of new kinds of learning environments within which new kinds of geopolitical subjects would be constituted. I have suggested that Aalto University as a co-functioning element within knowledge-based economization re-spatializes the "global" knowledge-based economy and its boundary-effacing pretensions. This mainly publicly funded and state-instigated but private-interest-driven institution thus illustrates the way in which transnational circuits of particular ideas – exemplified here by the discourse of knowledge-based economy – become entrenched in particular locales.

This chapter highlights that in the examined Finnish context these entrepreneurializing and internationalizing environments are generated to a significant extent through and by the state but at the same time enmesh intellectual, social and business interests. The re-casting of publicly funded institutions as learning environments where the constitution of entrepreneurial subjects takes place thus highlights one among the multiple ways that the state, by seeking to foster accumulation through new institutional arrangements, negotiates the instability and the persistent crises of capitalism. But in this case, agency is not reduced to the state as a homogeneous, stable actor; agency is rather distributed and emergent by nature.

Knowledge-based economization is a process that re-works political space. New kinds of borders and boundaries acquire salience in this process. That is, the examined case discloses selective investing in certain micro-spaces; it creates spatial exceptions presumed to be functional from the perspective of the present-day capital accumulation. This is also shown in the way in which processes of subjectification in knowledge-based economization place certain segments of population at the center of new system of capital accumulation and push others to its margins.

It is notable how little resistance and political tension these developments have generated in Finland, a country where the welfare state culture, and the related "social government", has been quite thoroughly institutionalized. Finland has been, however, demonstrated to be a fertile ground for the transfer of ideas on entrepreneurial university and on the importance of generating new geopolitical subjects that were discussed in Chapter 5. Something that has been touched upon briefly in this chapter, but that would also be crucial to focus on, are the resistances and contingencies which shape the meanings and impacts of higher education when these ideas arrive and are translated in a particular locale.

7 City geopolitics of knowledge-based economization

Cities and knowledge-based economization

It is beyond the scope of this book to evaluate whether the notion of the knowledge-based economy offers the most scientifically appropriate description of the nature of the contemporary political–economic condition. Rather, I draw from a body of research which suggests that since the 1990s the knowledge-based economy – both as an economic–political imaginary and as a set of practices – has emerged as a powerful discursive-cum-material phenomenon which provides a meaningful frame for political, economic and even cultural contestation across different geographical sites and within the different fields of social life. This phenomenon is arguably related to the rise of the competition state (Cerny 1990; Moisio 2008), neoliberal geopolitics of state space (Brenner 2004; Moisio 2011a) and the ostensibly geoeconomic visions and means in world politics (Moisio 2017; Sparke 2007). Whatever the best conceptualization may be, my perspective highlights both the fundamental role of sense making and meaning making in politics as well as related social relations and regulative structures in the context of the most recent iteration of capitalism (Jessop and Sum 2017; Jessop 2005). I have hence argued that knowledge-based economization is a process which brings together geopolitical subjects, objectifying calculative practices and, notably, geopolitical discourses.

The basic discursive tenets constitutive of the knowledge-based economization have been widely articulated and circulated in firms, business associations, international organizations, trade unions, cities, states and regions, as well as in a number of policy sectors from culture to science and health. These discursive tenets have a notable self-actualizing quality. Even if they represent the social world only partially and highly selectively with regard to territorial competition or the valuation of human capital, for instance, the discourses of the knowledge-based economy constantly contribute to the making of the knowledge-based economy in its own image. Moreover, the discourses of the knowledge-based economy carry with them a deep geopolitics, one which is predicated in particular on various discourses of global inter-spatial competition and territorial competitiveness. As suggested in Chapter 4, within such geopolitical discourses on "advanced nations" (e.g. Porter 2000, 15), global value chains emerge as a crucial political site which guides the strategic action and policymaking of states, cities and regions with regard to producing spaces and human capital.

It may be only a slight overstatement to say that since the 1990s the processes of financialization and knowledge-based economization have together established the urban as the unquestionable site of capital maximization (cf. Foglesong 2012). Knowledge-based economization can therefore be examined through the ways in which producers of urban space and experience – ranging from international organizations, firms and business associations to political leaders, state officials, urban planners, real estate developers and so on – define and articulate the strategic meaning of urban formations, infrastructures and environments vis-à-vis broader political–economic goals, in particular when these actors legitimize collective consumption in the production of these infrastructures and formations.

As a geopolitical process, knowledge-based economization has manifested itself in urban visions, branding and urban strategies in particular. Urban spaces, therefore, should not be treated as static sites of knowledge-intensive capitalism, but rather understood as spaces that are constitutive of knowledge-based economization.

The knowledge-based economy has become a significant meta-object of urban governance and planning. This kind of governance and planning rests on the assumption that urban infrastructures and built environments are important for engendering a culture of creativity, entrepreneurship and innovation, and, consequently, developing and maintaining territorial competitiveness of the nation state. Moreover, this kind of governance of competitiveness through cities has clearly become entangled with the mushrooming academic conceptualizations of urban attractiveness, urban amenities, smart urbanism, agglomeration economies, competitive cities and the like over the past two decades.

Importantly, knowledge-based economization has proceeded through a range of attempts to produce a novel spatial organization of the state through cities, city-regions and urban spaces more generally. These urban spaces are thus hoped to facilitate the circulation of knowledge-intensive capital and the production of surplus value. It seems clear, indeed, that the strategic role of cities and certain micro-spaces of cities has grown rapidly after the 2008 financial crisis, and that the mobilization of creative city, smart city, start-up city and eco-city imaginaries in crisis-ridden Europe and beyond stems from the efforts of political and economic actors to revitalize local as well as national economies through particular urban discourses of hope (also Rossi 2016). The phenomenon of knowledge-based economization thus refers to the increasingly salient and pervasive ways in which various actors think about cities and especially some locales of cities as well as city networks as pivotal spaces of value creation.

Particular urban singularities, such as business parks, signature buildings and so on, together form urban infrastructures or "spatial products" as Keller Easterling (2014, 12) would have it. These infrastructures are associated with economic growth not only locally but also nationally and even in the supranational context. Producing a competitive state spatially is therefore less about the territorial management of state space in its entirety, that is, connecting citizens to the land and state institutions in itself; it is more about maximizing the potential of places, micro-spaces and populace in the endless production of value in a transnational context. In such a context, cities and urban infrastructures within cities become crucial sites within which political–economic success or failure in the contemporary condition is being produced. Facilitating the circulation of capital in the upper tiers of global value chains and building urban infrastructures become two sides of the same coin.

The remainder of this chapter scrutinizes "city geopolitics", which is at the heart of the phenomenon of knowledge-based economization. The basic argument of the chapter is that the knowledge-based economy is not only predicated on particular urban imaginaries and the associated discourses on the inevitability of urbanization, but also practiced through cities and their micro-spaces. I begin with conceptualizing city geopolitics, before entering into a selected set of theories on the ways in which the knowledge-based economy, urban space and territorial competition come together. I scrutinize certain geopolitical narratives, such as the creative class and the creative city, which have been widely circulated and translated into policies in different geographical contexts as planning ideas within the past 15 years. Again, an analysis of these narratives and related ideas uncover the geopolitical in the context of knowledge-based economization. The analysis of the geopolitical narrative of the creative class and cities is followed by an examination of the recent Guggenheim Museum project in Helsinki, Finland. Finally, the role of urban projects vis-à-vis the imagined knowledge-based economy at the scale of the EU is briefly discussed.

On the concept of city geopolitics

Urban geopolitics is often used to denote the intertwining of cities, politics and conflicts, as they have manifested for instance in ethnically divided cities (see Fregonese 2009). It thus extends the concept of geopolitics from the realm of inter-state relations toward what could be called urban battlefields. The objective of urban geopolitics has therefore been to produce new insights on the fascinating yet potentially treacherous relationship between violent geopolitical processes and urban space (see, e.g. Rokem *et al.* 2017).

In their discussion of urban geopolitics, Rossi and Vanolo (2012) refer to the ways in which cities are commonly theaters of war across the globe, and how cities as geostrategic targets (including human capital and built environment) are destructed in the practices of warfare. They also associate urban geopolitics with the intensive governmentalization of urban experience, the neoliberal re-shuffling of the relationship between political authorities and citizens or urban communities, the rise of the so-called gated communities, the increasing demands for safety and security which have followed the terror attacks in the US in 2001 and the associated militarization of urban spaces as well as with the practices of criminalization in the context of neoliberal urban governance. Today, the concept of urban geopolitics is often used to denote militarization of urban space (see Graham 2010) and experience, and it therefore refers to the ways in which the security policies of the state, often articulated in terms of national security, have been urbanized and localized through new regulations, policies and related technologies of surveillance and control which have the potential to annihilate basic democratic rights.

In order to develop a geopolitical reading of urban space in the context of knowledge-based economization, I introduce the concept of city geopolitics, which resonates with the concept of urban geopolitics but also extends its meaning without falling into the trap of "methodological cityism" (for the concept, see Angelo and Wachsmuth 2015). The concept of city geopolitics covers at least four issue areas:

1   City geopolitics refers to the political processes of engineering cities through technologies of surveillance and discipline, and related systems of power. The increasingly pervasive surveillance and policing of urban spaces is connected to the "politics of fear" in the "age of insecurity" and "the war on terrorism", but it also reflects the various efforts to tackle crime and social deviance in urban space (Graham 2010; Rossi and Vanolo 2012).

2   City geopolitics stands for the political dimensions of urban infrastructure and built environments and the ways in which international politics penetrates or saturates urban space and experience. This alludes to how urban space not only mirrors but also becomes world politics. These urban infrastructures range from hard and soft infrastructures of "smart cities", "creative cities" and "start-up cities" to the more traditional geopolitical symbols which are situated in urban infrastructures. Urban infrastructure may thus signal both the conceivably fluid world politics of the knowledge-intensive mode of capital accumulation as well as the more traditional markers of geopolitics such as the West and East, "homeland" or "nation", among others. Urban infrastructure and built environments can thus be mobilized for various purposes, and the production and management of the urban built environment and related urban experience is inextricably connected to the issues of producing territories of wealth, power and competition.

3   City geopolitics refers to the historically contingent role of cities in the changing political strategies of the state more generally. City geopolitics signifies the positioning of cities in the geopolitical narratives and political–economic processes of the state. These narratives and processes can be nationalizing or globalizing, or both simultaneously. Cities and urban spaces, therefore, can be understood as having a historically contingent strategic position within the broader dynamics of state de- and re-territorialization. This dimension of city geopolitics can be interrogated through popular expert accounts, ideas and academic theories, as well as through urban projects (orchestrated by cities or the state) which seek to

establish correspondence between the conceived world political condition and the produced urban formations and experience.

4   City geopolitics denotes processes within which the urban built environment is produced as a resource system for the further production of value in a national as well as in an increasingly transnational context.

Points two, three and four are particularly relevant in an examination of the phenomenon of knowledge-based economization, for they disclose the geopolitical dimension of spaces such as innovative milieux, learning regions, national or regional innovation systems, triple helixes, clusters, ecosystems of innovations, smart cities, creative cities, compact cities and intercultural cities, to mention but a few. These are thus not "mere" urban ideas but carry a significant amount of geopolitics with them.

City geopolitics of spatial Keynesianism

During the peak of national welfare state construction in post-Second World War Europe, state development was characterized by territorialized and unified city spaces and urban networks in a predominantly national setting. This process is often dubbed spatial Keynesianism (see Brenner 2004) whereby territorial unification was accomplished through homogenizing and equalizing economic policies and hierarchic spatial planning practices (Table 7.1). Welfare statehood was thus produced and maintained through extending and generating state power through networks of interconnected cities and their "functional regions", thus connecting cities and the so-called hinterlands to form a nationalized spatial setting for national production, national consumption and national identity. By controlling the links between cities within its jurisdiction, and by protecting the commercial functions of inter-city relations, the state became a peculiar national mediator of socio-spatial relations. In this capacity, the state was both symbolically and in terms of institutional power located "above" cities (cf. Lefebvre 2003). This is one of the key constitutive elements of the so-called spatial Keynesianism that emerged in post-war Western Europe in particular: a historical epoch in which urban spaces and city governance were nationalized and statized through various techniques of "sovereign" government ranging from extensive spatial planning practices to systems of controlling the spatial distribution of public and, to a degree, private money. The state provided not only the necessary political and symbolic order but also, at least ideally, a uniform infrastructural basis and predictable operational environment for wide-ranging policymaking and market exchanges within the geographical boundaries of the state.

Toward a re-worked city geopolitics of state space

In some contexts, the key practices and geopolitical reasoning of spatial Keynesianism began to unravel already in the early 1980s. The uneasy

Table 7.1 From spatial Keynesianism to knowledge-based economization (modified from Brenner and Theodore 2002 and Moisio 2011b)

	Spatial Keynesianism	*Knowledge-based economization*
Regional structure	Even regional development, national integrity, decentralization in settlement and industrial policy	Economic development through major cities and metropolitan areas, regional concentration of economic and innovation activity, rise of metropolitan politics and city-regionalism
Forms of governance	Emphasis on "national", state-centered government, nationalization of the political	Internationalization of the national, de-nationalization, de-statization, diffusing system of economic governance, economization of the political
Purpose of the state	Economic growth, production and distribution of welfare, state ownership, provider of military security, transfers of income	Provider of conditions for effective competition, economic facilitator and supporter, creator of favorable conditions
Regulation	The Bretton Woods system, regulation by national central banks, public investments	Deregulation, freeing the financial market, enabling the (relatively) free movement of capital
Nodal scale	National	Overlapping of several scales, devaluation of the national, the increasing weight of the urban
Prevention of uneven regional development	Regional planning, transfers of income, dominance of homogenizing policies	Competitiveness and growth policy, innovation policies, region-led development through state income transfers, internationalization of places, specialization
Territory	Nationalization of territory, natural resources, economic growth, defense policies, societal order, sovereignty	Internationalization of territory, emphasis on attractive territorial qualities, economic growth through spatial centralization, partial suppression of territorial dimension of defense policies, movement from homogenization toward territorial specialization and spatial selectivity
City/state relations	Governing cities through nationalizing processes, managing and preventing competition between cities within a national city-hierarchy	Governing through cities, fostering inter-spatial competition, responsibilizing cities and city governments

Table 7.1 (Continued)

	Spatial Keynesianism	Knowledge-based economization
Urban symbolism and infrastructures	Nationalizing symbolism, major cities as national social and economic machines, industrial districts, technopoles	Mixture of nationalizing and globalizing symbolism and infrastructures, technopoles, the heightening role of spectacular architectural formations, "soft infrastructures" and learning environments (both higher education and start-up spaces), city as a multicultural and transnational hub
Characteristics of policymaking	The ideal of democracy and political representation and responsibility, the development of slow and long-term policies through inter-party and inter-ministerial consensus and collaboration	The growing role of consultants and economic agents in policymaking, fast policy formation, transnational policy mobilities and their translations

relationship between the knowledge-intensive form of capitalism and Fordist-Keynesian regional policies increasingly became a topic of debate (Jessop 1990). Spatial Keynesianism was gradually replaced by a reasoning according to which the new economy and related inter-state competition were equated with competition between cities.

In their work on the rise of technopoles, Castells and Hall (1994, 7) argued over 20 years ago that the role of cities in global politics is growing because – when compared to the state – cities "have a greater response capacity to generate targeted development projects, negotiate with multinational firms, foster the growth of small and medium endogenous firms, and create conditions that will attract the new sources of wealth, power, and prestige". In important ways, their formulation discloses the ways in which the economized geopolitical condition has embedded itself in policymaking in the context of both cities and states: the discourses of territorial competition and competitiveness instrumentalize the city as the pivotal site of inter-spatial competition in the age of knowledge-intensive capitalism. Castells and Hall perceive this inter-city competition as a productive one: it generates new growth because "such competition becomes a source of innovation, of efficiency, of a collective effort to create a better place to live and a more effective place to do business" (ibid., 7).

Many scholars, politicians, business people and lobbyists have from the 1990s onwards suggested that key cities and city-networks are somehow supplanting or at least challenging the territorial state both in terms of governance and market functions. They have postulated a declining role for the territorial state in the governance of both political and economic affairs, thus juxtaposing the state and the urban as competing scales of politics and governance (Brenner 1998).

Rather than embracing the above-mentioned hollowing out of the state argument, researchers in urban and regional studies have pointed out how contemporary state-orchestrated policies can be understood as spatially selective (Jones 1997), and thus significantly contribute to the increasingly city-centered image of the world. These policies challenge the decentralized and equalizing spatial formations of the state as sensible national expressions of public territorial sovereignty (Jonas and Moisio 2016). And, in consequence, the territorial logic of policies has been at least partially inverted. Brenner (2004, 16) argues exhaustively how "it is no longer capital that is to be molded into the (territorially integrated) geography of state space, but state space that is to be molded into the (territorially differentiated) geography of capital".

This new molding of state space into the geography of capital is practiced through policymaking which seeks to differentiate and segment state space in order to correspond to the conceived locational preferences of transnational capital within each national territory. This, in turn, can be understood as an effort to strategically position the state through its cities within the global circuits of knowledge-intensive capital. When we asked one of the leading officials of spatial development in the Finnish state about the strategic role of cities in the contemporary world, she responded revealingly how

> cities have agglomeration benefits in terms of economic activity and availability of skilled labor force. They are well connected with each other and internationally, and they attract students and working-age people with education and job opportunities. Cities are places for research, companies, and funding organizations working together to create value in the form of new products and services and well-being. Here, the role of the city is changing from service organizer and infrastructure builder to active and open platform developer.
>
> (Interview in 2016, Ministry of Economic Affairs and Employment, Finland)

The role cities play within the contemporary transnationalizing state apparatus is an intriguing geopolitical phenomenon. It seems evident that a pervasive reasoning of the colossal strategic role of major cities and their internal fabric in the production of vital, productive, prosperous, happy and innovative territorial polities is one of the constitutive elements of the process of knowledge-based economization. This kind of reasoning is premised on a particular geopolitical logic that discusses the role of cities in economic and state-centered terms, and it is not hard to find this pervasive logic in the mainstream academic discourse. Consider, for instance, some of the arguments presented by a well-known urbanist, influential neo-classical Harvard economist and widely read columnist Edward Glaeser (2012, 1, 6) in his bestselling *Triumph of the City*. The book is predicated on four central propositions which aptly disclose some of the geopolitical tenets of knowledge-based economization. Indeed, his work explicates how the territories of wealth and economic processes come together. First, cities, Glaeser argues, have for a long time been "engines of innovation"; second, "urban density provides the clearest path from poverty to [national] prosperity"; third, "proximity has become ever more valuable as the cost of connecting across long distances has fallen"; finally, industrial cities need to reconfigure themselves by "reinventing themselves" to meet the requirements of the new economy. Glaeser thus argues that

> A more connected world has brought huge returns to the idea-producing entrepreneurs who can now scour the earth in search of profits ... Cities are the absence of physical space between people and companies. They are proximity, density, closeness. They enable us to work and play together, and their success depends on the demand for physical connection. During the middle years of the twentieth century, many cities, like New York, declined as improvements in transportation reduced the advantages of locating factories in dense urban areas. And during the last thirty years, some of these cities have come back, while other, newer cities have grown because technological change has increased the returns to the knowledge that is best produced by people in close proximity to other people ... In America and Europe, cities speed innovation by connecting their smart inhabitants to each other.
>
> (Glaeser 2012, 5–7)

I would argue that this form of geopolitical reasoning, centered on the idea of the competitive city and echoing the nowadays popular "people go first, jobs follow" argument (Peck 2016, 6), has strengthened in the aftermath of the 2008 economic crisis. As a critical actor in this process, the state increasingly orchestrates territorial policies which are spatially selective – both within state territory and cities. Moreover, public investments in the structures of the puta-tive new economy have concentrated spatially during the past 20 years or so, and this pattern seems to be prevailing in the post-crisis setting and in fact may be invigorated by it. Today, a significant share of the private investments in innovation-driven development flow to and are being absorbed in major cities in different state contexts. This has prompted a kind of investment hunting as a key preoccupation of cities. This hunting results in a variety of attempts by cities to reinvent themselves by highlighting qualitative features of their urban spaces of production and consumption. Without such reinvention, cities are doomed to fail. As Glaeser (2012, 9) pronounces tellingly, "the age of the industrial city is over, at least in the West".

The creative class as a geopolitical theory

An attempt to produce value in places – be it a city, a region or a state – is at the heart of the process of knowledge-based economization. One of the driv-ing forces of such economization is an understanding that the world is divided between places in terms of their capacity to bring together particular types of economic agents and to aid them to produce economic value in the upper echelons of the production chain. Successful places are winners who produce a lot of economic value whereas other places are losers who are locked in the structures of the past and produce only a relatively limited amount of economic value (Florida 2004).

It is little surprise indeed that both the scholarly and more popular literature which discusses and explains the fragmentation and differentiation of the contemporary political–economic map with regard to economic value creation has emerged during the past two decades – thus in tandem with the process of knowledge-based economization. Literature on the spatial distribution and concentration of "creativity" in particular seeks to explain how some places are more successful than others in the knowledge-intensive form of capitalism.

I argue in the ensuing pages that this literature uncovers the ways in which the nature of territorial competitiveness is increasingly understood as if it were constituted through bringing together urban spaces and a particular type of geopolitical subjects. More specifically, I discuss one highly policy-relevant theory of economic and spatial development: the theory of the creative class which has been developed by the US-based Richard Florida in a series of writings from the early 2000s up to the present.

As Peck (2005, 740) argues, Florida's ideas have proven enormously seductive among civil leaders in different geographical contexts. These ideas have become the bread and butter of urban managers, planners, state officials and politicians who promote a kind of consumption city (Pratt 2008) and simultaneously seek to attract science, research and development and high-tech activities to locate in their city. Since the early 2000s, many cities which have or have not experienced large-scale loss of manufacturing jobs have jumped onto the creative city bandwagon and sought to create urban spaces and infrastructures to attract people with economically valuable ideas which can be utilized in the fields of nanotech, media, design, high-tech, bio-tech and other sectors. Creative city policies have also come to characterize knowledge-based economization because Floridean and related notions of creativity have seemed to offer quick solutions to complicated economic problems, solutions that can be fairly easily implemented by public authorities (Borén and Young 2013).

By way of simplifying the complex political–economic condition, the concept of the creative class and related concepts such as the creative city have shaped the ways in which a wide spectrum of actors view the world. Simultaneously, these concepts disclose the fundamentally place and urban-centered nature of knowledge-based economization. The theory of the creative class thus belongs to a wider genre of literature on the coming together of human capital and urban space in the generation of competitive advantage and territorial competitiveness (Moisio 2015).

Rather than treating the theory of the creative class as a mere elitist regional development theory of post-Fordism, I argue below that Florida's theory of the creative class is essentially geopolitical. The intellectual framing of creativity as a geopolitical phenomenon is in itself a striking phenomenon. Indeed, an analysis of the theory of the creative class nicely discloses some of the ways that geopolitical objects, subjects and discourses come together in the context of knowledge-based economization. Inter-spatial competition is the discourse and the "creative" segment of the population the subject. Furthermore, by way of tailoring indices, the literature on the creative class and the creative city (together with the related work of consultants) alters the city into a geopolitical object of competition that can be measured, analyzed and compared with other cities.

The theory of the creative class provides not only a subtext on the contemporary geopolitical condition but also an intellectual framework which identifies, privileges and normalizes certain issues which are then argued to explain how economic and political success can be engendered in the context of knowledge-intensive capitalism. Against this quality, it does not come as a surprise that the basics of this framework have been re-produced countless times in policy debates in different geographical contexts. In short, the theory of the creative class provides a particular ideational toolkit with which different kinds of actors in politics and administrations can circumnavigate the purportedly messy global capitalism.

When analyzed from a geopolitical perspective, the theory of the creative class is composed of five ideational elements (Figure 7.1). It is to these elements that I now turn.

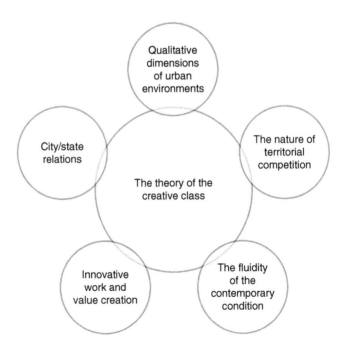

Figure 7.1 Constitutive elements of the theory of the creative class by Richard Florida.

The great epochal shift: creative class, value creation and territorial competition in the knowledge-based economy

Similarly to almost all theories of the knowledge-intensive capitalist economy, the creative class theory is premised on the view that there is presently an ongoing transition away from the manufacturing era toward an economy of innovations, especially in the most advanced parts of the world. Indeed, the theory of the creative class is premised on the assumption of an almost epochal shift in capitalism, and it is this piercing emphasis that connects Florida's theory to another set of influential theses that have emerged since the 1990s. One may argue that Florida's book *The Rise of the Creative Class* represents an influential body of "rise literature" which embodies knowledge-based economization. In particular, Florida's work resembles some of the ideas Castells (1996) developed in his *The Rise of the Network Society*, and in so doing highlights the role of high-paid professionals, innovative work and what Florida calls the creative sector of the economy.

The theory of the creative class does not seek only to analyze but also discursively construct a world in which creativity and knowledge replace the more traditional forces of production. The great epochal shift Florida portrays touches upon the ways in which economic growth "happens" and can be cultivated in different historical contexts. Whereas for most of human history economic growth derived "from a place's endowments of natural resources, like fertile soil or raw materials", today the key resource is a highly mobile creative populace and the resources they carry with themselves: creativity and "creative ethos" (Florida 2004, xix–xx, 21–43). In contemporary knowledge-intensive capitalism creativity plays a similar role to what coal and iron ore played in the era of steelmaking (ibid., 6). Creativity, in short, is not a tangible asset "like mineral deposits", but rather it is "something essential that belongs to all of us, and that must always be nourished, renewed, and maintained – or else it will slip away" (Florida 2007, 269). Accordingly, unlike the eras dominated by agriculture and manufacturing, today the key dimension of economic competitiveness is the ability to attract, cultivate and mobilize creativity as a resource (Florida 2004, xx).

Like many other theories of the knowledge-based economy, the creative class thesis is a theory of economic growth. The theory takes its inspiration from the issue of human creativity, which it treats as a resource, potential and economic force. Human creativity thus appears as a force of production that is crucial in the generation of value in the upper ladders of the value chain. Injecting what Florida calls "creative value" into the economic process thus makes local, regional and national economies grow. Human capital is something that is necessary for both wealth generation and inter-territorial competition. The theory of the creative class is thus premised on the ultimately instrumental nature of the concept of creativity. Florida narrows down, neutralizes, normalizes, economizes and, eventually, geopoliticizes creativity as a pivotal thing, ethos and process of post-Fordist capitalism.

This value creation is conceived of as happening primarily through the productive capacities of the creative class, which is composed of talented individuals. Florida (2004) associates the concept of the creative class with a relatively large group of people working in ostensibly creative jobs in science and engineering, design, education, architecture, the arts, music and entertainment. People working in these sectors hence form "a new social class" (obviously without class consciousness in its traditional sense). Accordingly, if "you are a scientist or engineer, an architect or designer, a writer, artist or musician, or if you use your creativity as a key factor in your work in business, education, health care, law or some other profession, you are a member" (Florida 2004, xxvii).

The creative class engages in work that seeks to create "meaningful new forms", and comprises two different groupings: the super-creative core (problem finding and problem solving) and creative professionals who work in various knowledge-intensive jobs – particularly in the high-tech sector. The creative class therefore produces value in a relatively limited spectrum of the economy. Florida (2004) defines certain occupations as essential agencies of economic growth, and locates a creative class with certain capacities and tastes at the heart of value generation. According to the theory of the creative class, it is the value that the work is producing which defines the success and failure of political communities at the contemporary conjuncture.

Resonating with the idea of Castells (1996) on the crucial role of a particular type of professionals in what he calls "informationalism", the creative class is itself a geopolitical subject that is needed to provide the framework conditions for engendering economic value. Florida's theory discloses how the process of knowledge-based economization is "peopled". The figure of the talented individual and the collective body of the creative class become the single most important geopolitical subject in determining the contemporary political economy of the purportedly advanced nations. Accordingly, creativity, more than any other force of production, positions cities, regions and nations vis-à-vis the knowledge-based economy, and in so doing determines their future in terms of wealth, prestige and resilience.

In sum, Florida's "value theory" is twofold. First, the creative class, through its fabulous capacity to create economic value, is both politically and economically indispensable. Second, the purported personal values of the creative class – tolerance, liberalism, celebration of cultural diversity and readiness to "take tremendous levels of risk" (Florida 2007, 244) – and the actual capacity to produce economic value through their creative ethos are two sides of the same coin. Creativity hence does not refer to such forms of "radical creativity" which would destabilize the existing political system. Rather, the liberal values of the creative class are understood as important components of establishing a firm economic and cultural base which attracts talented individuals to gather and produce even more economic value. Simultaneously, the central desires and values of the creative class – such as individualism, entrepreneurialism, meritocracy and willingness to engage in teamwork – may potentially spread to the rest of society (including some of the workers in the service sector and manufacturing), and in so doing eventually extend the economic base.

Geopolitical subtext: peaks, hills and valleys

> Superstar cities' expanding economies spur demand for more and better restaurants, theaters, nightclubs, galleries, and other amenities. Successful businesspeople and entrepreneurs endow their museums, concert halls, private schools, and universities … [Superstar cities] have unique kinds of economies that are based around the most innovative and highest value-added industries, particularly finance, media, entertainment and tech; businesses in superstar cities are formed and scaled up more quickly. All of this attracts still more industries and more talent. It's a powerful, ongoing feedback loop that compounds the advantages of these cities over time.
>
> (Florida 2017b)

According to the theory of the creative class, successful firms locate where the talent is. These are not the cheapest locations, but firms want to locate in them because of the availability of highly talented employees. Successful firms in the creative economy need highly specialized employees, who, according to Florida, tend to settle in cities or city-regions that offer the best quality of life.

As Castells (1996) reminded in his "rise book", creative knowledge workers are urbanized and mobile and value individuality, difference and merit. The theory of the creative class repeats the same message: because of their urban tastes, economically valuable individuals gather in cities. Following some of the Glaeserian tenets of urban economics, Florida argues that the productivity of people increases when they locate close to one another in cities and regions (Florida 2008, 6). The creative class is thus composed of a distinctive group of urban dwellers who are productive, passionate and embrace a particular modern urban lifestyle and associated active pastimes. They cherish urban amenities and value urban hustle and buzz. They thus express a proclivity for a "livable" urban environment which is loaded with cafes, boutiques and galleries, among other things.

The preferences of the creative class differ from those of the "old" middle class, characterized by suburban lifestyles. But the challenging thing with the creative class is that its representatives are hypersensitive and hence mobile, and they easily vote with their feet. The creative class do not therefore select their place of residence on the basis of the availability of jobs and thus on the basis of national and international labor markets (cf. Scott and Storper 2009). Rather, this class is not bound to any "nations" and is not restricted by state borders. It moves to cities in which they prefer to reside, and these preferences are based on quality-of-life perceptions (Houston *et al.* 2008).

In the theory of the creative class, place is the key economic and social organizing unit of the contemporary capitalist condition. Places are not only concentrations of creativity but also sites that nurture, manage and cultivate that creativity and the related "experiential life". Florida (2004, 166) argues that "the creative class lifestyle comes down to a passionate quest for experience. The ideal ... is to 'live the life' – a creative life packed full of intense, high-quality, multidimensional experiences". The power of place is therefore associated with its capacity to provide an environment for creative or experimental lifestyles through ecosystems (one of the catchwords which epitomize knowledge-based economization) which harness human creativity and turn it into economic value. Florida thus argues that building a particular "world class people climate" is absolutely essential in any attempt to attract or retain creative people (Florida 2004, 293).

By way of highlighting the connection between the generation of economic value and the urban lifestyles of the creative class, the theory of the creative class discloses how "metropolis" is seamlessly connected to biopolitics as a form of governmentality (see also Kivelä and Moisio 2017). As proposed by Agamben (2011), the concept of metropolis should not be understood as a mere "city" but rather linked to the emergence of a thoroughly economized urban fabric. The creative class theory indeed uncovers an urban-based view of the valorization of knowledge-intensive capital, and the associated governance to accommodate its lifestyles and things.

Because the concept of the creative class is predicated on a preference-centered economic model of human behavior, it highlights "underlying conditions", or what Florida (2004) eventually calls "ecosystem characteristics", which enable certain cities and city-regions to attract and mobilize creative people more effectively than their competitors. In so doing, a critical reading of the creative class theory exposes one of the central discursive tenets of knowledge-based economization: the emphasis on the "struggle" of major cities to compete for the highly mobile and de-nationalized creative class, international attention as well as a particular type of desirable investments. In such a view, urban space becomes not only a critical infrastructure in the production of economic value but also a crucial factor in inter-spatial competition.

All the above-mentioned issues of the theory of the creative class eventually boil down to the question of the nature of contemporary world politics. In the theory of the creative class, cities and city-regions are creative epicenters of national territorial economies, a kind of basic unit of competition. It is therefore unsurprising that the creative class theory has proceeded in tandem with the growing scholarly and practical interest toward what is customarily called the "creative city". This concept has its origins in the work of Jane Jacobs in the 1960s, but has been fundamentally re-animated as part of the process of knowledge-based economization since the 1990s (for an overview, see Borén and Young 2013; Scott 2014).

By way of highlighting the role and importance of urban experience in engendering value, wealth and prestige, the theory of the creative class destabilizes the cartographic image of the territorial state. Accordingly, whereas in the past the cities of one country or region competed for investment and talent with other cities in that same country or region, now locations all across the globe are competing with one another (Florida 2008, 28–29). The theory of the creative class thus reifies the geopolitical discourses of "global" territorial competition that were discussed in Chapter 4.

Florida (2008, 32) highlights that the emerging global politics is not a matter of competing states but rather competing metropolises. He divides the world into three groups of cities with regard to their economic performance: peaks, hills and valleys. Florida argues that talent, innovation and creativity are not distributed evenly across the world but tend to concentrate in specific locations. This makes global competition a harsh spatial game:

> When looked at through the lens of economic production, many cities with large populations are diminished and some nearly vanish. Three sorts of places make up the modern economic landscape. First are the cities that generate innovations. These are the tallest peaks; they have the capacity to attract global talent and create new products and industries. They are few in number, and difficult to topple. Second are the economic "hills" – places that manufacture the world's established goods, take its calls, and support its innovation engines. These hills can rise and fall quickly; they are prosperous but insecure. Some, like Dublin or Seoul, are growing into innovative, wealthy peaks; others are declining, eroded by high labor costs and a lack of enduring competitive advantage. Finally there are the vast valleys – places with little connection to the global economy and few immediate prospects.
>
> (Florida 2008, 48)

In such a view, the significant locations in the world economy remain limited in number. Florida presents provocative maps which show that there are roughly 25 places and regions worldwide that generate significant innovation. These are "mega-regions" which have ecosystems of leading-edge universities, high-powered companies, flexible labor markets and venture capital that are attuned to the demand of commercial innovation, and they produce the lion's share of the patents (Florida 2008, 25).

It is for this reason that global politics will, according to the theory of the creative class, hinge on the tensions brewing among different locations that are all seeking to navigate successfully in the global economic game. The main dividing line in global politics is now between the innovative talent-attracting "have" regions and the talent-exporting "have-not" regions. This is a world of both concentration of value, growth and success and potential marginalization of many places.

In the original treatment of the creative class concept Florida argues that "the real threat to American security is not terrorism, it's that creative and talented people may stop wanting to come here" (Florida 2004, xxiv). A few years later, he adds that "what we face is not a clash of civilizations but a deepening economic divide among the world's spikes and valleys" (Florida 2008, 32). This conception of territorial competition and national security is at the heart of knowledge-based economization, and it derives from an understanding of the restless mobility of investments, companies and talent, which has the potential to turn places and entire "nations" upside down.

The city and the state

According to the theory of the creative class, world-class cities benefit and prosper. Firms in the creative industry form weak and strong ties in urban environments and thereby support a process that attracts talented people to move to certain cities and city-regions. In such reasoning, cities must actively scan the horizon for investment, monitor competitors and emulate "best practices" (see Peck and Tickell 2002, 47), as well as re-structure themselves to respond to the creative class's needs just as companies have already done (Peck 2005, 742).

At first sight, the theory of the creative class does not appear to touch upon the state. The theory is premised on the view that the knowledge-based economy is characterized by a movement away from prosperity and wealth as understood in terms of homogenized state territories. Indeed, the second edition of the *Rise of the Creative Class* (Florida 2012) articulates the dysfunctional nature of the nation state when compared to local governments.

But upon closer inspection, "cities and regions" and city centers stand out in the theory of the creative class regarded as "a country's crucibles of competitiveness in the creative age" (Florida 2007, 258). Therefore it is only logical to propose that state-orchestrated urban policy must be "resurrected from the backwaters of social policy" to become "a cornerstone of national competitiveness planning" and a "strong innovation policy" (ibid., 259). The implicit emphasis on the state is not surprising given that "figuring out how to make national and regional economies grow and compete is the practical aspect" of Florida's work (2004, xxi). *The Flight of the Creative Class* (Florida 2007) includes explicit recipes for how nation states could renew their welfare, investment and education policies in order to strengthen their innovation capacities in global inter-territorial competition.

Rather than rejecting the role of the state in knowledge-intensive capitalism, the theory of the creative class can be understood as qualitatively reformulating state–city relations. And in this capacity it nicely articulates one of the basic elements of knowledge-based economization. By way of arguing that any country that does not constantly keep building its creative strengths will be left behind (Florida 2004, xxvi), the theory of the creative class articulates the city and city-region as crucial elements of state success as a territory of wealth. Ultimately, then, the theory of the creative class is concerned with inter-state rivalry. This same dimension has been similarly articulated by some of the most notable boosters of the creative city. To illustrate, Charles Landry suggests in his book *The Creative City* that

> When I first began talking about the Creative City idea around 20 years ago I did not think that it would take off as a concept. My original impulse

was to respond to the dramatic economic, social and cultural transformations happening in Europe at that time as our cities needed to restructure and rethink what their role and purpose were. Subsequently, these transformations have affected cities worldwide as cities everywhere have been drawn into the maelstrom of a reinvigorated globalization. In this process, cities have become the hubs of wealth creation and so increasingly more important than nation states; as a result, it is often cities that are competing as proxies for states.

(Landry 2009, xvii)

The theory of the creative class discloses the geopolitical reasoning inherent in knowledge-based economization whereby states appear as geopolitical agents of competition which compete through their cities. The theory of the creative class thus re-locates a territorial state in the framework of the conceived global competition, and represents the national state as being highly dependent on metropolises in particular as havens of jobs, talent and investment. These cities, rather than entire nation states, are styled as potential magnets for ambitious and highly skilled people (Florida 2008).

The most recent emphasis in the theory of the creative class articulates the growing interest in the so-called start-up cities and the related focus on city centers as micro-spaces in the valorization of capital. As such, it arguably points to some of the more recent developments of knowledge-based economization. Whereas the early ICT-driven entrepreneurial formation was still partly concentrated in outer areas in some of the major US cities – which was connected to what Florida (2007, 253) labels an "industrial-age materialist mind-set" – the recent development further highlights the role of dense urban space and urban lifestyle as well as the increasing role of "global start-up cities" (Florida 2013). This development stems from the putative creative ethos of ambitious start-up neo-entrepreneurs who concentrate in "superstar cities". These are "not just the places where the most ambitious and talented people want to be – they are where such people feel they *need* to be" (Florida 2017b, italics in original). Accordingly,

the most important and innovative industries and the most talented, most ambitious, and wealthiest people are converging as never before in a relative handful of leading superstar cities that are knowledge and tech hubs. This small group of elite places forge ever forward, while most others struggle, stagnate, or fall behind. This process is one I like to call winner-take-all urbanism.

(Florida 2017b)

This winner-take-all urbanism further highlights the role of major urban areas in the production of national success. Accordingly, super-star cities generate the greatest levels of innovation, and they also become proxies for the state to enter the sphere of global governance. These cities "control and attract the largest shares of global capital and investment, have huge concentrations of leading-edge finance, media, entertainment, and tech industries, and are home to a disproportionate share of the world's talent" (Florida 2017a). In such a view, the major metropolitan city-region is the most characteristic form of social organization of the current knowledge-intensive capitalism and a particular symbol of national economic growth. This ultimately geopolitical aspect of the theory of the creative class can be best summarized by referring to Florida's own phrasing, which comes in the context of comparison of nation states and major metropolises in terms of their role in world economy:

> Cities really are the new power centers of the global economy – the platforms for innovation, entrepreneurship, and economic growth. But when it comes to fiscal and political power, they remain beholden to increasingly anachronistic and backward-looking nation-states, which has become distressingly obvious with the rise of Trumpism in the United States and populism around the world. The greatest challenge facing us today is how to ensure that global cities have the economic, fiscal, and political power to govern themselves and to continue to be a force for innovation and human progress.
>
> (Florida 2017a)

Many local and state governments have taken their inspiration from the writings of Richard Florida and his fellow travelers, and a range of consultant companies have put these ideas into motion in different geographical contexts. But I have suggested in this section that an analysis of the theory of the creative class exposes the geopolitical that is built into knowledge-based economization. The relationship between major cities and their urban spaces and states has in fact become one of the key facets of the process of knowledge-based economization, and it is clearly a topic which merits further scholarly attention. It may be oversimple to argue that the enhanced political authority of "global city-regions" inescapably indicates a weakened sovereign political autonomy of the territorial state (cf. Soja 2011).

Finally, policy formation on the basis of ideas such as the creative class or the creative city can be understood as connected to one of the key geopolitical virtues of the state in the age of knowledge-intensive capitalism: its role not only as a facilitator and enabler of the production of economic value but also as a kind of "manager of mobility" which seeks to fix global movement to a national territory.

Guggenheim Helsinki and the limits of knowledge-based economization

> Every city of real ambition wants to move up the value chain and capture centrality for themselves and become a central hub of wealth creation by exporting, yet controlling from a distance, low-cost activities and attracting high-value ones to itself. These include research and knowledge

creation centres, headquarters, advanced manufacturing, or cultural and artistic creativity.

(Landry 2008, xvii–xviii)

The contemporary urban policy debates are littered with buzzwords like creativity, culture and livability and value-chain talk more generally. The same applies to the Helsinki city-region where imaginaries how the city-region is developing toward a world-class business and innovation hub whose success is based on the power of science, art, creativity and learning capacity have become increasingly visible in recent years. These debates highlight the potential role of culture in achieving non-cultural goals, and in so doing uncover one dimension of knowledge-based economization: the economization of culture. But these debates also disclose a somewhat narrow urban-policy repertoire based on central-city makeovers, place promotion, science and technology center construction and local boosterism.

Today, creative city developers constantly ask cities to do new things, to constantly revise themselves spatially, culturally and socially. This requires cities to constantly re-think their resources, weaknesses and assets vis-à-vis the knowledge-intensive form of capitalism. As Landry (2008, xvii) puts it, "cities have had to ask themselves: who am I; where do I go next; what is my identity; what is distinctive about me and what are my assets?"

The creative city is reinvented in many places at the same time, and it is above all fixated on enhancing the competitiveness of a given city in interspatial competition through value creation (cf. Peck and Tickell 2002). Arguments concerning how "super-star museums" are a sort of cathedral of the post-industrial age (for the logic, see e.g. Frey 2003) aptly disclose how spaces of culture and the valorization of capital are inextricably connected in knowledge-based economization. Those who highlight the link between urban density, urban amenities and productivity argue that successful cities are capable of attracting "smart entrepreneurial people" by "being urban theme parks" (Glaeser 2012, 11).

The term urban theme park is in reference to cultural infrastructures which occupy a specific function within knowledge-intensive capitalism, thus encapsulating the presence and availability of "urban culture" as a crucial dimension of knowledge-based economization. In this context, urban culture refers both to the qualitative aspects of urban space that are conceived to satisfy the needs of talented professionals as well as to the means through which cities try to develop their uniqueness. It is no surprise that since the 1990s in particular cities have sought to construct and develop facilities of culture in order to stand out favorably from other cities. Cultural infrastructures have thus taken on an integral role in developing knowledge-intensive economies in the so-called "ambitious cities". Landry (2008, xviii) argues revealingly that "the overall aim of ambitious cities is to increase their 'drawing power' and to get on the radar screen". In such process, local policymakers and leaders increasingly respond to an economic imperative that is instigated by global institutions, consultant companies, international organizations, state government or federal administration, for instance.

This section analyzes one particular dispute over cultural space in the City of Helsinki. More specifically, I elaborate upon the joint project by the city and the Solomon R. Guggenheim Foundation to construct a Guggenheim Museum in Helsinki. The project was initiated in 2011 by the City of Helsinki with the intention to raise the international profile of the city. The first official report (Drury *et al.* 2012) was commissioned by the City of Helsinki and was produced by the foundation with the help of consultant companies such as LaPlata Cohen, Boston Consulting Group, and Cooper, Robertson & Partners (with a price tag of two million Euros). The report included an idea to build a new building in the harbor area of downtown Helsinki.

The original plan did not gain majority backing in the city council, which put the project on hold. It is often suggested that the city council of Helsinki rejected the museum project because of financial concerns, particularly outside criticism of the proposed c. $30 million licensing fee for use of the Guggenheim name for two decades. This rejection was, however, followed by a revised proposal instigated by the Solomon R. Guggenheim Foundation in 2013. The new proposal included a reduced licensing fee, and a promise to assist local supporters in soliciting private donations through a newly formed local foundation. Even though the revised plan again sparked much political controversy, the City of Helsinki and the Guggenheim Foundation launched a competition over the architectural plan of the museum. In 2015, the results

Figure 7.2 The winning architecture of the Guggenheim Helsinki used with permission by Moreau Kusunoki Architects.

Figure 7.2 (Continued)

of the competition for the design of the Guggenheim Museum building were announced (Figure 7.2).

In the ensuing public debate, the price of the planned museum occupied a central role. *The New York Times* observed the situation from a distance and reported on how the City of Helsinki "has been bitterly divided over the project, largely because of concerns over its price of about $147 million" (Bogrebin and Carvajal 2015).

In 2016, the museum project was permanently shelved by the City Assembly. Throughout, the Guggenheim Helsinki project was characterized by twists and turns with respect to the actual implementation, division of labor, as well as funding and overall economic sensibility of the project. The confusion surrounding the funding of the museum is often mentioned as the primary reason why the project ultimately failed (e.g. Linko 2013). There are, however, a number of issues that connect the project with knowledge-based economization, issues that may help one to understand why the Guggenheim Helsinki did not materialize. The Guggenheim Helsinki in particular uncovers the uneasy entanglement of knowledge-based economization through mega-projects at the present political–economic conjuncture.

The following analysis of the project is not concerned with the economic difficulties and even oddities of the Guggenheim Helsinki, or the resistance to the project from different actors in the local art and political scene. I rather elaborate various ways through which the museum project and knowledge-based economization were entangled.

The following analysis of the Guggenheim Helsinki project is in two parts. I first dissect the different ways in which the museum project was connected to the production of urban experience by various stakeholders. In the second part, I interrogate the political coalitions and political dynamics which played a notable role in the debate surrounding the project, and discuss the role of the state in the Guggenheim Helsinki case.

Guggenheim Helsinki and the question of urban experience

> In the art and design world, the fate of the prospective museum has become a matter of global import: with everyone from the Louvre to the Hermitage looking to set up outposts abroad, Helsinki has become the latest battleground in an ongoing conflict over how—and whether—small cities and emerging countries should accommodate expansionist mega-museums.
>
> (Volner 2015)

The Guggenheim Helsinki mega-museum project did not take its inspiration from the so-called Bilbao model, which included a set of urban structural reforms and related experimentation – including the construction of a Guggenheim museum. The Guggenheim Helsinki was not about revitalizing declining industrial urban spaces. In contrast to the Bilbao case, the original and the revised plans located the museum in a historical neo-classical urban environment in Helsinki, which can be regarded as a peculiar spatial condensation of geopolitical symbolism of the Finnish state.

It may sound paradoxical – but not entirely surprising – that the public debate over the Guggenheim Helsinki was less about experiencing art and more focused on economic development through the production of urban experience. Accordingly, many stakeholders articulated the meaning of the museum vis-à-vis broader societal goals.

Observed from the perspective of the public debate and political debates in the City Assembly and Council, the proponents of the museum particularly articulated the meaning of the museum in terms of re-positioning the City of Helsinki (and Finland to a lesser extent) on European and global economic and political maps. In a similar vein, the transnational actors involved in the project portrayed the museum as if it were about re-situating Helsinki. It is notable how the Solomon R. Guggenheim Foundation linked the museum with the geopolitical location of Finland. In 2013, the CEO of the foundation, Richard Armstrong, explained that Helsinki was the only city with whom the foundation was negotiating because the "geographical location of Helsinki is unusual, between the East and West" (*Helsingin Sanomat* 16 May 2013), and the first official report of the museum included a detailed section on the geopolitical history of Finland and its recent identity as an "advanced nation" (Drury *et al.* 2012). *The New Yorker*, in turn, went so far as to connect the Guggenheim Helsinki to the issue of clarifying the geopolitical identity of the entire country:

> Finland is different: its language is like no other on earth, with only faint echoes in Estonian and Hungarian; its relationship with the rest of the West is exceptional, since it maintained cordial relations with Soviet Russia throughout the Cold War. In its nearly century-long history, Finland has managed to erect a social state as tolerant and egalitarian as any of its Nordic neighbors, but it has never attracted a substantial immigrant population, never become a major tourist destination—never, in short, figured out quite what its relationship with the rest of the world is meant to be.
>
> (Volner 2015)

In the early stages of this urban struggle in particular, articulations about the need to re-position Helsinki were high on the agenda. The proponents perceived the museum as a means to "internationalize" the City of Helsinki, and this form of reasoning was one of the key rhetorical devices of the local Guggenheim Helsinki foundation.

When examined through the public presentations and other articulations of the Solomon R. Guggenheim Foundation and the local proponents, the Guggenheim Helsinki case discloses a particular narrative of "cultural homogenization" with potential colonizing effects on the contemporary urban experience (see Rossi 2017). The potential colonizing repercussions of the museum were indeed vigorously taken up by the opponents of the project. Both in the public debate and in the political discussions, the museum was debated in terms of Americanization and harmful forms of globalization which would extend business logics to all sectors of cultural life. Local artists in particular resisted the museum as a space which would primarily serve the strategies of local and international urban elites. Accordingly, these elites are more concerned with urban attractiveness, place marketing and economic value, rather than local cultural institutions and inclusive artistic networks. They thus politicized the nature of the Guggenheim Museum as an elitist means to internationalize a place through mainstream cultural landscape branding.

From 2012 onwards, the Solomon R. Guggenheim Foundation together with local proponents articulated the meaning of the museum increasingly in terms of fierce global inter-spatial competition (Drury *et al.* 2012). The museum was represented as a magnet that would attract different forms of capital to an otherwise relatively peripheral city. In this context, the museum was explicitly articulated as a contributor to the knowledge-based economy. One of the supporters of the Guggenheim Helsinki wrote how in the new post-industrial era urban culture is a source of intangible capital that pulls in "real capital" from all over the world (Wilenius 2012). An expert report similarly argues explicitly how

> Helsinki is currently in the process of realizing its vision to be a dynamic world-class center for business and innovation. Its high-quality services, arts and science capabilities, creativity, and adaptability promote the prosperity of its citizens and bring benefits to all of Finland. Finland, the City of Helsinki, and the Guggenheim Foundation can certainly find a way for their respective missions to complement one another ... This project will allow Helsinki to grow strategically, creating room for continued expansion according to advanced principles of urban development.
>
> (Drury *et al.* 2012, 14–15)

This view of "advanced principles of urban development" has been repeated countless times since the 1990s in different geographical contexts as cities have sought to estrange themselves from their industrial past and move into the conceived new economy characterized by what Scott (2014) calls the cultural-cognitive form of capitalism. According to the nowadays mainstream urban development routines, ambitious cities and metropolitan areas need monuments, attractions, interesting creative spaces, signature architecture and other elements that would stimulate economic activity and distinguish the city from the identified competitor cities. The early phases of the Guggenheim Helsinki project aptly disclose this kind of urban development mantra.

The above comes not as a revelation given that the culture-reputation-economy nexus had been increasingly discussed in Helsinki since the 1990s and resulted in a growing interest toward what Zukin (1995) famously calls the symbolic economy of a city. One author wrote already in 1999 that "one major question facing Helsinki is how to maintain the relative advantage over competing cities and, in the long term, create a symbiosis between Helsinki (place), culture and economy" (Cantell 1999, xx). In 2000, the City of Helsinki officially declared that it is a "real" cultural city.

Closely resonating with these earlier debates, the Guggenheim Helsinki was increasingly represented as a reputational urban policy project for the City of Helsinki in 2013–2016. It was on numerous occasions connected to issues such as international recognition, attractiveness, and articulated as a means to prevent geographical marginalization.

It is, however, equally significant to notice that in the latter half of the campaign the Guggenheim Helsinki was tied to economic issues primarily through tourism and the accompanying local service economy. There remained only little evidence of articulations on how the museum would produce an emotionally stimulating city or how it would contribute to enhancing innovative capacities amongst the residents of Helsinki. In the local and national political campaigning, the Guggenheim Helsinki museum therefore became surprisingly thinly connected to concepts such as creative cities, urban amenities, innovative milieux or local buzz. It was no longer articulated as a crucial project of creativity that would stimulate innovative behavior on a grassroots level or beyond the somewhat narrow art and design circles.

The museum was thus not highlighted as a cultural space that would reach beyond "mere consumption"; it was not essential in the endeavor to create a more attractive urban space for the talented people working in various creative jobs beyond art and design. It did not therefore appear in political debates as a pivotal contributor to the local or national economic recovery that was sought after the economic hardships which ICT companies like Nokia faced in the aftermath of the 2008 economic crisis. Moreover, the museum was no longer explicitly represented as a piece of infrastructure that would help to re-territorialize global mobility and redirect flows of money, ideas and people related to the knowledge-intensive form of capitalism.

These silences are important, I believe, for they disclose the fact that the Guggenheim Helsinki was not strongly linked to the ICT sector (the representatives of the high technology industry remained largely silent throughout the process), to the emerging high-tech start-up scene, creative economy, cultural industry or any other main dimensions of new urbanism in the first place. Indeed, in the decisive phases of the struggle over the Guggenheim Helsinki, the economic articulation which sought to justify the construction of the museum remained utterly tourism and service centered and highlighted the direct revenue that the museum would generate locally.

If analyzed through the local and national political debates between the years 2013 and 2016 in particular, the Guggenheim Helsinki can of course be seen as an attempt instigated by the local elites to fill the void left by Nokia in a context of economic decline (Rossi 2017, 139). But more than that, these debates disclose the "contextual" limits of mega-projects, which are in the scholarly literature often associated with creative economy, creative cities and competitive urbanism. The case thus embodies how mega-projects such as the Guggenheim Helsinki are inescapably negotiated politically in local contexts and in particular historical conjunctures.

Transnational coalition, the decline of the "innovation right"

The Guggenheim Helsinki case exemplifies the interdependencies between local and transnational actors in attempts at constructing what is customarily known as new urbanism and related cultural mega-projects. These projects are often structured around an alliance of local government actors, local elites, business organizations, developers, transnational consultancies and others who join forces in an effort to expand the local economy and to generate surplus value.

A transnational coalition emerged in the context of the Guggenheim Helsinki. It played a decisive role in launching, maintaining and keeping the somewhat tumultuous museum project alive. It exerted significant pressure on local politicians and city officials over the developmental approval for the museum. This coalition was backed by notable auxiliary players such as the main local and national newspaper *Helsingin Sanomat* and the local chamber of commerce. Irrespective of the coalition's relatively strong line-up, the Guggenheim Helsinki Foundation was not able to convince the majority of the local and national political elites to channel public money into the project. As such, the Guggenheim Helsinki discloses the ways in which the effectiveness of transnational urban growth coalitions is in part dependent on their local and national ties and connections with political forces. As a related matter, the case also epitomizes how post-2008 austerity politics has influenced megaprojects such as the Guggenheim Helsinki.

From the beginning of the project, the local political sphere was divided on the issue. The Left Alliance was straightforwardly against the museum, which it perceived to be a symbol of harmful "American" globalization. The Social Democrats and the Greens were internally divided, and the right wing National Coalition Party was largely but not entirely supportive of the Guggenheim Helsinki. Focusing on mere party politics either on the local or national scale does not, however, produce a satisfactory picture of the difficulties that the Guggenheim Helsinki faced in tapping into the coffers of public money.

The ensuing paragraphs suggest that the progression of knowledge-based economization in the Finnish context since the 1990s has been based on the consolidation of what Teppo Eskelinen (2015) has called the "innovation right". This term refers to a political faction which embraces issues such as economic and political liberalism, internationalization and international competitiveness and knowledge-based and technical solutions to economic and social problems. This faction also stresses the role of innovation, the inevitable nature of urbanization, the strategic role of major cities as fundamental constituents of "national" success, a particular type of human capital, high-quality research and development, experimentation and charismatic "Steve Jobsian" leadership in the production of surplus value and political success. Moreover, the innovation right sees the role of the state and local government primarily as facilitators of the processes of innovation, and thus as essential providers of the related supporting infrastructures of learning and capacity building.

The innovation right emerged in Finland gradually in the 1990s. Its emergence was seamlessly connected to the rise of the Nokia Corporation as a national champion firm. The development of the innovation right in the late 1990s and in the early 2000s was not confined to the right wing political parties alone but gradually came to encompass nearly the entire political spectrum. In other words, the innovation right had its core in right wing economic liberalism, but enjoyed notable support among the center left political parties at a time when the annual national GDP growth of more than four percent was widely accepted as the result of the thriving innovation sector of the economy.

The innovation right had its peak momentum in the early 2000s when political elites across the political field, business firms in the ICT sector and beyond, as well as various Finnish and foreign experts of innovation formed strong coalitions. To illustrate the workings of this faction, a peculiar policy-network developed in the late 1990s based on the chance encounter between Pekka Himanen, a young Finnish philosopher interested in knowledge-intensive capitalism, and Manuel Castells. The pair went on to ingratiate themselves with key factions of the Finnish political elite and established a network of prominent individuals dealing with the knowledge-based economy. They thus began manufacturing what is today customarily known as the Finnish information society model, and successfully exploited the structures of the Finnish National Innovation System as well as publicly and privately funded think tanks clustered around the booming ICT sector.

In the early 2000s, the condensation of the power of the innovation right was based on its capability to bring into regular contact the government, its key ministries, various state-sponsored innovation funds, think tanks, private and public research institutes, multinational corporations and consultant companies. Contacts between these bodies were established through multiple official and unofficial learning events, such as seminars and major conferences in Finland and abroad, business site visits for politicians, officials and scholars to the various "model places" of the knowledge-based economy and various practices of evaluation, auditing and advocacy.

The innovation right demonstrates a particular fetish of expertise that has its roots in technological rationality, and introduces this rationality across policy fields. This faction frames the national interest as well as national identity against the purported needs of the global knowledge-based economy and portrays "national success" in biopolitical terms as if it were dependent on the attitudes and capacities of the populace. In its attempt to harness the intellectual, communicative and emotional capacities of individuals for the purposes of knowledge-intensive capitalism, the innovation right extends the sphere of the economy to all corners of social and cultural life. By encouraging individualism, creativity, a "global" entrepreneurial attitude, risk taking and internationalization, the innovation right thus expresses a will to develop a new innovative populace both for the needs of the nation and global capital. To illustrate, Castells and Himanen (2013) argue how the "renewed spiritual culture" of society would be the single most important factor in engendering economic success in Finland. The innovation right has therefore sought to further a transition from the purportedly passivating "welfare state of the industrial era" to the "welfare society of the information age" (Castells and Himanen 2013; Himanen 2007).

In the Finnish context, the innovation right figuratively uprooted and made Silicon Valley a referential component of the knowledge-based economy. In a number of reports, books, assessments, talks and informal events, the representatives of this faction have argued since the late 1990s that by selectively copying some economic, cultural and societal elements from Silicon Valley, Finland could be transformed into one of the "internationally most attractive concentrations of enriching interaction", a kind of "spiritual capital of the whole world" (Himanen 2010).

One peculiar outcome of the 2008 crisis was the internal unraveling of the innovation right, which has resulted in a decline of its relative importance as a political force in Finland. The center-left political forces have become less eager to circulate the faith of the innovation right in technological innovations and "global" entrepreneurial attitudes. Simultaneously, the relative power of the "conservative right" (Eskelinen 2015) has gradually grown stronger within right-wing politics – both at local and national scales.

The political reasoning of the conservative right resonates with what is customarily called austerity politics. This is a form of disciplinary governance which is based on entrepreneurship, an ethos of self-survival, positive understanding of hierarchic forms of economic and political organizations, valuing "hard work" and morality and resisting collective forms of political economy. The conservative right thus seeks to transform ostensibly "proletarianized" social structures into entrepreneurial ones (Bonefeld 2012). Moreover, the conservative right highlights "voluntary deflation" in which the economy adjusts through the reduction of wages, prices and public spending to restore competitiveness, which is supposedly best achieved by cutting the state's budget, debts and deficits. Doing so, the advocates of the conservative right believe, will inspire "business confidence" (see Blyth 2013).

The innovation right enjoyed much success in pushing through publicly funded projects in the early 2000s. However, the rise of the conservative right and the relative decline of the innovation right has from 2010 onwards meant that it is increasingly difficult to push through projects in the field of culture that are based on heavy public funding. Similarly, the gradual decline of the innovation right signals a weakening enthusiasm on the part of the key businesses in the technology industry to fund projects that are not explicitly associated with their global business interests.

The fact that the corporate fundraising of the museum project was tardy and lukewarm from the beginning clearly discloses the above-mentioned development. The key firms of the high-tech industry and related business associations did not make any direct commitments to the Guggenheim Helsinki. Only a handful of companies, operating primarily in the service sector (hotel chains, etc.), notably participated in the fundraising organized by the local Guggenheim Helsinki Foundation.

The rise of the conservative right was similarly visible in local politics. At decisive moments of the project, the conservative right highlighted the funding issues of the museum in particular, and in so doing made it practically impossible to treat public investments in the museum as if they were contributing to long-term "intangible capital".

Finally, the Guggenheim Helsinki case brings us back to the issue of the state and the role of government and public spending. The role of the Finnish government was singular throughout the Guggenheim Helsinki process. It was marked by notable strategic selectivities within the state apparatus. In the beginning, the museum was articulated as an economic and growth-oriented project to the extent that the Ministry of Culture and Education refused to get involved in the project because it considered it to be solely about economic affairs and local economic development (Linko 2013). The Ministry of Economic Affairs and Employment – a peculiar bastion of the innovation right – maintained a positive image of the museum throughout, whereas the Ministry of Finance (a stronghold of austerity politics) was more reserved about the public funding of the project.

Ultimately, the government refused to fund the project, which, in turn, made it impossible for the transnational coalition supporting the museum to rely on the state to push the museum through against local resistance. Even though the museum was articulated by its local supporters as a chance to demonstrate the skills, qualities and ambitions of the Finnish nation (Savolainen 2016), the government of Finland refused to channel public money into the museum project. The transnational coalition thus failed to scale the Guggenheim Helsinki as a national project. This together with the gradual consolidation of the politics of austerity after 2008, instigated in particular by the conservative right both nationally and locally, made the Finnish government reluctant to invest public money in the project.

With regard to state involvement, the Guggenheim Helsinki highlights the differences that exist among infrastructural projects central to knowledge-based economization. Some of these are more explicitly connected to reproducing human capital and the related crafting of geopolitical subjects, whereas others are more closely connected to the issue of exhibiting creativity. With regard to the former (see Chapter 6), the founding of Aalto University as the "MIT of Finland" in 2010 was heavily sponsored by local industry and foundations. It was a pet project of the innovation right. The local and national economic elites raised more than 200 million Euros of private money in less than a year, and the Finnish government invested another 500 million Euros to complement the generous private fundraising. The founding of Aalto University thus discloses the ways in which the growth strategies of the state and the local growth coalitions were seamlessly interlinked in a biopolitical attempt to produce human capital for "national" purposes but with a global focus.

The EU and knowledge-based economization: from regional to urban form of knowledge-based economization?

Since the 1990s, the process of European integration has been fundamentally predicated on an idea of economic competition between Europe, Asia and the

US. The formulation of such a space of competition was later accompanied by concrete policies which were structured around the issue of competitiveness. The debate on European economic competitiveness vis-à-vis its rivals brought together three powerful political ideas, two of which were geopolitical. First, the European single market policy was premised on the view that the European states were too small to compete on the global sphere in the age of globalization. Second, the diminutive size of European states was coupled with another political idea related to the need to qualitatively re-construct the entire economic structure at the scale of the EU. Since the 1990s the competitiveness problem of the EU has been articulated as a need to move toward a "knowledge economy" or even an "information society". Third, from the 1990s onwards, the European debate on competitiveness was predicated on the view that European competitiveness problems had to do with the territorial structures of the EU (Moisio, 2011b). The articulation of such a "European competitiveness problem" and the associated exercise of political power in the political–economic field since the 1990s has thus brought about the production of understandings of the EU as a territory of wealth with discernible supranational interests.

The EU as a regional knowlegdge-based economy

The decision in the 1990s to turn the EU into a world-class knowledge economy was a geopolitical one. As such it did not represent a predestined development path dictated by the conceived forces of globalization. Rather, the idea of the European knowledge-based economy was a selected and institutionally retained political choice, which was in the beginning in particular accompanied with the idea of a European social model. The EU-driven knowledge-based economization was wholeheartedly first instigated and later supported by notable political powers within the EU, by its member states, by the OECD and by large high-tech companies. Ever since, the European knowledge-based economization has been premised on an imagination of the EU as a territory of wealth, and rationalized by the fear of Europe losing its position in global competition.

The idea that the EU could be turned into an ideal type of knowledge-based economy culminated primarily in the launching of the so-called Lisbon Agenda at the EU Council Meeting in Lisbon in 2000. This summit on the Atlantic shore was a significant milestone in a process which had started already in 1993 with the publication of the White Paper on Growth, Competitiveness and Jobs issued by Jacques Delors as a response to the deepening employment crisis in Western Europe. The Lisbon meeting published a bold strategy which set for the EU the goal of becoming "the most competitive and dynamic knowledge-based economy in the world capable of sustainable economic growth with more and better jobs and greater social cohesion" (European Council 2000, 5). Since the Lisbon meeting, this overall economic goal has been among the leading political priorities of the EU. It has effectively subsumed other EU policies under its priorities and strategic aims. Indeed, the Lisbon Agenda and its follow-ups are predicated on the idea that a particular "European society" could be developed through the "European knowledge-based economy" (e.g. European Communities 2006).

Explicit instructions for organizing the European knowledge economy spatially were enshrined already in the European Spatial Development Perspective document (ESDP) published by the Commission of European Communities in 1999 (CSD 1999). The document identified the European competitiveness problem as partially a consequence of Europe's spatial disorder (Moisio 2011b, 21) and presented a set of guidelines which resonate explicitly with the later outlines of the Lisbon Agenda. These concerned issues such as how to organize European space to make better use of the economic potential of all of the EU's regions and how to guarantee parity of access to infrastructure and knowledge in different parts of Europe (CSD 1999, 20–30).

The alliance between the development of the EU as a regional knowledge-based economy and the spatial ordering of the EU has been further confirmed in the Territorial Agenda of the European Union, which was prepared in 2005–2006 and launched in 2007. The connections between the Territorial Agenda, the Lisbon Strategy and the ESDP are obvious since they all involved "regionalizing" policy priorities such as strengthening polycentric development through networking of cities around European mega-regions, and promoting regional clusters of competition and innovation in Europe (EU Ministers Responsible for Urban and Spatial Development 2007). The Lisbon Strategy was later replaced by the Europe 2020 strategy, published in 2010 (CEC 2010). This strategy further underscores the priorities of smart, sustainable and inclusive regional growth, which have been notable catchwords in the process of knowledge-based economization. In so doing, the strategy discloses the efforts to make the EU the world's leading knowledge-based economy. The same goal has been repeated numerous times in the follow-up documents (e.g. EU Ministers Responsible for Spatial Planning and Territorial Development 2011, 3).

All the above-mentioned political documents are premised on the geopolitical discourses of the knowledge-based economy. They articulate what kind of global position Europe and its populations are in, how they ought to be, where they ought to end up and what will happen if the chosen goal remains unattained (e.g. European Communities 2006, 19). In so doing, they expose one of the subtexts that the European policymakers ideally take into account when tailoring policies from the EU's point of view.

The above broadens the conventional analysis of the territorial features of the EU typically undertaken by border scholars (for a debate, see Moisio *et al.* 2013; Moisio and Luukkonen 2017). From the perspective of knowledge-based economization, the EU territory can be understood as a processual entity which brings together geopolitical discourses of global competition, segments of the population of the EU as geopolitical subjects and practices which produce the EU and its regions in particular as geopolitical objects of competition.

I have examined with Juho Luukkonen the ways in which the idea and ideal of transforming the EU into a "world class knowledge economy" has since the 1990s been envisioned and put into practice as a distinct territorializing strategy (see Luukkonen and Moisio 2016) which is geographically structured around regions in particular. In so doing, we have sought to demonstrate that the territory of the EU should not be comprehended as a distinctive set of policies but rather as a constituent and effect of the contemporary economic strategies which are implemented, analyzed and put in motion in professional networks within and beyond EU institutions. This perspective highlights the role of "expertize" (Kuus 2014) in imagining and implementing the connection between the knowledge-intensive form of capitalism and the EU's territorial structure. This expertize is in operation in different EU projects and discloses the complex agency of "EU power" (Moisio 2011b).

For instance, the so-called European Spatial Planning Observation Network (ESPON) framework has launched a number of scientific projects that have tasked European academics with measuring and quantifying the strength of the EU's knowledge-based economy in different corners of Europe. It can thus be understood as a concerted effort to produce European regions, networks, flows and spatial structures as calculable and comparable, and as if they represented the EU as a unitary space (Moisio and Luukkonen 2015). Another apt example is the European Regional Competitiveness Index (RCI) which was launched in 2010 by the European Commission to allow the European regions to monitor their development and make comparisons with other regions. Thus, the users of the RCI "can see easily where their region stands in innovation, governance, transport and digital infrastructure, and measures of health and human capital" (CEC 2017). The ESPON and the RCI thus disclose some of the ways in which the EU as a geopolitical unit of competition is constituted in calculative and objectifying social practices which render the EU thinkable in a particular spatial way.

The territorial construction of the EU-driven knowledge-based economization: from regions to urban spaces?

The territorial constitution of the EU has been intense in numerous other EU-funded projects since the 1990s, and most of these operate within the discursive and material structures of knowledge-intensive capitalism. These projects almost invariably locate spatial question at the core of the envisioned European knowledge-based economy. In this capacity, the projects on European regions and cities that have been initiated since the 1990s aptly uncover the coming together of the city, regions and the knowledge-based economy in the context of the EU's notable efforts to put together an ostensibly European system of economic value creation and related territory of wealth and power.

One may argue that since the 1990s the territorial construction of the EU has been based on privileging the regional scale over the urban scale, in particular when it comes to political–economic development strategies. Harding (1997) pointed out in mid-1990s how the political processes of the EU revolved around "Europe of regions" while "a Europe of the cities" was almost entirely confined to academic debates. Perhaps one of the long-term implications of such governing cities through regions is that the EU has launched only a limited number of projects that focus on the production of urban space and experience. Similarly, the EU-orchestrated discourses of the European knowledge-based economy have been predominantly region-centered since the 1990s.

However, one may also argue that the regional strategies of the EU as a knowledge-intensive economic territory have highlighted the role of cities as the fundamental backbone of regions and their competitiveness. From this per-spective, the urban-centered nature of the EU's regional development policies is not new. Since the 1990s, the EU has launched a series of "regionalizing" urban programs and town-twinning initiatives in order to enhance political integration and the valorization of capital at the same time. These initiatives have sought to make the EU more visible in localities and in local, national and regional expert networks. But I would argue that these "region-projects" also disclose the ways in which knowledge-based economization has been con-nected to cities in the context of the EU.

Indeed, most of the "city projects" of the EU operate through the discursive framings of the knowledge-based economy. One such example is the Urban Audit project, which was launched in 1997 by the European Commission and has continued up until recently under the auspices of Eurostat. From the beginning, the Urban Audit has been premised upon a need to compare cities and their spatial attributes at the European level. The earlier efforts to compare urban locations, and thus to bring these locations into the singular European spatial matrix, was, as one of the representatives of the European Commission stated in 2004, "fraught with problems due to differences in data collection methods and definitions" (Dijkstra 2004, 16). The Urban Audit was thus an attempt to solve these problems by generating a set of indicators that was based on primary data, aspects of urban life and urban space, from a number of large and medium-size cities primarily within the EU.

From the beginning, the Urban Audit was entangled with knowledge-based economization. It was a by-product of the policies of competitiveness that were officially articulated in the Lisbon Agenda in 2000. More precisely, the Urban Audit was predicated on conceiving urban space as a substance that can be fundamentally exploited for the needs of the EU-wide knowledge-intensive system of capital accumulation. Comparisons and related city statistics were generated at the level of the EU because an EU-wide urban network was comprehended as a resource, or indeed a prerequisite for the emergence of a new European economy:

> The *"Urban Audit"* data collection provides *information and comparable meas-urements on the different aspects of the quality of urban life in European cities.*

Improving the attractiveness of regions and cities is one of the priorities targeted by the renewed *Lisbon Strategy* and the EU's strategic guidelines for cohesion policy for 2007–13. Quality of life is crucial in attracting and retaining a skilled labour force, businesses, students, tourists and, most of all, residents in a city. Assessing the current situation is a prerequisite for any improvement, development and future monitoring. The *"Urban Audit"* is a response to this demand for assessment.

(CEC 2014, emphasis in original)

The Urban Audit discloses the breakout of the discourse of the knowledge-based economy in the 1990s as the primary growth and competitiveness strategy at the level of the EU. But it also reveals the endurance of this discourse as a crucial political substance in the wider European project. As such, the Urban Audit represents a wider re-territorializing discourse which couples particular urban qualities, urban problems and segments of population (particularly the highly educated) as strategic nodes in the genesis of the EU as the world's most competitive knowledge-based economy. A representative of the EU Commission states this revealingly:

The role of cities in reaching this goal is critical. Innovative knowledge-based firms tend to settle in cities and urban areas. Cities are major centres of employment, providing jobs for its residents as well as many commuters from the surrounding areas. However, cities often have important pockets of deprivation. These deprived urban neighbourhoods can be improved by reducing and preventing problems related to social exclusion, drugs and crime. Tackling these issues is necessary not only to create a more cohesive Europe, but also to make cities a better place to live and more attractive to investors.

(Dijkstra 2004, 16)

Another example of the EU-funded urban projects has been structured around the fashionable planning idea of the smart city. A considerable amount of the recent EU territory work has been clustered around the European Smart Cities Initiative which covers a broad range of issues ranging from transport infrastructures and soft infrastructures of innovation to digitalization and smart buildings. This initiative nicely uncovers the ways in which the attempt to produce the EU as a knowledge-based economy includes notable efforts to engender "smartmentality" (Vanolo 2014) at the scale of Europe and through European cities.

The imaginary of the knowledge-based economy almost invariably articulates certain substances of urban space as prerequisites for creative and thus putatively innovative human behavior. One of the key characteristics of this discourse has been the linking of cultural diversity with spaces of innovation potential and urban creativity, and translating this coupling into knowledge production. To illustrate, the Intercultural Cities project, jointly initiated by the European Commission and the Council of Europe, operates inherently on the basis of such understanding:

> Cities can gain enormously from the entrepreneurship, variety of skills and creativity associated with cultural diversity, provided they adopt policies and practices that facilitate intercultural interaction and inclusion. The Intercultural Cities programme supports cities in reviewing their policies through an intercultural lens and developing comprehensive intercultural strategies to help them manage diversity positively and realize the diversity advantage. The programme proposes a set of analytical and practical tools to help local stakeholders through the various stages of the process.
>
> (Council of Europe, 2014)

The Intercultural Cities project is structured around a discursive formation which brings together growth, characteristics of urban space, innovation and a particular breed of human capacity. The key aspects of the project boil down to the purportedly central role of "diversity" in the so-called creative city discourse whereby urban cultural diversity is perceived as an economic asset which fosters dynamism, innovation capacity, creativity and economic growth.

The Intercultural Cities project involves developing indices through which interculturality in a given European city can be measured and acted on in evidence-based policies. The *Intercultural Cities Index* is produced as a tool to rank cities within the EU and beyond according to their measured "intercultural performance". The *Intercultural Cities Index* reduces the mosaic of "cultures" to a governable sphere which is then articulated as a key domain of a concerted political project of the EU as a knowledge-based economy. The formation of scoreboards and charts conducted within the Intercultural Cities project is therefore not only a technical exercise. It rather presents difference and diversity management as pivotal political aspects of European territorial construction and the knowledge-intensive mode of accumulation. In this capacity, the Intercultural Cities project, together with many other similar projects, epitomizes that EU-funded projects have a proclivity to generate systems of comparison through which "knowledge-intensive" territorial developments within the EU can be represented and talked upon.

The urban focus has gradually strengthened in EU development policy-making since the economic crisis in 2008. The political elites of the EU have increasingly highlighted the role of cities as crucial sites in terms of innovation-led production and entrepreneurial development, and not just in terms of consumption. It would be tempting to argue that the change in perspective stems from the pervasive geopolitical discourses of knowledge-based economization in which cities appear as the key places of capital accumulation and geopolitical construction of competitive advantages. The gradual change toward more urban agenda in EU policy may also indicate the relative strengthening of the "European innovation right" which is primarily concerned with the city and the urban as a place of surplus value creation.

The most explicit manifestation of the gradually developing explicit urban rather than regionalizing focus of the EU-centered knowledge-based economization is the Urban Agenda (2014). It was launched only relatively recently after a CITIES forum organized by the EU Commission, the Commission's own Cities of Tomorrow project, and debates within the member states and beyond. This document highlights the need for a common EU urban policy, and denotes the increasing aspirations of the Commission's Directorate General for Regional and Urban Policy (until 2012 only regional policy was mentioned in its name) to produce an ideal European city model. The Commission indeed argues in the Urban Strategy that "in terms of aims, objectives and values, there already is an explicit agreement at the European level on the character of the European city of the future and the principles on which an ideal European city should be based" (CEC 2014, 6). It is illuminating to see that the list of policies which the Commission argues "explicitly target urban areas" is inextricably related to the process of knowledge-based economization that has been the topic of this chapter. The Commission lists the following EU policies:

> Energy, Information Society, Environment, Climate Action, Education and Culture, Transport, etc. support initiatives such as European Capital of Culture, Smart Cities and Communities European Innovation Partnership, Green Capital Award, Covenant of Mayors and Mayors Adapt.
>
> (CEC 2014, 7)

8 Coda

Geopolitics of the knowledge-based economy

In this book, I have elaborated the geopolitics of what is customarily called the knowledge-based economy, the knowledge economy, the information economy or even the new economy. This is a vast phenomenon, and I have chosen to focus on a specific aspect of it. A number of other connected issues could have been explored. Among these are, for example, the re-spatialization of the state in the discursive practices of "cyber security", the strategic use of "smart technologies" by national (Rodríguez-Bolívar 2018) and local governments (see e.g. Carrillo *et al.* 2014), and the gendered aspects of knowledge-based economization.

My analysis in the previous chapters has been premised on a view that the concept of the geopolitical is eventually about the production of territories of wealth and power. This production may take the form of territorial expansion, territorial contest, and war over geographical space. The twentieth century witnessed the centrality of such geopolitical contestation, and the more recent history indicates that this kind of Hobbesian geopolitics has not ceased to be important. I have however stressed that the geopolitical world of knowledge-based economization is also about producing territories of wealth and power, albeit with different spatial strategies (for these, see e.g. Thurow 1999). Chapter 2 thus elaborated the knowledge-based economy both as a capitalist social formation and an inescapably discursive political process which structures socio-spatial practices, related political decision-making and different kinds of strategy work across multiple scales and sites.

A major goal of the book has been to challenge the view that geopolitics belongs to the old twentieth-century world of territorial enmities, natural resources and the spatial consolidation of the nation state, as well as the view that it is not present or relevant in the contemporary knowledge-intensive capitalist development and its spaces of flows. This book is thus an effort to conceptualize the strategic and political nature of mastering space in the context of the knowledge-intensive form of capitalism. The point of departure has been the idea that the contemporary capitalism too encloses geopolitics which differs from the one we customarily associate with the concept.

In my perspective, the concept of the geopolitical refers to the production of territories of wealth, power, security and belonging, as well as to related social practices which are premised on ideas about how to best facilitate such production through mastering of space and population. I have developed the concept of knowledge-based economization as a process productive of a specific kind of spatial organization and related geopolitical subjects, that is, a historically contingent economic territory. Specific political forces seek to build a "new economy" which is based on innovations, high value, selective urban spaces and highly skilled "global entrepreneurs". This process is strategic in a dual sense. First, it is strategic in the sense of facilitating the circulation of capital in the contemporary historical conjuncture. Second, it is strategic in the sense of producing political territories of competition. In such a process, new geopolitical spaces and subjectivities are imagined and constructed, and new objectifying social practices are also tailored. In contrast to suggestions that globalization renders space and territory irrelevant, the concept of knowledge-based economization highlights the profoundly geopolitical nature of capitalist developments that have taken shape since the 1990s in particular.

Knowledge-based economization cannot be understood without its geopolitical element, its strategic spatial production which brings together political space, human subjects and capitalist valorization. Knowledge-based economization also transforms how politics and the political are understood. It entails what Michael Callon (1998) has called the technicalization of politics which emphasizes the growing importance of scientific and economic rationality, and the associated importance of expert knowledge in policymaking. I have suggested in the previous chapters that the 1990s and early 2000s mark the birth of a new body of academic work which is a constitutive element of knowledge-based economization. I have analyzed the ways in which the ideational frameworks generated by well-known academic figures such as Manuel Castells, Richard Florida and Michael Porter can be considered as disclosing some of the geopolitical elements of knowledge-based economization.

My point has not been to ask whether the academic theories of Castells, Florida and Porter hold water in terms of their capacity to explain patterns of migration, economic development, inter-spatial competition, the success of political communities or something else. It would, of course, not be difficult to argue that theories like the creative class are analytically flawed because they treat cities as unitary entities and homogenous actors who compete against each other, win or lose, succeed or fail as a result of policymaking (see Marcuse 2005). It would also be legitimate to claim that the policies that derive from ideas such as the creative class represent hegemonic projects which are "mobilized by politico-economic elites who are appropriating the socio-affective externalities of urban environments" (Rossi 2017, 74). These critiques are undoubtedly relevant. This notwithstanding, I have desired to highlight the ways in which the theory of the creative class, for example, frames the contemporary capitalist condition geopolitically, as a matter of territorial attractiveness and survival of political communities as territories of wealth in a world of flows and heightening inter-spatial competition in general. From my perspective, the theory of the creative class is a member of a wider family of ideas playing a constitutive role in the process of knowledge-based economization.

Table 8.1 summarizes the key features of the geopolitics of the knowledge-based economy vis-à-vis the geopolitics of territorial consolidation and control that characterized most of the twentieth century. I will discuss these

Table 8.1 Some features of the geopolitics of the knowledge-based economy

	Geopolitics of territorial condensation and control	Geopolitics of the knowledge-based economy
Ideologies	Nationalism, conservatism	Economic nationalism, liberalism
State strategies	Social and spatial homogenization	Selective opening and fragmentation of the state
Constitutive knowledge	Strategies of territorial management and sovereignty	Strategies of leadership, management, economic growth and competitiveness
Spatiality of state strategies	Control/management of topographical space	Managing the topological space of connectivity and "cognitive proximity"
Calculative practices of state success and strength	The size of territory, natural resources, population (growth), military power etc.	Competitiveness indices, creativity indices, innovativeness indices, indices on "connectivity" to "global networks"
Key transformative spatial imaginary	National cohesion/national space	Global networks/globalization
Underpinning spatial articulation	Nation state	Mega-regions, city-regionalism, hubs and spokes, global cities
Dominant geopolitical reasoning	Keynesian-Machiavellian, the potentiality of territorial enmities	Porterian-Floridean, the constitutive role of economic rivalries
Formative moment	War	Economic turmoil/crisis
Highlighted resource base	Tangible resources	Intangible assets
Targeted citizenship	Loyal national figure	Global entrepreneur
Nodal spatial strategies	Territorial equalization	Spatial selectivity
Exemplary institutions of higher education	Fragmented national university system	Globally competitive universities and related innovation centers
Nature of the state apparatus	Condensation of forces around national spatial fix	Diversification and transnationalization of state apparatuses; growing role of economizing Ministries, the ECB and related bodies; increasing power of business associations and firms to operate through the state

features through four and partly overlapping themes that merit further scholarly attention: the spatiality of knowledge-based economization; knowledge-based economization and the state; the relationship between neoliberalism and knowledge-based economization; and the emergence of socio-spatial divisions and hierarchies in the context of knowledge-based economization.

Spatiality of the process of knowledge-based economization

The processes that I have designated here as knowledge-based economization were underway prior to the early 1990s. In the 1980s, they took the form of national technology initiatives and programs in the OECD states. Yet, I have endeavored to highlight that knowledge-based economization took an increasingly geopolitical form in the early 1990s, an epoch characterized by the deepening crisis of Atlantic Fordism and the associated gradual dismantling of late Keynesian political structures. This involved re-imagining the nation state as a new kind of economic territory engaged in competition with other economic territories. With the notion of economic territory I have striven to highlight that knowledge-based economization has entailed new kinds of "national" economic imaginaries as well as urban visions and projects. It has proceeded as a spatial-strategic process manifest in locally orchestrated and spatially selective development visions and urban and regional projects. Again, this process has been most visible within the OECD sphere, but has not been confined to this context only.

If the Keynesian issue of social and spatial homogenization was still visible in the 1990s in some states which sought to generate innovation-driven growth, the contemporary knowledge-based economization is increasingly premised on a selective "opening" of the state in the name of both globalization and innovation (Moisio and Belina 2017). This raises the issue of the nature of knowledge-based economization with regard to what geographers customarily conceptualize as the distinction between relational and territorial spaces. If territorial geopolitics denotes topographical control and management of state space, knowledge-based economization is often taken to refer to spatial processes that seek to build strategic connections between the state and the "topological" space of "global" value chains. The Porterian and Floridean geopolitical rationalities are geared at producing this kind of an economic territory. In these texts, inter-state competition is not only represented in a new manner but is calculated through different kinds of indices measuring competitiveness, creativity, openness, innovativeness and so on. These indices "objectify" states, cities and regions as if they were units of global competition (for the disciplinary function of indices, see Kangas 2017). Such objectifying calculative practices produce the global as a meaningful political–economic territory or scale of competition (cf. Elden 2005; Larner and Le Heron 2002).

Knowledge-based economization is a process which transcends the territorial-relational dualism. It proceeds through the dynamics of re- and de-territorialization. In so doing, it highlights the overlapping spatial logics and processes of the contemporary capitalist condition and the related transnationalization of the state apparatus. In Chapter 6, I have interrogated the coming together of de- and re-territorialization in the context of institutions of higher education. These institutions can be regarded as being assembled geopolitically as units of competition in the process of knowledge-based economization. Furthermore, I sought to demonstrate that the construction of new kinds of state-orchestrated learning spaces is expected to produce novel transnational geopolitical subjects – a new generation of capitalist laborers with conducive minds and competences that meet the demands of the time. The geopolitics of the knowledge-based economy thus entails a state-orchestrated production of new professional citizen-subjects for the purposes of global knowledge-intensive capitalism.

Moreover, in the geopolitical imaginaries of urban economics the role of large cities and city-regions in the production of nation states as territories of wealth is highlighted (see, e.g. Glaeser 2012). Knowledge-based economization, as it unfolds today, is partly constituted through an emphasis on the role of metropolitan areas as epicenters of "national" productivity, innovation, prosperity, wealth and competitiveness. As a consequence, rural areas and smaller urban centers have been difficult to incorporate in policymaking, which takes its inspiration from the idea of innovation-led growth.

The transformation of urban politics in the age of knowledge-based economization is a notable scholarly issue that merits further scholarly attention. Knowledge-based economization, in its neoliberal form in particular, marks the generation of urban infrastructures as framework conditions for successfully defending national and local interests in the conceived global innovation game. One of the consequences is that the model of an innovative city becomes a powerful template that can be applied for regulating the entire state space. Exemplifying this process, most of the OECD states have launched urban strategies to retain or effect a link between creative economies, human capital and the state as a territory of wealth. Knowledge-based economization thus frames both the city and the urban in terms of their innovation capacities which in turn can be nurtured through urban amenities and more general cultural qualities of urban spaces.

Some reflections on the role of the state in knowledge-based economization

According to twentieth-century classical geopolitics, the territory of the state is understood as providing both "physical advantages" and setting possible limitations or material constraints on inter-state competition. Geopolitical struggle at the world scale revolves around attempts to control the distribution of natural and other material resources for the benefit of a territorially consolidating nation state. In territorial geopolitics, therefore, the government of the state is a crucial actor whose deeds are shaped by the state's geographical features and associated position in the capitalist world economy. By way of contrast, in knowledge-based economization the generation and utilization of technological, business and design innovations are pivotal constituents of the state as a territory of wealth, and determinants of its particular "location" in the global hierarchy of states.

Knowledge-based economization re-articulates the nature of inter-state competition and downplays the importance of the state as a bounded piece of land or physical territory. With respect to achieving success as a nation state, political virtues rather revolve around the capacity to re-work the state as an economic territory which is connected to the flows and streams of talent, money and ideas. In consequence, knowledge-based economization is premised on spatial selectivity rather than territorial maintenance, which aims at unifying state spaces through public investments.

The geopolitics of the knowledge-based economy is predicated on flow and network-articulations which highlight major cities not only as crucial circulatory infrastructures of contemporary capitalism but also as geographical sites within which the competitive advantages of nations are produced. Indeed, states play a key role in re-constructing urban spaces so as to meet the requirements for attracting and developing activities that belong to the upper tiers of value creation. Rather than "'freeing' of cities from containerization imposed by states" (Taylor 2004, 200), knowledge-based economization re-positions the city and even micro-scale urban fabrics vis-à-vis the conceived world political condition and the state's role therein. These attempts of re-positioning have been associated with twin developments. On the one hand, the spatial and symbolic structures of the state have been re-worked through cities. On the other hand, the symbolic, moral and ethical dimensions of national identities of given states have been reformulated, thus targeting nation-state citizens in the realm of their "being and subjectivity" (Ong 2006) by virtue of the constant attempts to enhance the national competitive advantage.

It must be highlighted that knowledge-based economization does not refer only to economic leverage but also to an active construction of institutional capacity. It is not least because of this issue that excavating the role of the state in the process of knowledge-based economization merits further study. Knowledge-based economization proceeds through what James Scott (1998) famously called state-led social engineering, and through related and increasingly transnational policy circuits. These circuits are mobilized by different kinds of actors ranging from international consultant companies to state and local authorities. These actors operate through different institutional capacities but are bound together in their efforts to produce innovation-led growth and economic value.

Neoliberalism and knowledge-based economization

Since the early 1990s, the process of knowledge-based economization has qualitatively changed. A gradual shift from the late Keynesian policies of technopolitization toward increasing neoliberalization has taken place. State apparatuses

have been increasingly transnationalized and coupled with a normative articulation according to which economic "strength" – understood as the main
issue behind the success of political communities today as well as in the future
– is dependent on the capacity of business firms to attract and produce winners and innovate. Talented individuals, business firms and private investors
are subjectified primarily as risk-takers and creative forces. Representatives of
the public, in turn, are responsibilized to align themselves with the former.
Accordingly, the role of the public sector in promoting innovation-led development has been actively dismissed since the early 2000s. The contemporary
knowledge-based economization, thus, highlights the role of the private sector
in determining the level of development among political communities. This
has unfolded irrespective of continuous public investments in the very basis of
the economy of innovations (cf. Mazzucato 2013).

In this book, I have also shown that one geopolitical outcome of knowledge-based economization is a heightened emphasis on new economic spaces,
start-up ecosystems and super-talented individuals in the overall social and
political developments of states. This resonates with the key characteristics
of the neoliberal project. Obviously, neoliberalization and knowledge-based
economization are intertwined and strongly co-constituted, both in terms of
their geopolitical and biopolitical features. Indeed, some scholars have explicitly linked the "language of innovation" with neoliberalism (Peck and Tickell
2002). Even though this link is not straightforward, the contemporary form
of knowledge-based economization is clearly premised on a neoliberal view
of the world, one which increasingly dominates the overall societal discourse.
Similarly to neoliberalization, the processes of knowledge-based economization are often re-cast as non-ideological and non-political economic problems
that necessitate meticulous "innovative" and "technical" solutions. This results
in policymaking which revolves around scientific and economic rationality
and unwavering belief in the potential of technological development, as exemplified by the mantra of digitalization, for example. Indeed, what lies at the
heart of the geopolitics of the knowledge-based economy is a strong belief in
economic and societal progress, which is taken to occur through the coming
together of science, rationality, markets, large-scale urbanization, "global men-
tality" and technology. As to the state, it is expected to exert its power in order
to foster and cultivate this meeting, and to act as a facilitator of knowledge-
intensive economic development – both socially and spatially – but otherwise
is expected to accept limited public authority and leave the field of knowledge-
intensive development to private actors (cf. Raco 2013). In the contemporary
form of knowledge-based economization, the state is thus charged with stepping aside and setting the field for market functions and private actors. But at
the same time, the state is activated to create a globally relevant business atmosphere that includes a political culture of competition and creativity within its
territorial jurisdictions (see Ahlqvist and Moisio 2014, 31).

Moreover, the contemporary neoliberal form of knowledge-based economization presumes that the state can facilitate private-sector-led innovations

primarily through subsidies, tax reductions and other means that increase the attractiveness of the economic territory of the state. For example, the Netherlands offers significant tax cuts to foreign "innovators". The French government, in turn, has launched a start-up visa program in order to kick-start its start-up economy with the help of a foreign talent pool. Indeed, the incorporation of foreign skilled labor recruitment into state territorial strategies is one important geopolitical dimension of knowledge-based economization.

Both knowledge-based economization and neoliberalization thus highlight the issue of the entrepreneurialization of society and the self. Similarly to neo-liberalization, in knowledge-based economization individuals and populations are taken up as economic resources with potentials that can be cultivated, mobilized and harnessed for profit making. Knowledge-based economization in its current form thus seeks to produce neoliberal subjects who apprehend themselves in an entrepreneurial, market-oriented and "post-national" manner, and who responsibilize themselves as creative and innovative economic agents. But what the literature on neoliberalism often leaves largely unaddressed is the fact that knowledge-based economization also highlights the co-consti-tution of the de-territorializing and globalizing of political geopolitical spaces (such as urban infrastructures and learning environments of higher education) and entrepreneurial social development as a territorial survival strategy of the nation state. Whether such an emphasis has implications with respect to the ways in which inter-state relations are organized is another matter entirely. But it seems obvious that because knowledge-based economization plays down the link between the state's physical territory and its political survival as a territory of wealth, it adds a new component to the ways in which inter-state com-petition and conflict are traditionally conceived in a geopolitical perspective. Be it as it may, the centrality of the discourses of territorial competition and competitiveness in knowledge-based economization signal a close relationship to neoliberalism. Neoliberalism and knowledge-based economization thus are in a productive interaction with each other (for a useful discussion on neolib-eralization, see Brenner *et al.* 2010); both designate a specific way of securing, enhancing and accelerating capital accumulation.

However, the relationship between the knowledge-based economization and neoliberalism is not straightforward. Peters (2009) stresses that not all of the key ideas of the knowledge-based economy are based on the tenets of neoliberalism. Jessop (2002) has made a distinction between the neoliberal, neo-statist, neo-communitarian and neo-corporatist ways of promoting the knowledge-intensive form of capitalism. Mazzucato's (2013) recent examina-tion of the role of the state in knowledge-intensive capitalism for instance exemplifies the evolving dispute on the appropriate ways of promoting the economy of innovations. Mazzucato (2013) seeks to promote innovation-led growth in a more inclusive manner than is currently the case. She provides an analysis of the undermined role of the state in the economy of innovations and points out that, contrary to the suggestions of neoliberal proponents of innovation-led growth, it has often been the state that has made the initial, absolutely crucial high-risk investments, the fruit of which business firms have later exploited. She underscores the collective character of innovations, proposes a Keynesian model of innovation-driven growth and calls for the need to end the large-scale privatization of profits which are generated partly through public investments. As such, her work demonstrates one of the ways in which the contemporary neoliberal mode of knowledge-based economization might become politically contested. The ways in which the Keynesian form of knowledge-based economization might challenge and alter the geopolitical features of contemporary knowledge-based economization nonetheless remain unclear in such otherwise notable academic interventions.

Toward a socio-spatial polarization?

The contemporary attempts to produce the state as a territory of wealth underscore the important role of a particular faction of population as well as the qualities of urban spaces in determining success in the global innovation game. The ways in which human capabilities and orientations are today valued in knowledge-based economization disclose clear connections with neoliberal dogma. Knowledge-based economization is about governing "living resources", and it gives and denies value to particular human conducts and human mentalities. In so doing, it involves defining valuable geopolitical subjects. As I have demonstrated through a reading of Manuel Castells' (1996) theory of the network society and Richard Florida's (2004) theory of the creative class, knowledge-based economization places a relatively narrow faction of population in the driver's seat of societal development. In other words, knowledge-based economization is not only characterized by the financial and political success of its "happy subjects" but also by its capacity to abandon certain populations and to situate them outside political normativity. Simultaneously, it is clear that as living resources the pivotal population factions, whether they are called creatives or something else, do not form a unitary group of people with a shared political identity or a similar economic status. It is not least for this reason that it would also be worthwhile to examine how knowledge-based economization is linked to democracy and socio-spatial-economic inequality – both crucial factors from the perspective of state transformation.

The potentiality of the knowledge-intensive form of capitalism to increase socio-spatial differentiation and uneven development has been recognized by some of the key geopolitical writers of the knowledge-intensive form of capitalism. Richard Florida (cited in Schell 2014), for instance, argues how

> I think I've been very unfairly criticized for not dealing with socioeconomic inequality. I think I've been one of the first urbanists, modern urbanists, empirical urbanists, to point to socioeconomic inequality. I said it was a direct outgrowth of the clustering of knowledge and creative workers, and their competition. In *Rise of the Creative Class*, I said that place would become the arena for class conflict in modern capitalism, and

I think I didn't quite know how that would play out. I cautioned city leaders and the creative class to be well aware over that contestation over space.

The interconnections between the contemporary form of knowledge-based economization and uneven geographical development require further scholarly attention. As Neil Smith (2005, 895) argues, socially divided societies reproduce their forms of social differentiation in geographical space and, by corollary, centrally produced hierarchic geographies reaffirm and reproduce social differences. The obvious socio-spatial unevenness inherent in the contemporary processes of knowledge-based economization inescapably has political implications which touch upon issues of socio-spatial justice, and which might manifest themselves in what Painter (2006) calls the prosaic geographies of stateness.

It is important in this context to re-think the means through which spatial justice can be engendered through public policies, and the ways in which policies are constrained by the current form of knowledge-based economization. This issue is pertinent not only in the context of states but also in the context of supranational political actors such as the EU. The Lisbon Strategy (2000) and the associated "knowledge-based economy talk" still dominate the so-called cohesion policies of the EU. Regions and cities are constantly encouraged to apply for EU funding in order to develop the territorial cohesion of the EU. But they are simultaneously forced to react to the tens of indices and metrics that have been developed after the launching of the Lisbon Agenda in order to measure the implementation of the Agenda and in order to develop the evidence-based policies of the EU (Moisio and Luukkonen 2015). This agenda, together with the recent proxy agenda of "smart specialization" (highlighting "smart growth" and "endogenous growth"), fundamentally structures and constrains the ways in which spatial policies can be imagined and practiced in the European countryside and in small and medium-sized cities and regions. It is clear that the Lisbon Agenda-driven regional policies of the EU favor major urban concentrations over smaller cities and their hinterlands – at a risk of furthering socio-spatial polarization in Europe. This is in stark contrast with the recent Urban Agenda of the EU which states that "small and medium-sized cities … form the backbone of Europe's territory and have an important role to play for territorial development and cohesion" (CEC 2014, 4).

Finally, the vulnerabilities of life and places as the processes of knowledge-based economization proceed will be pressing concerns in different corners of the OECD world and beyond. New social divisions, possible policy failures, the presence of symbolic violence, tensions, contradictions, crisis tendencies, conflicts over urban space and issues of socio-spatial inequality and uneven development are all crucial geopolitical issues of knowledge-based economization. Identifying and analyzing particular "cracks" inherent in the process of knowledge-based economization is an inviting challenge for scholarship and political action. An analysis of these cracks may increase the possibility of directing knowledge-based economization toward alternative projects which move it toward more progressive and inclusive forms that could de-stabilize the contemporary geopolitical discourses of inter-territorial competition and competitiveness. Developing new forms of knowledge-based economization would also require re-thinking the relationship between business firms and the public. It is not impossible that in the future knowledge-based economization might take a form that is more inclusive than its contemporary manifestations, and that its geopolitical constitution will be different compared to the current ones.

References

Acuto, M. and Curtis, S. (2013a). Assemblage thinking and international relations. In M.Acuto and S.Curtis (Eds.), *Reassembling International Theory: Assemble Thinking and International Relations* (pp. 3–15). Basingstoke: Palgrave Macmillan.

Acuto, M. and Curtis, S. (2013b). The carpenter and the bricoleur. In M. Acuto and S. Curtis (Eds.), *Reassembling International Theory: Assemble Thinking and International Relations* (pp. 17–24). Basingstoke: Palgrave Macmillan.

Addie, J-P., Keil, R. and Olds, K. (2015). Beyond town and gown: Universities, territoriality and the mobilization of new urban structures in Canada. *Territory, Politics, Governance*, 3, 27–50.

Agamben, G. (2011). *Metropolis*. Available at: http://www.generation-online.org/p/fpagambmen4.htm

Agnew, J.A. (2003). *Geopolitics. Re-visioning World Politics*. Second edition. London: Routledge.

Agnew, J.A. (2013). The origins of critical geopolitics. In K. Dodds, M. Kuus and J. Sharp (Eds.), *The Ashgate Research Companion to Critical Geopolitics* (pp. 19–32). Farnham: Ashgate.

Agnew, J.A. and Corbridge, S. (1995). *Mastering Space: Hegemony, Territory and International Political Economy*. London: Routledge.

Ahlqvist, T. and Moisio, S. (2014). Neoliberalization in a Nordic state: From cartel polity towards a corporate polity in Finland. *New Political Economy*, 19, 21–55.

Allen, J. (2011). Powerful assemblages? *Area*, 43, 154–157.

Allen, J. and Cochrane, A. (2010). Assemblages of state power: Topological shifts in the organization of government and politics. *Antipode*, 42, 1071–1089.

Alvesson, M. and Willmott, H. (2003). Introduction. In M.Alvesson and H.Willmott (Eds.), *Studying Management Critically* (pp. 1–22). Los Angeles, CA: Sage.

Anderson, B. and McFarlane, C. (2011). Assemblage and geography. *Area*, 43, 124–127.

Angelo, H. and Wachsmuth, D. (2015). Urbanizing urban political ecology: A critique of methodological cityism. *International Journal of Urban and Regional Research*, 39, 16–27.

Barry, A. (1993). The European Community and European government: Harmonization, mobility and space. *Economy and Society*, 22, 314–326.

Belina, B., Petzold, T., Schardt, J. and Schipper, S. (2013). Neoliberalising the Fordist university: A tale of two campuses in Frankfurt a. M., Germany. *Antipode*, 45, 738–759.

Bell, D. (1973/1999). *The Coming of Post-industrial Society*. New York: Basic Books.

Blyth, M. (2013). *Austerity. The History of a Dangerous Idea*. Oxford: Oxford University Press.

Bogrebin, R. and Carvajal, D. (2015). Guggenheim Helsinki unveils design. *The New York Times* 23.5. Available at: https://www.nytimes.com/2015/06/24/arts/design/guggenheim-helsinki-unveils-design.html?mcubz=1

Bonefeld, W. (2012). Freedom and the strong state: On German ordoliberalism. *New Political Economy*, 17, 633–656.

Borén, T. and Young, C. (2013). Getting creative with the 'creative city'? Towards new perspectives on creativity in urban policy. *International Journal of Urban and Regional Research*, 37, 1799–1815.

Brenner, N. (1998). Global cities, global states: Global city formation and state territorial restructuring in contemporary Europe. *Review of International Political Economy*, 5, 1–37.

Brenner, N. (2004). *New State Spaces*. Oxford: Oxford University Press.

Brenner, N. and Theodore, N. (2002). Cities and the geographies of "actually existing neoliberalism". In N. Brenner and N. Theodore (Eds.), *Spaces of Neoliberalism. Urban Restructuring in North America and Western Europe* (pp. 2–32). Oxford: Blackwell.

Brenner, N. and Wachsmuth, D. (2017). Territorial competitiveness: Lineages, practices, ideologies. In N. Brenner (Ed.), *Critique of Urbanization: Selected Essays* (pp. 85–111). Berlin: Bauverlag.

Brenner, N., Peck, J. and Theodore, N. (2010). Variegated neoliberalization: Geographies, modalities, pathways. *Global Networks*, 10, 182–222.

Bristow, G. (2005). Everyone is a winner: Problematizing the discourse of regional competitiveness. *Journal of Economic Geography*, 5, 285–304.

Bristow, G. (2010). *Critical Reflections on Regional Competitiveness. Theory, Policy, Practice.* London: Routledge.

The British Government (2016). *Success as a Knowledge economy*. Department for Business Innovations and Skills. Available at: https://www.timeshighereducation.com/sites/de fault/files/breaking_news_files/higher-education-white-paper-success-as-a-knowl edge-economy.pdf

Brown, W. (2006). American nightmare: Neoliberalism, neoconservatism, and de-democratization. *Political Theory*, 34, 690–714.

Browning, C.S. and de Oliveira, A.F. (2017). Introduction: Nation branding and competitive identity in world politics. *Geopolitics*, 22, 481–501.

Çalişkan, K. and Callon, M. (2009). Economization, part 1: Shifting attention from the economy towards processes of economization. *Economy and Society*, 38, 369–398.

Callon, M. (1998, Ed.). *The Laws of the Markets*. London: Blackwell.

Cantell, T. (1999). *Helsinki and a Vision of Place*. Helsinki: City of Helsinki Urban Facts.

Carrillo, F.J., Yigitcanlar, T., Garcia, B. and Lönnqvist, A. (2014). *Knowledge and the City. Concepts, Applications and Trends of Knowledge-Based Urban Development*. Routledge: London.

Carlaw, K., Nuth, M., Oxley, L., Thorns, D. and Walker, B. (2006). Beyond the hype: Intellectual property and the knowledge society/knowledge economy. *Journal of Economic Surveys*, 20, 633–690.

Castells, M. (1996). *The Rise of the Network Society*. Oxford: Blackwell.

Castells, M. (1997). *The Power of Identity*. Oxford: Blackwell.

Castells, M. (2005). The network society: From knowledge to policy. In M. Castells and G. Cardoso (Eds.), *The Network Society: From Knowledge to Policy* (pp. 3–21). Washington DC: Johns Hopkins Center for Transatlantic Relations.

Castells, M. and Hall, P. (1994). *Technopoles of the World. The Making of 21st Century Industrial Complexes*. London: Routledge.

Castells, M. and Himanen, P. (2004). *The Information Society and the Welfare State: The Finnish model*. Oxford: Oxford University Press.

Castells, M. and Himanen, P. (2013, Eds). *Kestävän Kasvun Malli: Globaali Näkökulma*. Helsinki: Valtioneuvoston kanslia.

Castree, N. and Spark, M. (2000). Professional geography and the corporatization of the university: Experiences, evaluations, and engagements. *Antipode*, 32, 222–229.

CEC (2010). Europe 2020: A strategy for smart, sustainable and inclusive growth. Communication from the Commission. Brussels, 3.3.2010. COM (2010) 2020.

CEC (2014). The Urban dimension of EU policies – Key features of an EU Urban Agenda. COM (2014) 490 final.

CEC (2017). European regional competitiveness index. Available at: http://ec.europa.eu/regional_policy/en/information/maps/regional_competitiveness/

Cerny, P. (1990). *The Changing Architecture of Politics. Structure, Agency, and the Future of the State*. London: Sage.

Clark, B.R. (1998). *Creating Entrepreneurial Universities*. Bingley: Emerald.

Clegg, S.R. and Palmer, G. (1996). Introduction: Producing management knowledge. In S.R. Clegg, and G. Palmer (Eds.), *The Politics of Management Knowledge* (pp. 1–18). London: Sage.

Council of Europe (2014). About Intercultural cities programme [WWW document]. Available at: http://www.coe.int/t/dg4/cultureheritage/culture/Cities/about_en.asp.

Cowen, D. and Smith, N. (2009). After geopolitics? From the geopolitical social to geoeconomics. *Antipode*, 41, 22–48.

CSD – Committee on Spatial Development (1999). *European Spatial Development Perspective*. Office for the Official Publications of the European Community, Luxembourg.

Dalby, S. (1990). *Creating the Second Cold War*. London: Pinter.

Dalby, S. (1991). Critical geopolitics: Discourse, difference, and dissent. *Environment and Planning D*, 9, 261–283.

Demirović, A. (2011). Materialist state theory and the transnationalization of the capitalist state. *Antipode*, 43, 38–59.

Dijkstra, L. (2004). European cities in a dynamic, knowledge-based economy. In J. Antikainen and T. Pyöriä (Eds.), *Kaupunkiseutujen Kasvun Aika* (pp. 16–19). Helsinki: Sisäasiainministeriö.

Dittmer, J. (2014). Geopolitical assemblages and complexity. *Progress in Human Geography*, 38, 385–401.

Drucker, P.F. (1969). Knowledge society. *New Society*, 13, 629–631.

Drury, T., Byers, H., Kingsley, L. and Wiseman, A. (2012). *Concept and Development Study for a Guggenheim Helsinki*. New York: Guggenheim Museum Publications.

du Gay, P. (1996). Making up managers: Enterprise and the ethos of bureaucracy. In S.R. Clegg and G. Palmer (Eds.), *The Politics of Management Knowledge* (pp. 19–35). London: Sage.

Dunning, J.H. (2000). Regions, globalization, and the knowledge economy. In J.H. Dunning (Ed.), *Regions, Globalization, and the Knowledge-based Economy* (pp. 7–41). Oxford: Oxford University Press.

Easterling, K. (2014). *Extra Statecraft. The Power of Infrastructure Space*. London: Verso.

The Economist (2013). Northern lights. Special report: The Nordic Countries. *The Economist*, Feb 2nd, 1–16.

Elden, S. (2005). Missing the point: Globalization, deterritorialization and the space of the world. *Transactions of the Institute of British Geographers NS*, 30, 8–19.

Elden, S. (2013). How should we do the history of territory? *Territory, Politics, Governance*, 1, 5–20.

Eskelinen, T. (2015). Talouskonservatiivit ja nelikenttä. Available at: http://www.poliitt inentalous.fi/talouskonservatiivit-ja-nelikentta/

European Communities (2006). *Creating an Innovative Europe. Report of the Independent Expert Group on R&D and Innovation Appointed Following the Hampton Court Summit and Chaired by Mr. Esko Aho*. Luxembourg: Office for Official Publications of the European Communities.

EU Ministers responsible for Urban and Spatial Development (2007). *Territorial Agenda of the European Union: Towards a More Competitive and Sustainable Europe of Diverse Regions*. Agreed on the occasion of the Informal Ministerial Meeting on Urban Development and Territorial Cohesion in Leipzig on 24–25 May 2007.

EU Ministers responsible for Spatial Planning and Territorial Development (2011). *Territorial Agenda of the European Union 2020: Towards an Inclusive, Smart and Sustainable Europe of Diverse Regions*. Agreed at the Informal Ministerial Meeting of Ministers responsible for Spatial Planning and Territorial Development, Gödöllő, Hungary 19 May 2011.

European Council (2000). *Presidency Conclusions of the Lisbon European Council*. 23 and 24 March. Lisbon: European Council.

Florida, R. (2004). *The Rise of the Creative Class*. New York: Basic Books.

Florida, R. (2007). *The Flight of the Creative Class. The New Global Competition for Talent*. New York: HarperCollins Publishers.

Florida, R. (2008). *Who's Your City? How the Creative Economy is Making Where to Live the Most Important Decision of your Life*. New York: Basic Books.

Florida, R. (2012). *The Rise of the Creative Class: Revisited*. New York: Basic Books.

Florida, R. (2013). The new global start-up cities. *The Atlantic Cities*, the 4th of June, 2013.

Florida, R. (2017a). The economic power of cities compared with nations. Available at: https://www.citylab.com/work/2017/03/the-economic-power-of-global-cities-com pared-to-nations/519294/

Florida, R. (2017b). Why America's richest cities keep getting richer? *The Atlantic Cities*, the 12 April, 2017. Available at: https://www.theatlantic.com/business/archive/2017/04/richard-florida-winner-take-all-new-urban-crisis/522630/

Foglesong, R.E. (2012). Planning the capitalist city. In S.S. Fainstein and S. Campbell (Eds.), *Readings in Planning Theory*. 3rd edition (pp. 132–138). Chichester: Wiley-Blackwell.

Fougner, T. (2006). The state, international competitiveness and neoliberal globalization: Is there a future beyond 'the competition state'? *Review of International Studies*, 32, 165–185.

Fregonese, S. (2009). The urbicide of Beirut? Geopolitics and the built environment in the Lebanese civil war (1975–1976). *Political Geography*, 28, 309–318.

Frey, B.S. (2003). *Arts & Economics: Analysis and Cultural Policy*. Berlin: Springer-Verlag.

Giroux, H.A. (2012). The militarization of US higher education after 9/11. In K. Gouliamos and C. Kassimeris (Eds.), *The Marketing of War in the Age of Neo-militarism* (pp. 236–261). London: Routledge.

Glaeser, E. (2012). *Triumph of the City*. London: Pan Macmillan.

Godin, B. (2006). The knowledge-based economy: Conceptual framework or buzzword? *Journal of Technology Transfer*, 31, 17–30.

Government of Canada (2016). *Maximizing Canada's Engagement in the Global Knowledge-based Economy: 2017 and Beyond*. Available at: www.horizons.gc.ca/eng/book/export/html/1623

Graham, S. (2010). *Cities Under Siege: The New Military Urbanism*. New York: Verso.

Guzzini, S. (2014). Revival of geopolitical thought in Europe. *Academic Foresights* 11. Available at: http://www.academic-foresights.com/Geopolitical_Thought.pdf

Hannah, M. (2001). Sampling and the politics of representation in the US Census 2000. *Annals of the Association of American Geographers*, 19, 15–34.

Harding, A. (1997). Urban regimes in a Europe of the cities? *European Urban and Regional Studies*, 4, 291–314.

Harland, T. (2009). The university, neoliberal reform and the liberal educational idea. In M. Tight (Ed.), *The Routledge International Handbook of Higher Education* (pp. 511–522). London: Routledge.

Harrison, J. and Hoyler, M. (2015, Eds.). *Megaregions: Globalization's New Urban Form?* Cheltenham: Edward Elgar.

Harvey, D. (1978). The urban process under capitalism: A framework for analysis. *International Journal of Urban and Regional Research*, 2, 101–131.

Harvey, D. (1985). *The Urbanization of Capital: Studies in the History and Theory of Capitalist Urbanization*. Baltimore, MD: Johns Hopkins University Press.

Harvey, D. (2001). *Spaces of Capital. Towards a Critical Geography*. Edinburg: University of Edinburgh Press.

Himanen, P. (2001). *The Hacker Ethic and the Spirit of the Information Age*. New York: Random House.

Himanen, P. (2007). *Suomalainen Unelma: Innovaatioraportti*. Helsinki: Teknologiateollisuuden 100-vuotissäätiö.

Himanen, P. (2010). *Kukoistuksen Käsikirja*. Helsinki: WSOY.

Hobsbawm, E. (1996). *The Age of Extremes. A History of the World, 1914–1991*. New York: Vintage.

Houston, D., Findlay, A., Harrison, R. and Mason, C. (2008). Will attracting the "creative class" boost economic growth in old industrial regions? A case study of Scotland. *Geografiska Annaler B: Human Geography*, 90, 133–150.

Howkins, J. (2001). *The Creative Economy. How People Make Money from Ideas*. New York: Penguin Books.

Jessop, B. (1990). *State Theory: Putting the Capitalist State in its Place*. Cambridge: Polity Press.

Jessop, B. (2002). *The Future of the Capitalist State*. Cambridge: Polity Press.

Jessop, B. (2004). Critical semiotic analysis and cultural political economy. *Critical Discourse Studies*, 1, 159–174.

Jessop, B. (2005). Cultural political economy, the knowledge-based economy, and the state. In A. Barry and D. Slater (Eds.), *The Technological Economy* (pp. 144–166). London: Routledge.

Jessop, B. (2007). From micro-powers to governmentality: Foucault's work on statehood, state formation, statecraft and state power. *Political Geography*, 26, 34–40.

Jessop, B. (2008). A cultural political economy of competitiveness and its implications for higher education. In B. Jessop, N. Fairclough and R. Wodak (Eds.), *Education and the Knowledge-based Economy in Europe* (pp. 13–39). Rotterdam: Sense Publishers.

Jessop, B. (2016). *The State: Past, Present, Future*. Cambridge: Polity Press.

Jessop, B. and Sum, N-L. (2017). Putting the 'Amsterdam School' in its rightful place: A reply to Juan Ignacio Staricco's critique of Cultural Political Economy. *New Political Economy*. DOI:10.1080/13563467.2017.1286639

Jonas, A.E.G. and Moisio, S. (2016). City regionalism as geopolitical processes: A new framework for analysis. *Progress in Human Geography*. DOI:10.1177/0309132516679897

Jones, M. (1997). Spatial selectivity of the state? The regulationist enigma and local struggles over economic governance. *Environment and Planning A*, 29, 831–864.

Jones, M. (2008). Recovering a sense of political economy. *Political Geography*, 27, 377–399.

Jones, R. (2012). State encounters. *Environment and Planning D: Space and Society*, 30, 805–821.

Jöns, H. and Hoyler, M. (2013). Global geographies of higher education: The perspective of world university rankings. *Geoforum*, 46, 45–59.

Kalska, T. (2013) Rockstars of entrepreneurship. *Aalto University Magazine* 6. http://www.aalto.fi/en/current/magazine/06/rockstars_of_entrepreneurship/

Kangas, A. (2013). Market civilization meets economic nationalism: The discourse of nation in Russia's modernisation. *Nations and Nationalism*, 19, 572–589.

Kangas, A. (2017). Global cities, international relations, and the fabrication of the world. *Global Society*, 31, 531–550.

Kangas, A. and Moisio, S. (2012). Creating state competitiveness, re-scaling higher education: The case of Finland. In P. Aalto, V. Harle and S. Moisio (Eds.), *Global and Regional Problems: Towards an Interdisciplinary Study* (pp. 199–224). Farnham: Ashgate.

Kantola, A. and Seeck, H. (2011). Dissemination of management into politics: Michael Porter and the political uses of management consulting. *Management Learning*, 42, 25–47.

Kelly, D. (1999). The strategic-relational view of the state. *Politics*, 19, 109–115.

Kerr, C. (2001). *The Uses of the University*. Cambridge MA: Harvard University Press.

Khanna, P. (2016a). A new map for America. *The New York Times* 15.4.2016. Available at: http://www.nytimes.com/2016/04/17/opinion/sunday/a-new-map-for-america.html?_r=1

Khanna, P. (2016b). *Connectography: Mapping the Future of Global Civilization*. New York: Random House.

Kitson, M., Martin, R. and Tyler, R. (2004). Regional competitiveness: An elusive yet key concept? *Regional Studies*, 38, 991–999.

Kitchin, R., Lauriault, T.P. and McArdle, G. (2015). Knowing and governing cities through urban indicators, city benchmarking and real-time dashboards. *Regional Studies, Regional Science*, 2, 6–28.

Kivelä, S. and Moisio, S. (2017). The state as a space of health. On the biopolitics and geopolitics of health care systems. *Territory, Politics, Governance*, 5, 28–46.

Knight, J. (2006). Internationalization: Concepts, complexities and challenges. In J.F. Forest and P.G. Altbach (Eds.), *International Handbook of Higher Education* (pp. 207–227). Dordrecht: Springer.

Koch, N. (2014). The shifting geopolitics of higher education: Inter/nationalizing elite universities in Kazakhstan, Saudi Arabia, and beyond. *Geoforum*, 56, 46–54.

Krugman, P.R. (1994). Competitiveness: A dangerous obsession. *Foreign Affairs*, 73, 28–44.

Krugman, P.R. (1996). Making sense of the competitiveness debate. *Oxford Review of Economic Policy*, 12, 17–25.

Kuus, M. (2007). *Geopolitics Re-framed: Security and Identity in Europe's Eastern Enlargement*. New York: Palgrave Macmillan.

Kuus, M. (2014). *Geopolitics and Expertize: Knowledge and Authority in European Diplomacy*. Chichester: John Wiley & Sons.

Laclau, E. (1990). *New Reflections on the Revolution of our Time*. New York: Verso.

Landry, C. (2008). *The Creative City. A Toolkit for Innovators*. London: Earthscan.

Larner, W. (2012). New subjects. In T.J. Barnes, J. Peck and E. Sheppard (Eds.), *The Wiley-Blackwell Companion to Economic Geography* (pp. 358–371). Chichester: Wiley-Blackwell.

Larner, W. and Le Heron, P. (2002). The spaces and subjects of a globalizing economy: A situated exploration method. *Environment and Planning* D, 20, 753–774.

Laukkanen, M. (2016). Uusi teollisuustuki ei suojele työpaikkoja. *Helsingin Sanomat* 26.9., A5.

Lefebvre, H. (1970/2003). *The Urban Revolution*. Minneapolis MN: University of Minnesota Press.

Lefebvre, H. (1991). *The Production of Space*. Oxford: Blackwell.

Lefebvre, H. (2003). Space and the state. In N. Brenner, B. Jessop, M. Jones and G. Macleod (Eds.), *State/space: A Reader* (pp. 84–100). Oxford: Blackwell.

Legg, S. (2005). Foucault's population geographies: Classifications, biopolitics and governmental spaces. *Population, Space and Place*, 11, 137–156.

Lemke, T. (2007). An indigestible meal? Foucault, governmentality and state theory. *Distinktion: Scandinavian Journal of Social Theory*, 8, 43–64.

Leslie, L. and Rantisi, N.M. (2012). The rise of a new knowledge/creative economy: Prospects and challenges for economic development, class inequality, and work. In T.J. Barnes, J. Peck and E. Sheppard (Eds.), *The Wiley-Blackwell Companion to Economic Geography* (pp. 458–471). Chichester: Wiley-Blackwell.

Liesto, M. (1988). *Teknillinen Korkeakoulu 1908–1988*. Hämeenlinna: Karisto.

Linko, M. (2013). Guggenheim Helsinki: Toimijatahot vastakkain. *Yhdyskuntasuunnittelu*, 51, 30–56.

Lundvall, B.A. (1992). *National Systems of Innovation: Towards a Theory of Innovation and Interactive Learning*. London: Pinter.

Luukkonen, J. and Moisio, S. (2016). On the socio-technical practices of the European Union territory. *Environment and Planning A*, 48, 1452–1472.

McCann, E.J. (2008). Expertise, truth, and urban policy mobilities: Global circuits of knowledge and the development of Vancouver, Canada's 'four pillar' drug strategy. *Environment and Planning A*, 40, 885–904.

MacKinnon, D., Cumbers, A. and Chapman, K. (2002). Learning, innovation and regional development: A critical appraisal of recent debates. *Progress in Human Geography*, 26, 293–311.

Magretta, J. (2012). *Understanding Michal Porter. The Essential Guide to Competition and Strategy*. Cambridge MA: Harvard Business Review Press.

Maier, C.S. (2016). *Once Within Borders: Territories of Power, Wealth and Belonging since 1500*. Cambridge MA: Harvard University Press.

Malkinson, T. (2003). The global engineer: Succeeding without boundaries. *ieee.USA Today's Engineers Online*. Available at: http://www.todaysengineer.org/2003/jun/global.asp

Marcuse, P. (2005). 'The city' as perverse metaphor. *City*, 9, 247–254.

Mayer, F.W. and Phillips, N. (2017). Outsourcing governance: States and the politics of a 'global value chain world'. *New Political Economy*, 22, 134–152.

Mazzucato, M. (2013). *The Entrepreneurial State: Debunking Private vs. Public Sector Myths*. London: Anthem Press.

Mead, W.R. (2014). The return of geopolitics. *Foreign Affairs*, 93, 69–79.

Meehan, K., Shaw, I.G.R. and Marston, S.A. (2013). Political geographies of the object. *Political Geography*, 33, 1–10.

Mezzadra, S. and Neilson, B. (2013). *Border as a Method, or, the Multiplication of Labor*. Durham, NC: Duke University Press.

Miettinen, R. (2002). *National Innovation System: Scientific Concept or Political Rhetoric*. Helsinki: Edita.

Miller, P. (2001). Governing by numbers: Why calculative practices matter. *Social Research*, 68, 379–396.

Ministry of Education (2007). Teknillisen korkeakoulun, Helsingin kauppakorkeakoulun ja Taideteollisen korkeakoulun yhdistyminen uudeksi yliopistoksi. *Opetusministeriön Työryhmämuistioita Ja Selvityksiä* 16/2007.

Ministry of Education and Culture (2012). *Suomi Osaamispohjeiseen Nousuun. Tutkimus- ja Innovaatiopolitiikan Toimintaohjelma*. Helsinki: Opetus- ja kulttuuriministeriö.

Ministry of Education and Culture (2014). University reform. Available at: http://www.minedu.fi/OPM/Koulutus/koulutuspolitiikka/Hankkeet/Yliopistolaitoksen_uudistaminen/?lang=en

Ministry of Employment and the Economy (2008). *Proposal for Finland's National Innovation Strategy*. Available at: http://ec.europa.eu/invest-in-research/pdf/download_en/finland_national_innovation_strategy.pdf

Mitchell, K. (2003). Educating the national citizen in neoliberal times: From the multicultural self to the strategic cosmopolitan. *Transactions of the Institute of British Geographers*, 28, 387–403.

Moisio, S. (2008). From enmity to rivalry? Notes on national identity politics in competition states. *Scottish Geographical Journal*, 128, 78–95.

Moisio, S. (2011a). Beyond the domestic-international divide: State spatial transformation as neoliberal geopolitics. In P. Aalto, V. Harle and S. Moisio (Eds.), *International Studies: Interdisciplinary Approaches* (pp. 149–177). Basingstoke: Palgrave Macmillan.

Moisio, S. (2011b). Geographies of Europeanization: The EU's spatial planning as a politics of scale. In L. Bialasiewicz (Ed.), *Europe in the World: EU Geopolitics and the Transformation of European Space* (pp. 19–40). Farnham: Ashgate.

Moisio, S. (2013). The state. In K. Dodds, M. Kuus and J. Sharp (Eds.), *The Ashgate Research Companion to Critical Geopolitics* (pp. 231–246). Farnham: Ashgate.

Moisio, S. (2015). Geopolitics/critical geopolitics. In J. Agnew, V. Mamadouh, A. Secor and J. Sharp (Eds.), *The Wiley Blackwell Companion to Political Geography* (pp. 220–234). Chichester: Wiley-Blackwell.

Moisio, S. (2017). Towards geopolitical analysis of geoeconomic processes. *Geopolitics*. DOI :10.1080/14650045.2017.1326481

Moisio, S. and Paasi, A. (2013). From geopolitical to geoeconomic? Changing political rationalities of state space. *Geopolitics*, 18, 267–283.

Moisio, S. and Luukkonen, J. (2015). European spatial planning as governmentality. An inquiry into rationalities, techniques and manifestations. *Environment and Planning C: Government and Policy*, 33, 828–845.

Moisio, S. and Kangas, A. (2016). Reterritorializing the global knowledge economy: An analysis of geopolitical assemblages of higher education. *Global Networks*, 16, 268–287.

Moisio, S. and Belina, B. (2017). State (the). In D. Richardson, N. Castree, M.F. Goodchild, A. Kobayashi, W. Liu, R.A. Marston (Eds.), *The International Encyclopedia of Geography: People, the Earth, Environment, and Technology*, Vol. XIII (pp. 6798–6808). Chichester: Wiley-Blackwell.

Moisio, S. and Luukkonen, J. (2017). Notes on spatial transformation in post-Cold War Europe and the territory work of the European Union. In P. Vihalemm, A. Masso and S. Operman (Eds.), *The Routledge International Handbook of European Social Transformation*, pp. 224–238. Abingdon: Routledge.

Moisio, S. and Jonas, A.E.G. (2018). City-regions and city-regionalism. In A. Paasi, J. Harrison, M. Jones (Eds.), *Handbook on the Geographies of Regions and Territories*. Cheltenham: Edward Elgar Publishing.

Moisio, S., Bachmann, V., Bialasiewicz, L., dell'Agnese, E., Dittmer, J. and Mamadouh, V. (2013). Mapping the political geographies of Europeanization: National discourses, external perceptions and the question of popular culture. *Progress in Human Geography*, 37, 737–761.

Mulgan, G. (2009). *The Art of Public Strategy: Mobilizing Power and Knowledge for the Common Good*. Oxford: Oxford University Press.

Müller, M. (2008). Reconsidering the concept of discourse for the field of critical geopolitics: Towards discourse as language *and* practice. *Political Geography*, 27, 322–338.

Müller, M. (2011). Education and the formation of geopolitical subjects. *International Political Sociology*, 5, 1–17.

Müller, M. (2015). Assembling power: Assemblages, actor-networks and politics. *Geography Compass*, 9, 27–41.

Müller, M. and Schurr, C. (2016). Assemblage thinking and actor-network theory: Conjunctions, disjunctions, cross-fertilizations. *Transactions of the Institute of British Geographers*, 41, 217–229.

Nordin, A. and Sundberg, D. (2014). The making and governing of knowledge in the education policy field. In A. Nordin and D. Sundberg (Eds.), *Transnational Policy Flows in European Education* (pp. 9–20). Oxford: Symposium Books.

OECD (1996). *The Knowledge-based Economy*. Paris: OECD.

OECD (2012). A guiding framework for entrepreneurial universities. Available at: http://www.oecd.org/site/cfecpr/guiding-framework.htm

Ohmae, K. (1993). The rise of the "region state". *Foreign Affairs*, 72, 78–87.

Olds, K. (2007). Global assemblage: Singapore, foreign universities, and the construction of a "global educational hub". *World Development*, 35, 959–975.

Ong, A. (2006). *Neoliberalism as Exception. Mutations in Citizenship and Sovereignty*. Durham, NC: Duke University Press.

Organization of American States (2014). Knowledge-based society. Available at: http://www.oas.org/en/topics/knowledge_society.asp

Orta, A. (2013). Managing the margins: MBA training, international business, and "the value chain of culture". *American Ethnologist*, 40, 689–703.

Ó Tuathail, G. (1992). The Bush administration and the "end" of the Cold War: A critical geopolitics of US foreign policy in 1989. *Geoforum*, 23, 437–452.

Ó Tuathail, G. (1996). *Critical Geopolitics*. London: Routledge.

Ó Tuathail, G. and Agnew, J.A. (1992). Geopolitics and discourse. Practical geopolitical reasoning in American foreign policy. *Political Geography*, 11, 190–204.

Painter, J. (2006). Prosaic geographies of stateness. *Political Geography*, 25, 752–774.

Peck, J. (2005). Struggling with the creative class. *International Journal of Urban and Regional Research*, 29, 740–770.

Peck, J. (2016). Economic rationality meets celebrity urbanology: Exploring Edward Gleaser's city. *International Journal of Urban and Regional Research*, 40, 1–30.

Peck, J. and Tickell, A. (2002). Neoliberalizing space. *Antipode*, 34, 380–404.

Peck, J. and Theodore, N. (2015). *Fast Policy. Experimental Statecraft at the Thresholds of Neoliberalism*. Minneapolis, MN: Minnesota University Press.

Pekkarinen, J. (1990). *Corporativism and Economic Performance in Sweden, Norway and Finland*. Helsinki: Labor Institute for Economic Research.

Pellinen, T. (2013). Insinöörikoulutuksen uudistaminen. Available at: http://www.infrajohtaminen.fi/File/346/f-terhipellinen-aalto-1230.pdf

Peters, M.A. (2007). Knowledge societies and knowledge economies. In M.A. Peters (Ed.), *Knowledge economy, Development and Further of Higher Education* (pp. 17–30). Rotterdam: Sense Publishers.

Peters, M.A. (2009). Introduction: Knowledge goods, the primacy of ideas, and the economics of abundance. In M.A. Peters, P. Marginson and P. Murphy (Eds.), *Creativity and the Global Knowledge Economy* (pp. 1–22). New York: Peter Lang.

Pike, G. (2012). From internationalism to internationalization. The illusion of global community in higher education. *Journal of Social Science Education*, 11, 133–149.

Porter, M. (1980). *Competitive Strategy*. New York: Free Press.

Porter, M. (1985). *Competitive Advantage*. New York: Free Press.

Porter, M.E. (1990). The competitive advantage of nations. *Harvard Business Review*, 68, March–April, 73–93.

Porter, M. (1998a). *The Competitive Advantage of Nations*. 2nd edition. Basingstoke: Macmillan.

Porter, M. (1998b). Clusters and the new economics of competition. *Harvard Business Review*, 76, November–December, 77–90.

Porter, M. (2000). Location, competition, and economic development: Local clusters in a global economy. *Economic Development Quarterly* 14, 15–34.

Porter, M. (2008). *On Competition (Updated and Expanded Edition)*. Cambridge, MA: Harvard Business Press.

Pratt, A.C. (2008). Creative cities: The cultural industries and the creative class. *Geografiska Annaler B: Human Geography*, 90, 107–117.

Prime Minister's Office (2011). *Programme of Prime Minister Jyrki Katainen's Government*, Helsinki: Valtioneuvoston kanslia.

Prime Minister's Office (2013). Government report on the future. Well-being through sustainable growth. *Prime Minister's Office Publications* 20/2013.

Prince, R. (2012). Transnational elites and the geographies of power. *Geopolitics*, 17, 423–428.

Prince, R. (2015). The spaces in between: Mobile policy and the topographies and topologies of the technocracy. *Environment and Planning D: Society and Space*, 34, 420–437.

Raco, M. (2013). The new contractualism, the privatization of the welfare state, and the barriers to open source planning. *Planning, Practice and Research*, 28, 45–64.

Read, J. (2009). A genealogy of homo-economicus: Neoliberalism and the production of subjectivity. *Foucault Studies*, 6, 25–36.

Roberts, S. (2003). Global strategic vision: Managing the world. In W. Perry and B. Maurer (Eds.), *Globalization Under Construction* (pp. 1–38). Minneapolis, MN: University of Minnesota Press.

Rodríguez-Bolívar, M.P. (2018). *Smart Technologies for Smart Governments. Transparency, Efficiency and Organizational Issues*. Cham: Springer.

Rokem, J., Fregonese, S., Ramadan, A., Pascucci, E., Rosen, G., Charney, I., Paasche, T.F. and Sidaway, J.D. (2017). Interventions in urban geopolitics. *Political Geography*. DOI:10.1016/j.polgeo.2017.04.004

Rossi, U. (2016). The variegated economies and the potential politics of the smart city. *Territory, Politics, Governance*, 4, 337–353.

Rossi, U. (2017). *Cities in Global Capitalism*. Cambridge: Polity Press.

Rossi, U. and Vanolo, A. (2012). *Urban Political Geographies*. Thousand Oakes: Sage.

Rossi, U. and Di Bella, A. (2017). Start-up urbanism: New York, Rio de Janeiro and the global urbanization of technology-based economies. *Environment and Planning A*, 49, 999–1018.

Salter, B. (2009). State strategies and the geopolitics of the global knowledge economy. China, India and the case of regenerative medicine. *Geopolitics*, 14, 47–78.

Sassen, S. (2005). When national territory is home to the global: Old borders to novel borderings. *New Political Economy*, 10, 523–541.

Sassen, S. (2008). *Territory, Authority, Rights. From Medieval to Global Assemblages*. Princeton, NJ: Princeton University Press.

Sassen, S. (2013). When territory deborders territoriality. *Territory, Politics, Governance*, 1, 21–45.

Savolainen, J. (2016). Helsinki tarvitsee Guggenheimin. *Helsingin Sanomat* 24.1.2016, C 28.

Saxenian, A. (1994) *Regional Advantage: Culture and Competition in Silicon Valley and Route 128*. Cambridge, MA: Harvard University Press.

Schell, E. (2014). The creativity bubble. *Jacobin* 15/16. Available at: https://www.jacobinmag.com/2014/10/the-creativity-bubble/

Scott, A. (2001). Globalization and the rise of city-regions. *European Planning Studies*, 9, 813–816.

Scott, A. (2014). Beyond the creative city: Cognitive-cultural capitalism and the new urbanism. *Regional Studies*, 48, 565–578.

Scott, A.J. (2017). *The Constitution of the City. Economy, Society, and Urbanization in the Capitalist Era*. Cham: Palgrave Macmillan.

Scott, J. (1998). *Seeing Like a State. How Certain Schemes to Improve the Human Condition Have Failed*. New Haven, CT: Yale University Press.

Sellar, C., Lan, T. and Poli, U. (2017). The geoeconomics/politics of Italy's investment promotion community. *Geopolitics*. DOI: 10.1080/14650045.2017.1350171

Smith, N. (2005). WHAT'S LEFT? Neo-critical geography, or, the flat pluralist world of business class? *Antipode*, 37, 887–899.

Soja, E. (2011). Regional urbanization and the end of the metropolis era. In Bridge, G. and Watson, S. (Eds.), *The New Blackwell Companion to the City* (pp. 679–689). Oxford: Wiley-Blackwell.

Sparke, M. (2007). Geopolitical fears, geoeconomic hopes, and the responsibilities of geography. *Annals of the Association of American Geographers*, 97, 338–349.

Sparke, M. (2017). Globalizing capitalism and the dialectics of geopolitics and geoeconomics. *Environment and Planning A*. DOI: 10.1177/0308518X17735926

Stalder, F. (2006). *Manuel Castells. The Theory of the Network Society*. Cambridge: Polity Press.

Statistics Finland (2015). Annual statistics. Available at: http://www.tilastokeskus.fi/til/index.html

Storper, M. (2000). Globalization and knowledge flows. In J.H. Dunning (Ed.), *Regions, Globalization, and the Knowledge-based Economy* (pp. 42–62). Oxford: Oxford University Press.

Storper, M. and Scott, A.J. (2009). Rethinking human capital, creativity and urban growth. *Journal of Economic Geography*, 9, 147–167.

Ståhle, P. (2016). Aineettoman pääoman kehitys taantuu Suomessa. *Helsingin Sanomat* 30.5., B 10.

Sum, N-L. and Jessop, B. (2013). *Towards a Cultural Political Economy. Putting Culture in its Place in Political Economy*. Cheltenham: Edward Elgar.

Taylor, P.J. (2004). *World City Network: A Global Urban Analysis*. London: Routledge.

Taylor, P.J. (2011). World city networks: Measurement, social organization, global governance, and structural change. In M. Amen, N.J. Toly, P.L. McCarney and K. Segbers (Eds.), *Cities and Global Governance* (pp. 201–216). Farnham: Ashgate.

Thinkers50 (2015). Thinkers50 ranking of management thinkers announced. Available at: http://thinkers50.com/wp-content/uploads/Thinkers50-2015-Rankings-Press-Release-November-9.pdf

Thrift, N. (2000). It's the little things. In K. Dodds and D. Atkinson (Eds.), *Geopolitical Traditions: A Century of Geopolitical Thought* (pp. 380–387). London: Routledge.

Thrift, N. (2005). *Knowing Capitalism*. London: Sage.

Thrift, N. and Olds, K. (2004). Cultures on the brink: Re-engineering the soul of capitalism – on a global scale. In A. Ong and S. Collins (Eds.), *Global Anthropology: Technology, Governmentalities, Ethics* (pp. 270–290). Malden, MA: Blackwell.

Thurow, L. (1992). *Head to Head: The Coming Economic Battle Among Japan, Europe, and America*. New York: Morrow.

Thurow, L.C. (1999). *Building Wealth. The New Rules for Individuals, Companies, and Nations in a Knowledge-Based Economy*. New York: HarperCollins Publishers.

Tremblay, G. (1995). The information society: From Fordism to Gatesism. *Canadian Journal of Communication*, 20, 461–482.

Van Ham, P. (2001). The rise of the brand state: The postmodern politics of image and reputation. *Foreign Affairs*, 80, Sep–Oct, 2–6.

Wahlström, N. (2014). The changing role of the state in a denationalised educational policy context. In A. Nordin and D. Sundberg (Eds.), *Transnational Policy Flows in European Education* (pp. 159–182). Oxford: Symposium Books.

Walters, W. (2012). *Governmentality. Critical Encounters*. London: Routledge.

Vanolo, A. (2014). Smartmentality: The smart city as disciplinary strategy. *Urban Studies*, 51, 883–898.

Vartiainen, J. (2011). The Finnish model of economic and social policy – from Cold War accumulation to generational conflicts? In L. Mjøset (Ed.), *The Nordic Varieties of Capitalism* (pp. 53–87). Bingley: Emerald.

Volner, I. (2015). Can the Guggenheim charm Finland? *The New Yorker*, 12.5. Available at: http://www.newyorker.com/culture/culture-desk/can-the-guggenheim-charm-finland

Webber, A.M. (1993). What's so new about the new economy? *Harvard Business Review*, 71, Jan-Feb. Available at: https://hbr.org/1993/01/whats-so-new-about-the-new-economy

Webster, F. (2006). *Theories of the Information Society*. 3rd edition. London: Routledge.

Welzel, C. and Inglehart, R. (2010). Agency, values, and well-being: A human development model. *Social Indicators Research*, 97, 43–63.

Wilenius, M. (2012). Kulttuuri on vankka pääoma. *Helsingin Sanomat* 14.1.2012. Available at: http://www.hs.fi/mielipide/art-2000004850825.html

World Economic Forum (2016). The Global Competitiveness Report 2015–2016. Available at: http://reports.weforum.org/global-competitiveness-report-2015-2016/

Virkkunen, H.(2010). Suomen korkeakoulutus ja tutkimus on liian pirstaleista. *Kanava*, 2010/1, 4–9.

Välimaa, J. (2004). Nationalisation, localization and globalization in Finnish higher education. *Higher Education*, 48, 27–54.

Zukin, S. (1995). *The Cultures of Cities*. Oxford: Blackwell.

Index

For Product Safety Concerns and Information please contact our EU
representative GPSR@taylorandfrancis.com
Taylor & Francis Verlag GmbH, Kaufingerstraße 24, 80331 München, Germany

www.ingramcontent.com/pod-product-compliance
Ingram Content Group UK Ltd.
Pitfield, Milton Keynes, MK11 3LW, UK
UKHW021611240425
457818UK00018B/496